# CULTURE AND THE DEATH OF GOD

# CULTURE
## AND THE
# DEATH OF GOD

TERRY EAGLETON

YALE UNIVERSITY PRESS
NEW HAVEN AND LONDON

For information about this and other Yale University Press publications, please contact:

U.S. Office: sales.press@yale.edu    www.yalebooks.com
Europe Office: sales@yaleup.co.uk    www.yalebooks.co.uk   .

Set in Arno Pro by IDSUK (DataConnection) Ltd
Printed in the United States of America

Library of Congress Cataloging-in-Publication Data

Eagleton, Terry, 1943
    Culture and the death of God/Terry Eagleton.
       pages   cm
    ISBN 978–0–300–20399–8 (cl: alk. paper)
1. Religion—History.   2. God.   3. Enlightenment.
4. Religion and culture.   I. Title.
    BL98.E24 2014
    200—dc23                                                        2013041989

A catalogue record for this book is available from the British Library.

10 9 8 7 6 5 4 3 2 1

For Denys Turner

# Contents

# PREFACE

THOSE WHO FIND religion boring, irrelevant or offensive need not feel too deterred by my title. This book is less about God than about the crisis occasioned by his apparent disappearance. In pursuit of this subject, it begins with the Enlightenment and ends with the rise of radical Islam and the so-called war on terror. I start by showing how God survived the rationalism of the eighteenth century, and conclude with his dramatic reappearance in our own supposedly faithless age. Among other things, the narrative I have to deliver concerns the fact that atheism is by no means as easy as it looks.

Religion has been one of the most powerful ways of justifying political sovereignty. It would be absurd, to be sure, to reduce it to such a function. If it has provided a craven apology for power, it has also acted from time to time as a thorn in its side. Yet God has played such a vital role in the maintenance of political authority that the waning of his influence in a secular age could not be greeted with equanimity even by many of those who had not the faintest belief in him. From Enlightenment Reason to modernist art, a whole range of phenomena therefore took on the task of providing surrogate forms of transcendence, plugging the gap where God had once been. Part of my argument is that the most resourceful of these proxies was culture, in the broad rather than narrow sense of the term.

All of these stopgaps had other business in hand. They were not just displaced forms of divinity. Religion has not survived simply by assuming a number of cunning disguises, any more than it has been secularised away. Yet despite the fact that art, Reason, culture and so on all had a thriving life of their own, they were also called on from time to time to shoulder this ideological burden, one to which they invariably proved unequal. That none of these viceroys for God turned out to be very plausible is part of my story. The Almighty has proved remarkably difficult to dispose of. Indeed, this is perhaps the most extraordinary aspect of the narrative the book has to tell. Again and again, at least until the advent of postmodernism, what seems like an authentic atheism turns out to be nothing of the kind.

Another recurrent feature of my argument is the capacity of religion to unite theory and practice, elite and populace, spirit and senses, a capacity which culture was never quite able to emulate. This is one of several reasons why religion has proved easily the most tenacious and universal form of popular culture, though you would not suspect so by leafing through a few university cultural studies prospectuses. The word 'religion' crops up in such literature about as often as the sentence 'We must protect the values of a civilised elite from the grubby paws of the populace.' Almost every cultural theorist today passes over in silence some of the most vital beliefs and activities of billions of ordinary men and women, simply because they happen not to be to their personal taste. Most of them are also ardent opponents of prejudice.

## Preface

This book began life as the Firth Lectures of 2012 at the University of Nottingham, and I would like to thank Professor Thomas O'Loughlin, who organised the event, for being such a genial and efficient host. I am also grateful to John and Alison Milbank for their friendship and hospitality during my stay in Nottingham. Peter Dews and Paul Hamilton read the typescript with their customary insight and acuity, and contributed some helpful suggestions.

TE

CHAPTER 1

# THE LIMITS OF ENLIGHTENMENT

SOCIETIES BECOME SECULAR not when they dispense with religion altogether, but when they are no longer especially agitated by it.[1] In a British survey of 2011, 61 per cent of the respondents claimed to have a religion, but only 29 per cent of them claimed to be religious. Presumably they meant that they belonged to a religious group but were not especially zealous about the fact. As the wit remarked, it is when religion starts to interfere with your everyday life that it is time to give it up. In this, it has a certain affinity with alcohol. Another index of secularisation is when religious faith ceases to be vitally at stake in the political sphere, not just when church attendance plummets or Roman Catholics are mysteriously child-less. This need not mean that religion becomes formally privatised, uncoupled from the political state; but even when it is not, it is effectively taken out of public ownership and dwindles to a kind of personal pastime, like breeding gerbils or collecting porcelain, with less and less resonance in the public world. In elegiac mood, Max Weber notes that in the modern era, 'the ultimate and most sublime values have retreated from public life either into the transcendental realm of mystic life or into the brotherliness of direct and personal human relations'.[2] It is as though the kingdom of God gives way to the Bloomsbury Group.

In this sense, religion follows the trajectory of art and sexuality, those other two major constituents of what one might call the symbolic sphere. They, too, tend to pass out of public ownership into private hands as the modern age unfolds. The art which once praised God, flattered a patron, entertained a monarch or celebrated the military exploits of the tribe is now for the most part a question of individual self-expression. Even if it is not confined to a garret, it does not typically conduct its business amidst the bustle of court, church, palace or public square. At the same time, Protestantism finds God in the inmost recesses of the individual life. It is when artists, like bishops, are unlikely to be hanged that we can be sure that modernity has set in. They do not matter enough for that. In England after 1688, the church-and-state settlement was such that religious disputes could be conducted for the most part without fear of political recrimination or loss of personal liberty. Ideas that might prove seditious in Paris could be freely aired in London. Religious fervour would pose no challenge to the foundations of the state. *Pas de zèle* was the watchword. Nor were religious sceptics inclined to act in a treasonable way. Hence the markedly non-militant character of the English Enlightenment, such as it was, which by and large remained comfortably ensconced within the social and political establishment.

Philosophically speaking, its background was empiricist rather than rationalist, Locke rather than Spinoza. It was the radical, semi-underground Enlightenment which would find its inspiration in the latter, while the mainstream culture of the so-called Glorious Revolution took its cue from the former. For a patrician Whig like the Earl of Shaftesbury, the deity was essentially an English gentleman. He was certainly not the curmudgeonly old fanatic worshipped by some ranting seventeenth-century plebeian foaming at the mouth, with what one commentator has dubbed the 'psychopathy of enthusiasm'.[3] 'They give the name of infidel to none but bankrupts,' Voltaire observed of the English.[4] The same shyness of religious ardour exists in England today. One would not expect the Queen's chaplain to inquire whether one had been washed in the blood of the Lamb.

The privatisation of the symbolic sphere is a strictly relative affair, not least if one thinks of the various Victorian contentions over science and religion, the culture industry, the state regulation of sexuality and the like. Today, one of the most glaring refutations of the case that religion has vanished from public life is known as the United States. Late modernity (or postmodernity, if one prefers) takes some of these symbolic practices back into public ownership. This includes religion, which in the form of the various revivalisms and fundamentalisms becomes once more a political force to be reckoned with. The aesthetic, too, is reclaimed from the social margins to extend its influence over daily life. Sexuality also becomes political once more, not least in the shape of the women's movement and the rise of militant sexual minorities. High modernity, by contrast, is marked by a divorce between the symbolic and the politico-economic, one which frees symbolic activities for new possibilities while relegating them to the sidelines. There is thus loss and gain at the same time. If the purity police no longer break down your bedroom door, it is partly because sexuality in an individualist culture is nobody's business but your own.

The eighteenth-century Enlightenment in France, Germany, Holland and elsewhere in continental Europe was certainly agitated by questions of religious faith.[5] As such, it was a continuation by more pacific means of the ferocious sectarian conflicts which had left the Continent torn and bleeding in the preceding centuries. Now, however, it was an issue of faith versus Reason rather than Catholic versus Protestant, a matter of polemics rather than pitched battles. It is a cliché of intellectual history that though the Enlightenment was much preoccupied with science, Nature, Reason, progress and social reconstruction, what lay closest to its heart was the subject which caused it the most rancour and moral outrage, namely religion. Jonathan Israel maintains that the Enlightenment's 'chief preoccupation during its first century and a half, and the theme with which it was most preoccupied in print, was its relentless war on ecclesiastical authority, theological ways of viewing the world, and religion seen as an instrument of social and political organisation and oppression.'[6] Frank Manuel remarks that 'in both their belief and their disbelief, men of the Enlightenment were profoundly agitated by religion as an exploration of human nature.'[7] J. G. Cottingham holds that 'the coherence, as well as the confidence, of the Enlightenment, rested on religious foundations.'[8] All history was the history of secular struggle against a priestly, power-hungry caste. Hegel notes in the *Phenomenology of Mind* that the abiding concern of the Enlightenment is the battle against religion – though he also insists that since religious faith has in any case been reduced to propositional status, as a body of theoretical knowledge or science of the deity, it has grown every bit as impoverished as the rationalism which lays siege to it. We shall be returning to this theme later in the chapter.

In his magisterial account of the radical Enlightenment, Jonathan Israel observes that 'theological debate lay at the heart of the early Enlightenment'. It was, he considers, 'neither science ... nor new geographical discoveries, nor even philosophy as such, but rather the formidable difficulty of reconciling old and new in theological terms, and finally, by the 1740s, the apparent collapse of all efforts to forge a new general synthesis of theology, philosophy, politics, and science, which destabilised religious beliefs and values, causing the wholly unprecedented crisis of faith driving the secularisation of the modern West'.[9] This spiritual crisis, Israel points out, has its roots in a thoroughly material history – the expansion of European commercialism and imperialism in the late seventeenth and early eighteenth centuries, the rapid growth of the great international monopolies, the dislocating effects of diaspora, a new social fluidity and diversity, the impact of new technologies, the partial dissolution of traditional social hierarchies and their accompanying symbolic systems and the like.

The Enlightenment may have been troubled by the question of faith, but it was not especially anti-religious. 'It is doubtful,' writes Ernst Cassirer, '... [that] we can consider the Enlightenment basically as an age irreligious and inimical to religion ... the fundamental objective (especially in the German Enlightenment) is not the dissolution of religion but its "transcendental" justification and foundation.'[10] We should recall that the word 'atheism' did not enter modern European languages until the sixteenth century, and that for some considerable time afterwards it was doubted whether such a position was actually tenable. As Malcolm Bull wryly puts it, 'at the same time that atheism was everywhere denounced, its existence was held to be impossible'.[11] (Despite this, one might point out, the House of Commons in 1666 could cite Thomas Hobbes's atheism as a cause of the fire and plague of London.)[12] Many of the so-called atheists denounced from the pulpit and burnt at the sake were not really godless at all. As Bull notes, it was a century after the term originated that the first indisputable modern atheists arrived on the scene, and it was well into the eighteenth century that the word 'atheism' became commonplace usage. Atheism, he points out, arose well before atheists, rather as the idea of anarchism was invented long before real-life anarchists began to emerge, and as nihilism predated the appearance of nihilists.

It would be curious, then, if the Enlightenment had taken the form of an aggressively secular movement, as some of its modern apologists assume. When it came to religion, a good deal of this audacious intellectual project landed us back on a spot not far from where we were in the first place, furnished with a new, more plausible set of rationales. The task was not so much to topple the Supreme Being as to replace a benighted version of religious faith with one that might grace coffee-house conversation in the Strand. For the most part, it was priestcraft rather than the Almighty that the movement had in its sights.[13] Radical objections to Christianity came to a head in a hostility to the role of the church in politics.[14] Indeed, Peter Harrison claims that the concept of religion as a system of social practices is itself a product of the Enlightenment. Traditionally, and certainly in medieval times, the relevant term was not 'religion' but 'faith'. The very concept of religion as we have it, then, emerges in the context of an institutional inquiry. It is a sociological phenomenon to be scientifically investigated from the outside, as well as to be approached comparatively (the comparative study of religion was central to Enlightenment thought).[15] The very term holds the thing off at judicious arm's length. In this sense, the modern idea of religion, and a rational inquiry into its historical origins and effects, are twinned at birth.

It was religion in this institutional sense that most of the *philosophes* took as their target. It is a familiar fact that there were relatively few outright atheists among their ranks. For it to have been otherwise would be as surprising as if hordes of Europe's premier intellectuals today turned out to be Trotskyists. It is true that there were some rank unbelievers among the intelligentsia. Godwin, Holbach, Helvetius, Diderot, La Mettrie, Montesquieu, Benjamin Franklin and (perhaps) Hume are cases in point. Yet many other thinkers were not so convinced of the vacuity of faith. If the Holbachians saw religion as a mania or contagious pestilence, there were others who insisted on its civic necessity, or even on its benevolence. A spontaneous atheism was typical of the naturalistic social order to which the Enlightenment helped to give birth, but not of the movement itself. As far as the common people were concerned, we are speaking of a world in which almost everyone believed in angels and hardly anyone in atheism. (Fewer, however, believed in witches as the eighteenth century drew on.) A general loss of belief was to follow in the wake of the Enlightenment, but not in the main because of it. Such scepticism has its foundation in social conditions. Modern societies, as we shall see later, are faithless by their very nature. It is the convictions or lack of them embodied in their everyday practices that matter, not what archbishops or militantly secular scientists might argue. Lucien Goldmann claims that the middle class represents for the first time in history 'not merely a class that has generally lost its faith, but rather one whose practice and whose thought, whatever its formal religious belief, are *fundamentally* irreligious in a critical area [i.e. the economy], and totally alien to the category of the sacred'.[16]

As Nietzsche recognised, it was middle-class society itself that, contrary to its own best intentions, succeeded in bringing religion into disrepute. In this respect, science, technology, education, social mobility, market forces and a host of other secularising factors played a more vital role than Montesquieu or Diderot. That this was the case was not generally apparent to the *philosophes* themselves, who tended to attribute the failure of their anti-clerical onslaughts to the vested interests of the clergy and the ignorance of the *canaille*, rather than to the fact that pieties and principles embedded in age-old forms of life are not to be uprooted by a few eloquent polemics. In its campaign against the churches, the Enlightenment could be hampered by its naively rationalist faith that ideas are what men and women live by. It was also thwarted by the fact that the social forces making for secularism were still at an early stage of evolution.

All the same, though ideas do not alter history in isolation, there are few more compelling examples of their social impact than the period in question. As Jonathan Israel writes, 'the trends towards secularisation, tolerance, equality, democracy, individual freedom, and liberty of expression in western Europe and America between 1650 and 1750 were powerfully impelled by "philosophy" and its successful propagation in the political and social sphere'.[17] These ideas, he argues, nurtured a newly insurgent rhetoric intent on arousing the common people against authority and tradition. The Enlightenment was a political culture, not just a set of philosophical texts. The name of the dreaded Spinoza, a byword for socially subversive godlessness, was lauded and detested far beyond scholarly circles. The movement may not have been capable of extirpating religious belief, or even of desiring to do so, but neither was it simply a minor coterie of dissident intellectuals.

The majority of these zealots of Reason still held to some form of religious faith. Newton and Joseph Priestley were Christians, while Locke, Shaftesbury, Voltaire, Tindal, Toland, Paine and Jefferson were Deists. The Scottish Enlightenment was for the most part hostile to both atheism and materialism.[18] Rousseau was a theist, while Gibbon, despite his notorious religious scepticism, held that aspects of religion could prove productive for social life, not least as a bulwark against the likes of the godless Jacobins. He was even rumoured to have returned to the religious fold in his final days.[19] Herder, though a cleric, rejected the idea of a personal God and was a Spinozist of sorts, steering between supernaturalism on the one hand and materialism on the other. Despite this, he considered religion to lie at the very core of a culture.[20] Pierre Bayle, scourge of prejudice, superstition and priestly despotism in his *Historical and Critical Dictionary*, viewed actually existing religion as a species of psychopathy, believing that the 'the terror-stricken savage and the pagan of antiquity were both psychically ill'.[21] Yet he accepted the existence of God. Kant, the greatest *Aufklärer* of all, was no enemy of religion.

The Enlightenment sought to reconstruct morality on a rational basis, but as Alasdair MacIntyre has pointed out, the morality in question remained largely Christian in provenance.[22] John Gray, a doughty critic of Enlightenment thought, remarks that in Nietzsche's view the 'project of unifying all values under the aegis of a rational reconstruction of morality is merely a long shadow cast in the slow eclipse of Christian transcendental [*sic*] faith'.[23]

This rationalist ethics retains the universal, foundational character of Christian moral doctrine, along with its appeal to absolute truth and supreme authority. Nietzsche, as Gray appreciates, held that God had survived his apparent assassination at the hands of secular society. He had gone into hiding under a number of aliases, one of which was morality.

In a similar way, Friedrich Jacobi recognised that the Enlightenment conception of Reason has a prehistory, one which includes elements of the very Christianity it challenges. In our own time, Jürgen Habermas has also claimed that the values of freedom, autonomy, egalitarianism and universal rights derive from the Judaic ethic of justice and the Christian ethic of love.[24] Autonomy may be a cherished modern value, but it is one with a venerable theological pedigree, since God himself is traditionally seen as pure self-determination. The parallel between an autonomous Reason and a self-sufficient deity is already being noted as early as ancient Stoicism. 'Let reason search into external things,' urges Seneca, '... yet let it fall back upon itself. For God also, the all-embracing world and the ruler of the universe, reaches forth into outward things, yet, withdrawing from all sides, returns into himself.'[25]

Gotthold Lessing, along with many another savant, argued for a union of Reason and revelation. The Gospel of the future would be based upon Reason, but was prefigured in grosser, more primitive form by both Old and New Testaments.[26] Despite this, Lessing was a Christian of a kind, and an admirably tolerant one for whom religion was a matter of inner conviction rather than rational demonstrability.[27] A whole range of thinkers preached the virtues of natural religion, of which Christian revelation was simply one somewhat redundant expression. As one commentator wryly remarks, such thinkers are among those who 'believe that Christianity is true precisely to the extent that it is superfluous'.[28] The Deists in particular were reluctant to pay excessive heed to the word of a scruffy, plebeian, first-century Jew in an obscure corner of the earth. J. G. Fichte was to inherit this prejudice. The title of Matthew Tindal's best-known study, *Christianity as Old as Creation*, appears to inflate the claims of Christianity while in fact diminishing them. Christian doctrines are simply one version of certain imperishable human truths accessible to the light of Reason. Edward Herbert of Cherbury believed that the Ten Commandments could be deduced from rational principles.

Polite eighteenth-century circles found such a toothless brand of Christianity far preferable to the sectarian rancour of the previous century – what one seventeenth-century commentator describes as 'the general increase of open libertinism, secret atheism, bold Arminianism, desperate Socinianism, stupid Anabaptism'.[29] The Earl of Shaftesbury put in a plea for what he called 'complacency, sociableness, and good humour in religion', which would hardly be to the taste of Oliver Cromwell.[30] David Hume, probably an atheist or diluted Deist and certainly a full-blooded naturalist, rejected even this thoroughly anthropologised version of religion. He had no such faith in the resources of Reason, maintaining that it is powerless to penetrate metaphysical mysteries.[31] If Reason in Hume's eyes could not come up with a watertight account of the nature of causality, it was unlikely that it could shed much light on the Archangel Gabriel. Knowledge could not extend to the objects of faith, not least because in Hume's view knowledge itself was simply a kind of faith. It was the product of habit and custom. Morality, likewise, was simply a set of human contrivances, with no metaphysical foundation. Hume also upbraided natural religion for assuming that there was a common human nature. In this respect at least, such rationalism was not sceptical enough.

\* \* \*

The Enlightenment's assault on religion, then, was at root a political rather than theological affair. By and large, the project was not to replace the supernatural with the natural, but to oust a barbarous, benighted faith in favour of a rational, civilised one. It was the role of ecclesial power in consecrating the *ancien régimes*, the unholy alliance of throne and altar, which scandalised these scholars most deeply, as the intellectual avatars of an emergent middle class. Some of them were less philosophers in the modern sense of the word than ideologues and intellectual agitators. They were public intellectuals, not cloistered academics. If the version of rationality they promoted could be antiseptic enough, they were admirably fervent in its cause. The impulse which inspired them was as much practical as intellectual. What seized their imagination was the Baconian project of harnessing knowledge and power, placing the findings of scientific reason at the service of social reform and human emancipation. The apostles of Enlightenment could take a lofty enough view of Reason, but their brand of rationality was for the most part pragmatic and mundane. Reason was to be autonomous not in the sense of being quarantined from worldly affairs, but in the sense of being absolved from sinister vested interests. Even epistemology could be pressed into the cause of human welfare. John Locke's doctrine that the mind is originally a *tabula rasa* could be used to banish the spectre of Original Sin, thus countering a view of men and women as innately depraved with a sanguine trust in the power of social engineering to mould them into virtue. What was sin for the Christians was error for the Deists.

All the same, the view that the Enlightenment held a universally positive estimate of humanity, in contrast to the Christian doctrine of moral corruption, is as much a myth as the assumption that it was militantly irreligious. It is true that some of its thinkers could be complacent enough about human corruption. Francis Hutcheson, a Presbyterian clergyman, claims that the human mind reveals a strong bias 'towards a universal goodness, tenderness, humanity, generosity, and contempt of private goods'.[32] Yet Swift and Gibbon would have regarded such a view as sentimentalist fantasy. Henry Fielding seems to hold that when human beings act virtuously, they do so naturally and spontaneously, but that virtue is nonetheless in drastically short supply. It is in our nature to be good, but most of us are unnatural. Immanuel Kant certainly believed in progress, but had no bright-eyed view of his fellow creatures. David Simpson is not far from the mark when he remarks of Kant's writings on history and society that they reveal a pessimism closer to the spirit of Schopenhauer than to that of any other of Kant's successors.[33] In his *Religion within the Limits of Reason Alone*, Kant speaks of the propensity to evil as natural to humanity.[34]

The Deists, with their drawing-room creed of Man as naturally sociable, reasonable, affectionate and good-natured, formed a minority among Enlightenment thinkers, and are mercilessly sent up by Fielding in the figure of Dr Square in *Tom Jones*. Nor were all of these thinkers unequivocally committed to the idea of progress –'this gloomy beacon', as Baudelaire was later to call it, 'licensed without guarantee of Nature or God – this modern lantern [that] throws a stream of darkness upon all the objects of knowledge'.[35] It is, he considered, 'a grotesque idea that has flourished on the rotten ground of modern self-complacency'.[36] It is true that some Enlightenment thinkers were perfectibilists, assured of the inevitability of a future state of bliss. Godwin, Turgot and Condorcet ranked prominently among them. Joseph Priestley held that the final state of humanity would be 'glorious and paradisical', a remarkable belief for one who spent a fair amount of his life in Birmingham.[37] Condorcet, who preached the virtues of universal suffrage, equal rights for women, non-violent political revolution, equal education for all, free speech, the welfare state, colonial emancipation, religious tolerance and the overthrow of despotism, also believed in the infinite perfectibility of humankind.[38] It is one of the choicer ironies of intellectual history that he wrote his great sketch of human utopia while on the run from those practical purveyors of the stuff, the Jacobins. There were those for whom evil was a consequence not of human degeneracy but of the observer's myopia. If only one could view it in a cosmic context, one would recognise its necessity. Writers like Mandeville, Spinoza, Alexander Pope and Adam Smith acknowledged the power of self-interest, but saw it as contributing in the long run to the common good. Theodicy, or the justification of evil, was one current of theological thought which many in the Enlightenment were reluctant to abandon. Whereas Darwinism sees randomness in apparent order, the Enlightenment did the reverse.

Others, however, were less persuaded of human perfectibility, and thus less at loggerheads with orthodox religion. It was not an article of faith to be found among many English thinkers of the eighteenth century. Not all *philosophes* were fetishists of the future. Voltaire regarded history as little but savagery. It was a chronicle of how the rich grew bloated on the blood of the poor. Adam Ferguson had a similarly bleak view of the human saga. Both Holbach and Diderot denied that humanity was inherently improvable. Alexander Pope's *Essay on Man*, with its Leibnizian vision of a beneficent universe, is strikingly untypical of English letters. Jonathan Swift's response to such cosmic Toryism, as it has been aptly called, was to tell Pope that he had not known he was so deep in metaphysics. It was not intended as a compliment. Swift himself has been described with some justice as a rationalist who did not believe in Reason. The same might be said of Sigmund Freud. Samuel Johnson held that history was decaying rather than ascending, and that all change was a great evil. It was England that produced one of the few great tragedies of the period, Samuel Richardson's novel *Clarissa*.

For Hume and Gibbon, civilisation was a fragile phenomenon, besieged by irrational forces and governing passions. The fact that they were both reasonably satisfied with their own civilised circumstances made no particular dent in this anxiety. If ancient Rome had perished, why not modern Europe? Whatever drove the course of history, it was certainly not Reason. Indeed, in Gibbon's view Reason is very often rationalisation, in the Freudian sense of lending a specious air of plausibility to some discreditable motive. In equally gloomy spirit, Kant thought a certain overweening impulse to be inherent in human reasoning.[39] Herder, one of the great founders of nationalism, historicism, culturalism and Romanticism, as well as a prime agent of the linguistic turn in philosophy, saw progress in history but pluralised it. Nations evolved at their own pace in their own distinctive style. There was no uniform, linear improvement. Each *Volk* would pursue self-realisation in its own unique way. Hans Blumenberg suggests that though progress was indeed an Enlightenment value, it became unduly inflated by being forced to inherit something of the function of Christian eschatology. It is as though it was never intended to answer the question of the meaning of history, but came perforce to perform that task.[40]

Most Enlightenment thinkers, as Carl Becker points out in *The Heavenly City of the Eighteenth-Century Philosophers*, failed to break decisively with a religious world-view, lambaste it though they might. 'They put off the fear of God,' Becker comments, 'but maintained a respectful attitude to the Deity.'[41] As his suavely ironic book title suggests, Becker is scarcely an unbiased commentator, and the word of an author who writes of Marxism that 'the stars in their courses, rather than the puny will of man, will bring about a social revolution'[42] is not exactly to be treated as gospel. Even so, he is mischievously alert to the inconsistencies of the *philosophes'* religious views. Some of them, he comments, ridiculed the biblical doctrine of Creation, yet believed that the universe revealed a beautifully articulated design which testified to the presence of a Supreme Being. It is indeed true that some Enlightenment figures turned from God to Nature, only to discover there the signs of an intelligence that turned them back to God again. Critics of religion, Becker points out, dismissed Eden as mythical, but looked back wistfully to a golden age of Roman virtue. Some adhered to an all-powerful, self-founding, self-determining power, but its name was now Reason rather than God. They renounced the sovereignty of church and Scripture, but betrayed a naive trust in the authority of Nature and Reason. They dismantled heaven but looked forward to a perfect human future; spoke up for tolerance but found the sight of a priest hard to stomach; scoffed at miracles but believed in the perfectibility of the human race, and substituted a devotion to humanity for the love of God. They also replaced divine grace with civic virtue. For all their brave talk of hanging the last king in the entrails of the last priest, 'there is more of Christian philosophy in the writings of the Philosophes,' Becker remarks, 'than has yet been dreamt of in our histories.'[43]

There is some truth in all this, as well as a degree of special pleading. Becker's account underplays the boldness and originality of the Enlightenment project, while properly highlighting some of its ideological limits. Because the doctrine of Reason was still in the first flush of youth, it was militant, robust and admirably ambitious; but for just the same reason the established order could prove too redoubtable for it, forcing it to comply with some of its own assumptions. Isaiah Berlin, despite his nervousness of the 'totalitarian' bent of the Enlightenment, strikes the appropriate note of praise when he observes that 'the intellectual power, honesty, lucidity, courage, and disinterested love of truth of the most gifted thinkers of the eighteenth century remains to this day without parallel.'[44] This extraordinary current of thought played its part in revolutionising America and France, as well as in shaping the course of modern history. Its ideologues were capable of stirring both fear and fury in the custodians of the status quo. Yet it was largely the product of a monarchical, mob-fearing intelligentsia who continued to believe for the most part in the providential design of Nature, the value of social hierarchy and the bovine resistance of the common herd to their own speculations.

The Newtonians, for example, formed a patrician culture, one well entrenched at court. In a notable irony, their mechanical theory of the universe could be used to buttress spiritual authority. If matter was, in Newton's phrase, 'brute and stupid', then it could be set in motion only by the divine will. Spiritual forces ruled Nature from above rather as kings and despots governed their states. Descartes, Leibniz and Newton were all champions of the established churches of their nations, and for the most part of monarchy as well. As Margaret Jacob comments, 'the major seventeenth-century proponents of the mechanical world picture were quite willing to see their scientific principles and methodological insights enlisted in the ideological service of strong and authoritarian forms of government and in support of New Testament orthodoxy'.[45] If Spirit and Nature were distinct, then the former was free to exert its sway over the latter. Mechanistic materialism and the imperious will were ideological bedfellows. Materialists such as Spinoza and Diderot, by contrast, argued that if matter was itself dynamic there was no need to posit a transcendence beyond its borders. The radical Enlightenment took its cue from the pantheistic determinism of Spinoza, probably the most reviled philosopher of eighteenth-century Europe. If Nature and Spirit were one, there was no need to imagine an all-powerful will lording it over the material world. Pantheism thus linked arms with political radicalism.

Social background played a part in the Enlightenment's conservatism. Most of its apologists were of high or high-to-middling social rank. Holbach and Montesquieu were barons, Condorcet was a marquis and Condillac an *abbé*. Voltaire sprang from the minor gentry, grew immensely rich and lived like an aristocrat. Helvetius, the son of a millionaire who moved in courtly circles, made a fortune as a tax farmer; Bentham lived off inherited income;

Gibbon was a Member of Parliament and the son of a prosperous landowner. They were, as Peter Gay remarks, 'a solid, respectable class of revolutionaries',[46] who denounced civilisation in the most urbane of tones. Rousseau and Diderot were two of the few figures of modest stock among these noblemen and *haut bourgeois*. The other most notable thinker to hail from the common people was Thomas Jefferson. The contrast with the German Idealist and Romantic thinkers we shall be examining later is sharp: the social provenance of Kant, Schiller, Novalis, Herder, Hegel, Hamann, Fichte, Jacobi, Tieck and Hölderlin is considerably more humble. The readers of the *Encyclopaedia*, the primary document of the French Enlightenment, were for the most part aristocrats, landowners, higher clergy, provincial dignitaries, lawyers, administrators and the like.

There is, to be sure, no simple relation between social class and political outlook. Rather as the English Revolution was in part the work of a progressive wing of the landowning class, some of whose descendants would give voice to the interests of the industrial middle class, so the Enlightenment in France was largely the product of a progressive wing of the nobility and *haute bourgeoisie*, men who spoke up in abstract terms for notions of liberty and equality which others would later take to the streets. Like the English Revolution, however, their project was incomplete. It has been claimed that they represent the point at which, for the first time in Europe, a secular intelligentsia becomes an independent political force.[47] Even so, most of these scions of the ruling order were hardly out to abolish the very popular ideology (religion) which helped to legitimise their power. They wished rather to reconcile religion with a new, secular form of rationality, as well as to detach the whole business of divinity from its role in promoting political autocracy. Or, at least, from those forms of despotism of which they disapproved. Some of them were not averse to hiring themselves out as apologists for rather milder versions of it.

Some of the enlightened intelligentsia hoped to refashion the governing class in their own image; but for a governing class to hold one world-view, while its underlings hold another, is scarcely conducive to political stability. It is imprudent for the rulers to worship Reason while the masses pay homage to the Virgin Mary. There were those, then, who thought it desirable to enlighten the masses as well. The problem with this, however, was that the common people were widely considered to be impervious to Reason. The more radical *Aufklärer* like Paine and Godwin held to the possibility of general enlightenment, but this faith was conspicuously lacking among their more conservative colleagues, some of whom accordingly settled for what has been called the 'double truth' thesis.[48] According to this doctrine, the scepticism of the educated must learn not to unsettle the superstition of the populace. It must be sequestered from the common folk, for fear of the political unrest it might incite. There can be no common ground between the more rational and more barbarous species of religious faith. This was thought true of the relations between eighteenth-century gentlemen and the pagan hordes of antiquity, as it was between these men and their less privileged contemporaries. Others took a less jaundiced view of the past, seeing the prelapsarian Adam and Eve as essentially eighteenth-century rationalists without clothes. Even so, they had spawned down the ages a monstrous progeny of idolaters, crafty clerics, brutal zealots and crazed mystics.

John Toland, despite being portrayed in Irish legend as the bastard offspring of a priest and a prostitute, takes a dim view of the common people in his *Pantheisticon*, urging the need to keep the truths of Reason and the *doxa* of the mob rigorously distinct. There must be one God for the rich and one for the poor. There is a genteel religion of love, justice and the adoration of the Supreme Being, and then there is the benighted, bloodthirsty cult of the priests. Orthodox religion is a matter of primitive terror and a priestly lust for power. Hume is another who insists on the gulf between the reasons for religious faith advanced by the learned and those offered by the ignorant.[49] Even so, the two camps must learn to live cheek by jowl, neither interfering with the other, if the truths of Reason are to be protected from the myths of the populace, and the piety of the people preserved from the subversive truths of Reason. As Charles Taylor observes, 'for [the common people], a little superstition could be a good thing, satisfying their religious impulses without inculcating rebellion'.[50] Thomas Jefferson considered that there could be no republican virtue among the masses without a belief in God, a belief he signally failed to hold himself. One may contrast this divided vision with the republican views of Baruch Spinoza, who held that the common folk labour in delusion but wished to illuminate them. Spinoza believed that the people were educable, that their desires were malleable enough to be remoulded, and that this, rather than the fostering of consoling lies and politically convenient fictions, was the task of the philosopher.

For Toland, by contrast, truth, which in rationalist style is plain and lucid, must darken if it is to preserve itself from the grubby paws of the unlettered. This is one reason among several why Toland's writings are such an extraordinary melange of rationalism and esotericism – why an author whose most renowned work is entitled *Christianity Not Mysterious* also produced a *History of the Druids* and probably belonged to a secret Dutch society known as the Knights of Jubilation. It is a mixture of the hermetic and exoteric which can also be found in Freemasonry. Only a coterie of cognoscenti can be entrusted with the most momentous truths. The freethinker, a title which Toland is said to have invented, thus enjoys something of the privilege of the very clerics he detests.

Condorcet abhorred this intellectual double dealing, though he located it in the benighted past rather than the enlightened present. 'What morality can really be expected,' he asked, 'from a system one of whose principles was that the morality of the people must be founded on false opinions, that enlightened men were right to deceive others provided that they supply them with useful errors, and that they may justifiably keep them in the chains that they themselves knew how to break?'[51] In his view, it was both inevitable and desirable that progressive principles should gradually penetrate 'even into the hovels of . . . slaves, and inspire them with that smouldering indignation which not even constant humiliation and fear can smother in the soul of the oppressed'.[52] This, one might note, is the voice of a movement decried by some postmodern thinkers as a lamentable outbreak of authoritarianism.

Not all of Condorcet's *confrères* endorsed his views. A.O. Lovejoy remarks that 'since the Deists had joined ranks in a war against credulity, they were often involved in a war against the people'.[53] Schiller, who was rattled by the prospect of popular sovereignty, was also deeply pessimistic about the prospect of *Bildung* or spiritual education for the masses. He reacted with scepticism to the outbreak of the French Revolution, and doubted that the populace in their current state were capable of the civic virtue required for a republic. As one commentator astutely remarks, Schiller 'intended his aesthetic education not only to stabilise revolution but to replace it'.[54] Voltaire held that the multitude would always be benighted. It would be impossible to civilise them without subverting the state. Indeed, he doubted whether they were worthy of such a favour in the first place. Swift held much the same opinion.

Reason, then, was supposedly universal, but was incapable of universalising itself even within a single nation. It was an unfathomable source of wisdom, yet the credulous folk were an embarrassing reminder of its fragility. Popular gullibility might help to sustain your rule, but it was also an affront to the values by which you aspired to govern. Even so, though religion might be intellectually offensive, it was a vital source of hope and comfort, and in that sense could prove politically essential. 'The tragedy,' writes Frederick Nietzsche, 'is that we cannot believe the dogmas of religion and metaphysics,' yet continue to 'need the highest means of salvation and consolation.'[55] 'Keep your reasons secret!' he appeals to the so-called 'higher men' in The Joyful Wisdom.[56] There is no point in striving to bring Reason to bear on the masses, who hold their beliefs without reason and whose views are thus immune to being refuted by it. The populace 'ever lieth', and will merely be unsettled by a parade of rational arguments. Better to let them stew in the juice of their ignorance. At least this is likely to stifle dissent. Perhaps the basis of enlightenment for some is enslavement for others, a case which Nietzsche shamelessly advocates. If it takes generations of toil and wretchedness to produce the Übermensch, well and good. Only this magnificent animal can confront the brute absurdity of existence, a horror necessarily hidden from the meaning-craving, metaphysically minded masses. The people would simply perish with the truth, a view that some of Ibsen's spiritual aristocrats were to inherit.

There was, then, a clear dilemma. You could opt for a politically docile populace, whose backward religious views implicitly questioned your own faith in the universality of Reason; or you could plump for a rational-minded citizenry who might confirm your own faith in the scope of Reason, but only at the cost of potential political disaffection. Were the savants to see themselves as a vanguard, safeguarding truths which in time would become available to all, or as an elite, shielding such doctrines from the common herd?

'They courageously discussed atheism,' Carl Becker comments tartly of some Enlightenment thinkers, 'but not before the servants.'[57] Voltaire was notoriously nervous of the effects of his own heterodoxy on his domestic staff. Religion, for him as for many of his colleagues, was a useful device for preserving morality, and to that extent social harmony. The Enlightenment yearned for universal illumination, yet desired nothing of the kind. Diderot, who probably ended up as an atheist, wrote scurrilously that if Jesus had fondled the breasts of the bridesmaids at Cana and caressed the buttocks of St John, Christianity might have spread a spirit of delight instead of a pall of gloom.[58] Yet he supported natural religion on account of its socially unifying effects. Montesquieu, similarly, did not believe in God himself, but considered it prudent that others should do so.

Perhaps the dangers of mass infidelity were exaggerated. Hume considered that religion had much less of an everyday influence than was commonly assumed.[59] He was not prepared to settle for a rational version of Christianity, trusting as he did neither in reason nor in Christianity. In fact, he regarded almost all religion as actively inimical to political virtue, a view also taken by Shaftesbury in his *Inquiry Concerning Virtue*. Virtue must be autonomous, not strategic. Religion corrupted morality by fostering self-interest (fear of punishment, the desire for immortality), as well as by eroding the natural sources of our passion for justice and sense of benevolence. For one commentator, religion in Hume's estimate posed a grave danger to society.[60] Yet he also seems to have held that a moderate, non-superstitious version of it is an aid to political stability. As with many an Enlightenment sage, religion is judged primarily in terms of its utility. It is acceptable only if it promotes the kind of morality one would still endorse without it. This, for Hume, was 'true' religion, which could only ever be that of a cultivated minority, as opposed to what he derided as the sick dreams of the masses. When it came to social utility, Hume's social conservatism trumped his intellectual scepticism. Indeed, he himself acted out a version of the double truth thesis in his everyday life, famously setting aside his subversive anti-foundationalism for the sake of social convention.

Holbach concurred with Hume's low opinion of religion's value as political ideology, observing that it is the hangman rather than the priest who underpins the social order. In any case, he scornfully inquired, who reads the philosophers? Joseph de Maistre also maintained that public order depended in the end on a single figure: the executioner. His Holy Trinity was said to consist of Pope, King and Hangman. Since he held that human beings were evil, aggressive, self-destructive, savagely irrational creatures in need of being terrified into craven submission by an absolute sovereignty, the public executioner played no mean role in his political imagination. He even had a sneaking admiration for the Jacobins' guillotine, believing as he did that all power was divine. With his lauding of instinct, prejudice, war, mystery, absolutism, inequality and superstition, de Maistre is a graphic example of everything the Enlightenment set out to eliminate.[61]

Perhaps society had need of a civic religion, though Gibbon thought that Islam might fill the bill more effectively than Christianity. He, too, considered religion largely in the light of social utility, as a celebrated sentence from his work suggests: 'The various modes of worship which prevailed in the Roman world, were all considered by the people as equally true; by the philosophers, as equally false; and by the magistrates as equally useful.'[62] The more radical of the *philosophes*, by contrast, insisted on a complete divorce of religion and morality, maintaining that an atheistic society might prove more morally admirable than a Christian one. Perhaps a group of atheists could consort more amicably together than a bunch of stiff-necked believers. In the long run, the Enlightenment's fear of a domino effect – that the collapse of religion would topple morality as well, which in turn would fatally undermine political cohesion – was to prove groundless. Belief, whether religious or otherwise, is not what welds liberal capitalist societies together. As Marx points out, the dull compulsion to labour is generally sufficient for that. Religious faith survived into later modernity, and continued to flourish among sectors of the common people. Politically speaking, however, it was reduced often enough to a spot of window dressing for secular governance, more facade than foundation. Its status in this respect was more that of a monarch than a prime minister.

\* \* \*

True to its Baconian bent, the Enlightenment could lay claim to some formidable practical achievements. Quite apart from its incalculable influence on the course of modern civilisation, it had a hand in a range of political revolutions, played a role in the abolition of serfdom and slavery, helped to unseat colonial powers, and through the political economists of the Scottish Enlightenment left an enduring mark on the British polity. Jeremy Bentham's Utilitarianism was to become a cornerstone of the ruling ideology of nineteenth-century England. Enlightened thinking also transformed the public sensibility and filtered down into everyday life. Pub wisdom such as 'Everyone's entitled to their own opinion', 'It'd be a funny world if we all thought the same' or 'It takes all kinds to make a world' (a motto which Ludwig Wittgenstein considered 'a most beautiful and kindly saying') are informal testimony to its influence.

The philosophers themselves were simply illustrious names in a broader maelstrom of ideas. The Enlightenment thrived as an entire culture, and not one confined to polite society. It also harboured a radical underground, with its intellectual capital in The Hague, in which notions of Reason and Nature merged with pantheism, Neoplatonism, hermeticism, Freemasonry, Spinozism, naturalism, millenarianism, republicanism and a host of other heterodox tendencies. As Margaret Jacob writes, 'before there was a High Enlightenment in Europe, there was a Radical Enlightenment.'[63] This turbulent subculture owed more to the egalitarianism of the Diggers than it did to the epistemology of Locke. In Spinozist fashion, it insisted that Nature itself was alive with spirit, as the

Idealists and Romantics were later to do. Thomas Paine's best-selling *The Rights of Man* gives the lie to the assumption that the Enlightenment was the monopoly of scholars and noblemen. It also served to discredit a prejudice we shall be encountering later – that the common people are able to grasp ideas only if they are first converted into iconic or mythological terms.

Something of the distinctive flavour of this revolutionary underworld is captured in the extraordinary career of John Toland, a man who began life as an Irish-speaking shepherd in Donegal and ended up as a potent influence on the European Enlightenment, respected by Leibniz and admired by Voltaire.[64] Toland became a militant Presbyterian in Glasgow, a consort of freethinkers in Leiden, an intellectual bruiser in the coffee-houses of Oxford, a literary hack and habitué of radical circles in London and a protégé in Dublin of Robert Molesworth, patron of the Irish intellectual left. It is also possible that he had an affair with the sister of George I. Bumptious, intemperate and pathologically indiscreet, a champion of Judaism and an apologist for Islam, he probably invented the term 'pantheist' along with the title 'freethinker'. He also dabbled in occultism, reputedly mastered some nine languages and roamed at large in a louche underworld of radical republicans, religious dissidents and shady political operators. Despite posing from time to time as *plus Anglais que les Anglais*, he was a considerable Celtic scholar impressively learned in Irish letters, ancient history and archaeology. Among the Celtic manuscripts on which he worked was one stolen from a Paris library by a defrocked clerical crony. Exile, vagrant, turncoat, picaro, heretic and adventurer, this former Roman Catholic, probably the offspring of an ancient bardic family, urged that sectarian conflict in his native land should be sedulously fostered in the interests of Protestant ascendancy.

Toland lived it up in Berlin at the court of the Electress Sophia, and may have been employed as a secret agent. As a mercurial fantasist or traditional Irish trickster, he glided between a number of identities and allegiances. He admired Milton, Harrington, Giordano Bruno and William of Orange, regarded Moses as a republican and was a passionate Commonwealth man and philosophical materialist. He kept one foot in the world of Whig realpolitik, while the other remained planted in more crepuscular circles. He was also entrusted to carry the Act of Succession to Hanover, thus playing a modest but historic role in securing the British throne for Protestantism.[65]

It was the fate of the Enlightenment to help usher in a civilisation which in its pragmatism, materialism and utilitarianism tended to discredit some of the very exalted ideals which presided over its birth. There can be hymns to Liberty, but hardly to proportional representation. If the history of the middle classes is part comedy and part tragedy, it also betrays a touch of bathos. The critical, rationalist views of the *Aufklärer* involved an abrasive assault on the old order, but they were scarcely the kind of ideas that could easily legitimise a new regime. For that, as we shall see later, there was need for more affective, affirmative values. Rationalism was able to damage the credibility of the clerics, but not to step into their ideological shoes. Hegel found the whole outlook too critical and destructive, marked by a 'colourless, empty' brand of reason which assumed 'a purely negative attitude to belief'.[66] It was a style of thought too thin in emotional and imaginative resources, too shorn of a symbolic dimension, to provide modernity with an assured means of self-legitimation. It could not engage the allegiance of the masses, who were more interested in religious consolation than cosmic harmony. As Cardinal Newman writes of liberalism, 'it is too cold a principle to prevail with the multitude'.[67] The God of the philosophers and the God of the masses were dangerously distinct sorts of being.

It is not true, then, that as one commentator suggests, 'Deism is raising the kind of questions that the common man is likely to ask'.[68] Nobody was likely to sacrifice their lives for such a cerebral creed, as they might at a pinch for the Christian Gospel. The Epistles of St Paul might move them to sobriety and subservience, but hardly the physics of Newton or the theodicy of Leibniz. Johann Georg Hamann, the ne'er-do-well son of a Königsberg bath-keeper, rails with lower-class *ressentiment* against what he sees as the smug, arrogant, over-civilised, typically Gallic form of rationality at work in Enlightenment thought. 'What is this highly praised *reason*,' he sneers, 'with its universality, infallibility, overweeningness, certainty, self-evidence? It is a stuffed dummy which the *howling* superstition of reason has endowed with *divine attributes*.'[69] It is, he maintains with some justice, a form of rationality unable to acknowledge failure, disorder, irregularity or idiosyncrasy. Hamann himself turned from such high-flown discourse to the Pietist faith in which he was reared, disowning all general truths for the irreducibly specific. He would not have been impressed by Francis Bacon's dictum that a little philosophy makes men atheists, while a great deal of it reconciles them to religion. This may have been the case with some Enlightenment savants, as it was with some of the Idealist and Romantic thinkers who followed in their wake. It was not true for the likes of Hamann and Jacobi.

A rational religion, one based on a vision of a universal human nature, could be pressed into the service of political reconciliation, undercutting sectarian squabbling with its few simple, fundamental, imperishable truths. Such a conception harked back to the universalism of the ancient Stoics. It was a matter of sweet reasonableness against raucous dissent. Yet as Bishop Butler complained, such a rational faith dispels the mystery of God with its intolerable mathematical clarity, and thus tends to undermine piety, reverence and humility as well. This is one of several ways in which the gentrification of religious belief could backfire. It was not always in the interests of the governing order for the esoteric truths of religion to be dragged unceremoniously into the light of day, any more than Burke judged it in the interests of political stability to probe pruriently into the traumatic primal scene of civilised society. In Dublin, Bishop Berkeley and his fellow divines, confronted with a permanently disaffected Irish populace, protested in the same vein against those who would strip the decorous drapery from these sublime matters and haul them naked into the public square. To demystify divine truths was also to demystify the authority of those who proclaimed them, as Berkeley and Toland, from their different sides of the Irish theological barricades, were both aware. Plainness and lucidity were qualities of a rational (and thus more plausible) brand of Christianity, but they were also virtues which could spread disquiet among the simple faithful, or be turned against the intimidating mysteries of establishment Christianity by the radical Dissenters.

By the end of the eighteenth century, Enlightenment rationality stood unveiled for many a fearful observer as dark, satanic and pathological, as God himself is thought by some to have a demonic aspect. The Terror in France was enough to discredit the claims of Reason for many a European thinker. An excessive degree of light dazzles and obscures, as Reason goes on the rampage and capsizes into its opposite. A glut of infinity can drive men mad, as Swift was sourly aware. Once Reason cuts loose from the sensuous constraints of the body, it turns on humanity like a lunatic and tears it limb from limb. A rationality unhinged from human fleshliness is a Lear-like form of insanity. Rather as God is portrayed by the Hebrew Bible as a destructive force, burning up all idols and pious illusions with his intolerably unconditional love, so reason can murder and maim with its elegant abstractions. One can kill for all sorts of motives, but killing on a spectacular scale is almost always the consequence of ideas. Enlightenment Reason lacked a body, and so, it was considered, could not feel the sentiments of those it subjugated. As the emphasis shifted from ideas to affections in the trek from Enlightenment rationalist to Romantic artist, it was the body that would become the model of a more sensuous, intuitive sort of rationality, so that the feel of a rose leaf or the odour of woodsmoke was akin in its very immediacy to one's grasp of the Absolute. In this sense, the rational or discursive was bypassed in two directions at once, one cutting below it and the other soaring above it. The body was a form of knowledge, but not of the kind that Holbach or d'Alembert would recognise. One does not need to employ a map or pocket compass to know where one's left foot is located.

If the Enlightenment was never a question of the death of God, neither was it a matter of culture. In its universalism and cosmopolitanism, it paid too little heed to the fact that local customs, pieties and affections are the places where power must embed itself if it is to flourish. Otherwise, it will prove too abstract and remote to be assured of its subjects' allegiance. There can be no effective sovereignty without a foundation in lived experience, which is one reason why Reason feels the need for a kind of supplement or prosthesis known as the aesthetic. For the most part, Enlightenment Reason lacked a corporeal presence, which the German Idealists and Romantics would seek to restore.

In the meanwhile, however, it could act as a plausible deputy for an increasingly absentee God, one who was every bit as bodiless as itself. Just as we cannot ask where the Almighty comes from, so for a certain vein of rationalism we cannot raise questions about the provenance of Reason.[70] Reason on this view does not have a history, as it does for Herder and Hegel. Indeed, we would need to appeal to Reason to judge the validity of our conclusions about its nature and origin, and would thus stand convicted of a *petitio principii*, presupposing what we were out to prove. God, truth and Reason would all appear to be bottom-line or end-stopping terms, impossible by definition to delve beneath. It is for this reason that, in his polemic against rationalism, Friedrich Jacobi, for whom Reason did indeed have a history, argues for a distinction between knowledge and truth, insisting that there is something epistemologically primitive and irreducible about the latter. 'I understand by "the true", he writes, 'something which is prior to and outside knowledge; that which first gives a value to knowledge and to the faculty of knowledge, to reason.'[71] Reason cannot demonstrate the very truth it is bound to presuppose.

The God of Scripture has the distinct advantage of being in some sense personal, whereas Reason is distinctly un-godlike in its impersonal hauteur. As Edmund Burke suggests of our attitude to the law, we may revere such an authority, but it is hard to love it. Reason cannot offer us ecstatic fulfilment, a sense of community or wipe away the tears of those who mourn. In nineteenth-century England, Utilitarianism and scientific rationalism would thus need to be supplemented by some less emotionally anaemic creed, one which lay near to hand in the legacies of Idealism and Romanticism. Many a thinker, from Carlyle to T.S. Eliot, would turn back to the ancient or medieval past for resources to refurbish the present. As Fredric Jameson comments, the capitalist system reveals 'an urgent need to reinvent older forms of coding to supplement its impoverished structures'.[72]

When human reasoning becomes autonomous, it approaches divine status; but a rationalised world is also one in which God's presence gradually dwindles, so that he grows remote from rationality and becomes accessible only through faith and feeling. In this sense, the other face of rationalism is fideism. A rigorously rational world, one able to operate without the intervention of the Almighty, gives rise, ironically, to an arbitrary and irrational God. The more translucent reality becomes, the more impenetrable its Creator comes to appear. To banish him to the periphery of his own cosmos is to treat him as largely dispensable, but also to deepen his mystery. Reason extended too far can thus end up undoing itself. As with Pascal, a darkly unfathomable God is an ominous reminder of the limits of rationality. We are also reminded of those limits by the fact that when rationality becomes for the most part instrumental, a matter of calculation and cause and effect, it risks emptying social existence of meaning and value. As such, it can provide it with no plausible justification. Society is accordingly divided between a mode of calculative or pragmatic reasoning which reflects what its members actually do but fails to validate it in any more edifying terms, and a form of belief, religious or otherwise, which might offer such legitimacy but which increasingly fails to reflect men and women's actual behaviour. It is because Reason is no longer able to link fact and value, as an older version of it aspired to do, that this dilemma arises.

The problem is that any effective ideology must accomplish both tasks at once. In order to be credible, and thus to win general consent, it must be rooted in what men and women actually do; but in a society driven by appetite and self-interest it is therefore in danger of reflecting all the most disreputable kinds of value, and thus of failing to legitimise the social order. Perhaps religion in a rationalised society can survive by reflecting the reified logic of everyday life, as in the Enlightenment's 'natural' or 'rational' religion. It does so, however, only at the risk of depleting its own symbolic resources. Alternatively, it can retreat into *Schwärmerei* or fanaticism, cults of sentiment and the beautiful soul, mystical ravings, anodyne dreams of universal benevolence or plunge into the abyssal depths of the self.[73] If religion chooses this path, it preserves its symbolic resources, but must accept that they have less and less bearing on social existence as a whole. In the modern period, art is plagued by a similar dilemma.

Some Enlightenment thinkers reduced the God of Abraham to a rational abstraction, while others like Kant thrust him beyond the bounds of reason and the senses into the trackless spaces of the sublime. Either way, there is an ideological problem. To treat the deity as a rational entity is to salvage him from superstition only at the cost of banishing him from the realm of the sensible altogether. As a Newtonian kind of deity, his presence may be discerned in the miraculous design of the cosmos, as well as in the providential march of history; but it is not to be found in the secret recesses of subjectivity, as Pietists like Hamann and Jacobi complain. Yet if God transcends Reason rather than finding himself reduced to it, a problem of a different kind arises. The Almighty's decrees remain absolute, but his remoteness from humanity renders them less and less intelligible. We are now expected to obey him not because his commands make some rational or experiential sense, but because they are, when all is said and done, his commands. Like the rules of a game, they combine their absoluteness with a certain arbitrariness, hence inflicting the worst of both worlds on those who seek to conform to them. God's decrees, like the moral law as Kant first conceived it or the Reason of the rationalists, become entirely self-legitimising. It is, to be sure, part of Christian doctrine that God is a law unto himself, but this is not an autonomy which is meant to estrange him from his creatures. On the contrary, their own power of self-determination is one of the ways in which they are most akin to him. Their dependence upon him takes the form of personal freedom.

Rationalised societies tend not only to impoverish their symbolic resources, but to pathologise them as well. If a religion grounded in Reason is tepid, one without such a grounding tends to be torrid. The former risks weakening its authority, while the latter may stir a dangerously anarchic 'enthusiasm' among the masses. 'God is pure, unlimited, free Feeling,' gushes Ludwig Feuerbach,[74] but politically speaking such feelings can be hard to control. Louis Dupré claims that religion can be seen either as explanation or experience; but whereas the scientific rationality of the Enlightenment threatens to strike the former superfluous, it tends equally to undermine the credibility of the latter.[75] You can either rationalise religion, as in some of Fichte's more audacious writings,[76] or expel it from the sphere of Reason altogether, as in the various currents of fideism; but the former is unlikely to gratify the masses, and the latter is unlikely to satisfy the elite. Rational propositions are poor ways of inciting men and women to virtue, while faith as inner sentiment smacks of the intellectually disreputable. Either way, the ideological power of religion is undermined. It is a Hobson's choice between Socinianism and Pietism, John Locke and John Wesley.

One can, to be sure, combine religion as explanation with religion as experience, as Samuel Johnson, one of the greatest of all English *Aufklärer*, did to some extent. So in a different way did Shaftesbury before him, with his coupling of a Neoplatonic vision of order with an immediacy of moral sentiment. In Shaftesbury's view, all moral action must be mediated through the affections, and what is not thus mediated is simply non-moral.[77] Yet his Neoplatonism, with its absolute law of Reason, was enough to guard his case against mere sentimentalism. As one commentator remarks, 'virtue [for Shaftesbury] required an interior motion or affection and, ultimately, a rational recognition of the good'.[78] In general, however, explanation and experience were becoming harder to reconcile. A rift was opening up between religion as rational totality and religion as inward vision – or, in philosophical terms, between Hegel and Kierkegaard. The latter, for whom Christian faith is scandal, folly and sheer rational impossibility, an affront to all civilised mores and gentrified reason, is one of the greatest of all scourges of Enlightenment thought.

Friedrich Jacobi recognises that the two camps, rational and experiential, are for the most part speaking past each other. In his view, the Enlightenment's abstract conception of God can teach the believer nothing. The human subject of the Enlightenment is simply not the kind of creature who could be significantly addressed by the God of Abraham, or who could conceivably have faith in him. Only a subject who was rather more than a thinking substance or point of pure consciousness could do that. The God of the *philosophes* is the kind of rational construct that such an eviscerated subject could indeed believe in, and so much the worse for him. As Max Horkheimer and Theodor Adorno write in *Dialectic of Enlightenment*, the reified thought of scientific rationalism cannot even pose the question of the existence of God.[79] Or, at least, it can pose it only in the same way that one can inquire after the existence of the Yeti or the Loch Ness monster. By and large, faith for the Enlightenment meant subscribing to a proposition despite the fact that it could not be rationally demonstrated, which is not at all what the word signifies for Judaism, Islam or Christianity. The passionate, needy, vulnerable subject of Romanticism, by contrast, is a being capable of faith in the authentic sense of the term; but by this time the process of secularisation has done its work, so that as the subject of faith re-emerges, the God of Abraham and Jesus gradually fades from view.

To sever religion from Reason is to render it immune to rational criticism. Since such a faith is scarcely propositional at all, it is not the kind of phenomenon to which judgements of truth and falsehood could apply. If religion is feeling, as it is for Rousseau and Schleiermacher, passionate inward conviction, as it is for Lessing, Hamann and Kierkegaard, or essentially a form of symbolic practice, as it is for Emile Durkheim, it is hard to see how it can be argued against, any more than one can argue against arthritis or a hurricane. Yet that this is so is not wholly to its advantage. Conviction or experience is likely to be valued in an individualist society which prizes such interiority, but it can scarcely provide the kind of common foundation which religious faith needs if it is to be ideologically effective. It is too close to the vagaries of taste to secure a social consensus. What one would need is an equivalent of Kant's aesthetic judgements, which are both subjective and universal, a question of personal assent but also of universal agreement.

It is true that feeling and fellowship can also be linked. If religion is primarily a matter of the heart, as it is for the likes of Jacobi and Jean-Jacques Rousseau, then these simple, universal, spontaneous feelings are more likely to bring individuals together than a set of abstruse truths. The more one casts these affections into conceptual terms, the more divisive they threaten to become. By contrast, the natural religion of love and benevolence of Rousseau's Savoyard vicar can be shared by both untutored peasant and urbane scholar. Yet this cannot make up for the fact that the affections in themselves are too fragile a foundation for social cohesion. They are a necessary but not sufficient condition of political unity. For that one also requires articulate belief, which mediates between the affective and the cognitive.

In one sense, feeling is the most incontrovertible of grounds, while in another sense it is a notoriously slippery one. To base morality in the body is to lend it as firm a foundation as one might wish, leading thinkers like Francis Hutcheson to feel as repelled by a vicious action as they would by a foul stench. A feeling-based faith has something of the sureness and immediacy of the body, and as such is a good deal more dependable than ideas. Laurence Sterne recommends virtue as a kind of spiritual tonic which purges the system, leaving you both cheerful and prosperous.[80] The Man of Feeling finds in Sterne's phrase a 'glorious lust' in doing good, so that virtuous behaviour comes to resemble nothing quite so much as chewing a leg of roast chicken or downing a fine glass of port. It is a far cry from Kant. In the blithe Hellenism of a newly self-satisfied middle class, at ease in the coffee-houses of eighteenth-century England, charity and clubbability, the benevolist and the bon viveur, are becoming hard to tell apart. For a moralist like Hutcheson, the good and the sensuous are closely interwoven: benevolence is a kind of bodily pleasure, in which one savours the moral delectability of others as one might smack one's lips over a succulent dish of prawns. It is not for nothing that Hutcheson, for whom virtue is in a sense comedy, wrote a treatise on laughter, not the most popular of literary forms among Ulster Protestants.[81] It even contains some tolerably good jokes.

Yet in an empiricist world, bodily experience is irredeemably private, which is not how religion or morality will best serve the cause of political consensus. Religious belief is not to be stripped to private sentiment, not least in a fragmented civilisation in pressing need of some stouter social bonds. The passionate devotion of a Kierkegaard will have no truck with such suburban matters as social mores or political stability. The inwardness of Protestant faith reflects an individualist society, but it also disdains the abstractions upon which such an order depends. Faith as private experience is too closely allied with a politically disruptive individualism for which the self is purely autonomous. It was one of the .errors of some Enlightenment thought to view human dependency as a defect, and some Idealist thought will repeat the error. In a tirade against Fichte's Idealism, Friedrich Jacobi rejects the autonomy of the self as sheer pride, countering it with what he calls the dependency of love. 'Transcendental philosophy,' he announces, 'shall not wrest this heart from my breast and put a pure drive for *selfhood alone* in its place.'[82] If the highest condition that philosophy can imagine is that pure, naked, empty thing it calls the self, then, so Jacobi declares, it ought to curse its own existence.

Benevolism and sentimentalism were useful correctives to an arid ethical rationalism. Yet the cult of sentiment, in purging religion of its more rebarbative dogmas, threatened at the same time to eviscerate it, and in doing so to lessen its ideological force. In the eighteenth century's own aesthetic idiom, it was too beautiful and too little sublime. It lacked the sanctions, taboos and superegoic sadism associated with sublimity, which religion jettisoned at its political cost. As Edmund Burke recognised, we must seek to love the Law, but we also take a masochistic delight in being terrorised by it.

Moral rationalists like Richard Price were dismayed by this aestheticising of ethics. 'Our ideas of morality, if this account is right,' he complains of the benevolists and sentimentalists, 'have the same origin with our ideas of the sensible qualities of bodies, the harmony of sounds, or the beauties of painting and sculpture ... Virtue (as those who embrace this scheme say) is an affair of taste.'[83] The kind of morality Price has in his sights can stir men and women to action, but it is perilously reliant on sentiment, intuition or moral sense. By contrast, a morality based on Reason is solidly founded, but lacks the power to motivate. Hume famously denies that Reason can furnish a source of motivation. Indeed, the more you ground morality in Reason, the more it may rob you of initiative. If the moral order is divinely manufactured, built into the mighty design of the cosmos itself, it is likely to appear as deterministic as the laws of gravity, and thus as indifferent to the individual will. One is accordingly in danger of being caught between what Seamus Deane has called the 'smiling lunacies of the Man of Reason and the sodden effusions of the Man of Feeling'.[84]

Eighteenth-century moral rationalists such as Samuel Clarke and William Wollaston hold that the good must be grounded in a Reason independent of sentiment, if the vital domain of morality is to be insulated from the vagaries of subjectivism. Yet these thinkers, so the empiricists, sentimentalists and 'moral sense' theorists riposte, are unable to say why it is good to obey the dictates of Reason in the first place. As such, their case is simply question-begging. If Reason does not already include an idea of the good, in the manner of Plato or Aquinas, there is a problem about why one should commend it. A purely technical rationality can have nothing to say about questions of value. Francis Hutcheson holds that you cannot give a rational justification for accepting a moral viewpoint. The moral sense must be prior to reasoning, a kind of Heideggerian pre-understanding which we are unable to think ourselves behind, a capacity which must always already be in place if a piece of language is to count as a moral argument in the first place.[85] Moreover, if Reason signifies the rational design of the universe, then there is no compelling argument as to why one should obey it in the sense of living in conformity with this order, as Friedrich Nietzsche was later to point out.

Secular social orders thus have a problem with their moral rationales. As the rationalising process comes to infiltrate the cultural and religious spheres, as with the mechanistic world of

Deism or the legalistic nature of some Protestant doctrine, these realms become less hospitable to questions of fundamental value, and thus less capable of underpinning political power. Yet if they play no part in this process, they are in danger of losing all public significance. Religion is either too mundane or too otherworldly, too complicit with the logic of this world or too aloof from it. God is either too immanent, as with Spinoza, or too ineffably transcendent, as with Kant. He is either absorbed into Nature or History or expelled beyond the frontiers of Reason. The inner tension of orthodox Christianity – that the kingdom of God is both present and absent, immanent in human history yet a form of transcendence still to come – is fatally relaxed. It will be left to the German Idealists to repair this disabling duality.

# CHAPTER 2

# IDEALISTS

THE HISTORY OF the modern age is among other things the search for a viceroy for God. Reason, Nature, *Geist*, culture, art, the sublime, the nation, the state, science, humanity, Being, Society, the Other, desire, the life force and personal relations: all of these have acted from time to time as forms of displaced divinity.[1] 'It is certain that in our time,' writes Fredric Jameson, 'religion is so vague and tenuous a discursive field that its vocabulary can itself be appropriated by other causes.'[2] If the religious spirit of modernity can indeed be vague, it is among other things because a diluted brand of faith is more to the taste of a sceptical age than a doctrinal one. Suitably degutted of its dogma, it is then easily wedded with secular modes of thought, and as such can fill ideological gaps and offer spiritual solutions more persuasively than orthodox religion itself.

Alain Badiou, perhaps the most eminent philosopher of our time, fervently embraces the death of God, but refuses to give up on the ideas of infinity and the void, both of which have a theological pedigree. 'The death of God,' as Peter Hallward comments of Badiou's work, 'implies ... the rigorous affirmation of our *own* infinity.'[3] It is hard to see how this, as it stands, differs from the nineteenth-century Religion of Humanity, a school of thought we shall be glancing at later. In Badiou's judgement, it is hermeneutics, with its passion for sense-making, which has tried to fill the shoes of divinity, since religion in his view is essentially a desire to invest reality with a degree of meaning.

The modern age, then, has been heedless of the warning not to make graven images of the godhead. None of the divine deputies it has come up with, needless to say, is reducible to that role. They are all phenomena in their own right, not simply a locum tenens or camouflaged version of something else. Yet religion has played such a key ideological role in human history that once it begins to fall into disrepute, that function cannot simply be abandoned. Instead, it must be taken over by various secular styles of thought, which then unwittingly help to keep divinity alive in a more clandestine way.

'Theology has been so long a queen,' remarks a character in Iris Murdoch's novel *The Time of the Angels*, 'she thinks she can still rule as a queen in disguise.' Some would even detect a form of ersatz religion in psychoanalysis, with its high priests, rituals of confession, consciousness of Original Sin, ontological guilt, numinous Law, sectarian schisms and quasi-theological probings into the sublimely unfathomable unconscious. Walter Benjamin found a suitably profane version of religious experience in Surrealism, judiciously mixed with a little hashish. Our own era has been a trifle less high-minded in its pursuit of second-hand gods. The contemporary version of religion is sport. It is sport, with its sacred icons, revered traditions, symbolic solidarities, liturgical assemblies and pantheon of heroes, which is the opium of the people. It is also the culture of the people, in both major senses of the word: a communal form of life, but also a chance to display or appreciate the kind of artistry from which the mass of citizens are otherwise largely excluded.

Perhaps the most successful understudy for a discredited deity has been the idea of culture. We shall be examining this topic in a later chapter. In the meantime, however, we may turn our attention to the German Idealist philosophers, who retain all the universal scope and totalising drive of the Enlightenment, along with its search for sturdy foundations, but who put Spirit in place of Reason as the mainspring of human history. This synoptic vision of science, art, Nature, history and politics represents one of the most astonishing intellectual syntheses of the modern era, shot through with the buoyancy and elan of a revolutionary age. Somewhere in its obscure depths, a number of motifs which will become staples of modern thought can already be felt germinating.[4] Nicholas Boyle writes of German philosophy in this period as 'the principal form of secularised theology'. The German university, he comments, 'gave birth to systematic idealist philosophy as a secular, state-centred substitute for religion'.[5]

Poised on the threshold of the industrial-capitalist age, Idealist thought finds itself cusped between traditional Christian doctrine and the creeping secularisation of the modern era. As Andrew Bowie writes, 'the need for such a system [of Idealism] results from the awareness that the decline of religion creates a deficit that must be overcome if a new place for humankind in the order of things is to be rationally negotiated'.[6] 'Hegel,' remarks Jürgen Habermas, 'completed the philosophical appropriation of the Judeo-Christian tradition as much as was possible under the conditions of metaphysical thinking.'[7] Transcendence is now, so to speak, more horizontal than vertical – more a question of a history which is perpetually in excess of itself, en route to some future *pleroma* or state of fulfilment, than of a God who lies in the silent spaces beyond his own universe.

Whereas some Enlightenment savants sought to reconcile Reason and revelation, the Idealists and Romantics are in pursuit of a natural supernaturalism, to borrow the title of a classic study of the period.[8] Both projects involve a rewriting of religious faith in secular terms. It is not hard, for example, to see Spirit as a surrogate for God, and this in a fairly exact sense. Spirit, or freedom, is the foundation of the world, but it cannot be reckoned up within it or captured in a graven image; and although it lies at the source of the self, it is also infinitely transcendent of it. For a range of thinkers from Herder to Hölderlin, rationalism is in danger of bleaching the world of inherent value. The problem is how to restore that value without excessive recourse to the very religious notions that rationalism itself is busily undermining. The Enlightenment's turn to the sciences and natural philosophy has left its mark, not least on the *Naturphilosophie* of Friedrich Schelling. One must avoid mechanical materialism, but not at the price of a false transcendence. *Geist* must be rescued from both, and in the form of intersubjectivity installed, as with Hegel, as the prime mover of human history. Since eternity is in love with the products of time, it is of the nature of transcendence to be immanent. There is no ultimate conflict between Spirit and Nature, as there is no contradiction between the Father who is Spirit and the Son who is flesh and blood. If the mind can remake reality from the ground up, a capability sensationally manifested by the French Revolution, it is because the world is secretly made up of its own stuff.

One problem for Enlightenment thinkers is how this lordship of the mind over Nature was not to leave Man estranged from reality at the very apex of his sovereignty over it, monarch of a lifeless cosmos incapable of conversing with him and thus of confirming his centrality. What meaning it possessed was simply what he himself had invested in it, and to glimpse nothing but your own visage wherever you turn is a kind of madness. To pass money from one of your hands to another does not constitute a financial transaction, as Wittgenstein reminds us. The consequence of power is thus an implosion of the self. This absolute ruler becomes in Kierkegaardian phrase 'a king without a country, [who] really rules over nothing'.[9] This need not be so, however, if Nature itself is alive with vital forces, as it is for Hegel and Schelling. The mind can then turn to reality without fear of being annulled by it. The world becomes active enough to strike up a fruitful dialogue with humanity. Schelling believed that Nature must be converted from an It to a Thou, transformed from an object to a subject.[10]

Men and women may accordingly feel anchored in the world without finding their autonomy undercut. Freedom is simply the distinctive way in which they participate in this magnificently self-moving whole. They represent that outcropping of it where it has become conscious of itself, and can therefore share in its inner life through the dignity of a free decision, as daisies and earthworms cannot. The rifts which Kant has introduced into our existence may thus be repaired. We can nestle in the bosom of Nature without fear of being locked into some soulless determinism, assured that the self is securely founded – but founded on a principle which is the very essence of liberty, and thus with no detriment to our flourishing as free agents.

Like much Idealist and Romantic thought, this is a covertly theological vision. For orthodox Christianity, God is the ground of all being, the condition of possibility of anything at all, so that to fall out of his hands would be to fall out of existence. Yet since he is unconditional freedom, humanity's dependence on him, which is what is meant by its createdness, is what allows it to be fully itself. God is the source of human freedom and autonomy, not what suppresses them. It is through the dependency of grace that men and women achieve their self-determination, as they do through their dependency on language and culture. The Enlightenment was aware of this paradox in its own way. God was the author of both Nature and Reason, but he had fashioned them so as to be self-determining. In this sense, at least, the sacred and the secular were not at loggerheads. If the autonomy of the universe springs from its sharing in the life of its Creator, faith is no enemy of science.

The problem, not least for some Romantic thinkers, is that if there is indeed a foundation beneath our feet, it is hard for us to have any exact knowledge of it. It would seem more a matter of faith than cognition. As with the Almighty, there is a ground to our subjectivity which cannot be represented there – one which is closer to us than breathing, yet which must necessarily elude our conceptual grasp if we are to function as self-governing subjects. In this sense, the absence of God is not a deficiency to be regretted, but what makes us the free agents we are. We can, to be sure, seek to turn back on ourselves to steal a glimpse of whatever it is that puts us in place, haul ourselves up by our bootstraps so as to see ourselves from some vantage-point beyond subjectivity itself. But all we will find is yet more subjectivity. If the principle of being is itself a subjective one, there can be no peering behind it to see what it, in turn, might be resting on, since we would remain within the frame of subjectivity in the act of doing so. We cannot think ourselves outside thought. No doubt this is what Schelling has in mind when he comments that 'self-consciousness is the source of light for the entire system of knowledge, but it shines only forward, not backward'.[11]

Like the turtles on which the world supposedly stands, then, subjectivity goes all the way down. It also goes all the way back. In this sense, not least with Fichte, the subject is transcendent in much the same way that God is traditionally thought to be. God cannot be included in his own cosmos, any more than the eye can figure as an object in its own field of vision without the aid of a reflection. He cannot be reckoned up alongside created things, since it is he who brought them into existence in the first place. He is not an item either inside or outside the universe. In a similar way, the whole of reality now has its origin, goal and *raison d'être* in this enigmatic non-entity, the subject; but the subject itself would seem eternally exiled from that reality, and as such appears to lapse out of existence. As soon as we try to close our fist over this mercurial stuff, it gives us the slip. What makes the subject so remarkable – the fact that in godlike fashion it is eternally prior to the world it generates – is also a kind of lack. Banished from the phenomenal world, it can be known only as an eloquent silence at the heart of it. To reckon subject and object up together would be as much a category mistake as to imagine that God and the universe make two. The source of all knowledge cannot itself be known. There are limits to our self-reflexivity. We are dealing with a theology of the subject, not simply a philosophy of it.

So it is that freedom, or subjectivity, is one of the myriad secular names for God. 'Freedom,' writes Schelling, 'is the one-principle upon which everything is supported.'[12] It can meet with no material obstacles in the long run, since the material world is secretly its own product. Being, as Schelling sanguinely remarks, is simply 'freedom suspended'. Yet if the ground of being is pure freedom, the faintest attempt to conceptualise it risks being self-defeating. To objectify this point of pure self-determination, this mercurial thing sprung perpetually from its own loins which is no thing at all but sheer act or process, would be to risk striking it dead in the very moment of cognition. Like the unconscious for Freud, Spirit must fall outside the purview of human consciousness if that consciousness is to perform its proper work. 'The unground of eternity,' writes Schelling, 'lies this close in every person, and they are horrified by it if it is brought to their consciousness.'[13] There is a smack of the Lacanian Real about this concealed horror, as well as of the fearful void of the sublime. For Fichte, Schlegel and Schleiermacher, there can be no conceptual knowledge of this ground because pure freedom is sheer vacancy or negativity, which means that there is no object to be known. In a similar way, God cannot be known for Judaeo-Christian theology – not simply because our minds are too feeble to comprehend such an exalted entity, but because he is no kind of entity in the first place.

The most vital principle of middle-class civilisation, freedom, is thus at risk of being struck alarmingly indeterminate. The subject would seem an elusive spectre which is gone as soon as we give it a name. We are constituted by what must necessarily remain opaque to us. It is true that though the Absolute may not be within reach of common reasoning, it can yield itself up *à la* Hegel to dialectical thought. It can also be known in practice (Fichte) or prove accessible to intuition (Schelling) in a way that reflects the immediacy of

God's own knowledge of things. There are also those thinkers for whom its presence can be felt in the very act of trying unavailingly to pin it down. Even so, the elusiveness of this principle is a cause for disquiet. If the subject is now raised up to infinite status, harbouring within its breast a boundless energy, one might equally claim (since infinity is sheer negativity) that there is a terrifying nothingness at its core. There is no end to its self-expression; but it is precisely for this reason that it cannot signify itself as such in any of its individual works. Infinity is both our triumph and our undoing. Subjectivity, like the divinity whose place it is now stealthily usurping, is an unfathomable abyss, a thought which is as alarming as it is exhilarating. In what sense can an abyss serve as a foundation?

If the subject is proving so difficult to snapshot, it is largely because there is a form of subjectivity abroad which threatens to break the bounds of traditional thought in its unsearchable depths, perpetual motion, infinite will and dynamic self-fashioning. Very little, to be sure, is ever entirely new, and this conception of humanity has a distinguished pedigree; yet it is not the kind of entity that Voltaire or James Boswell would readily have recognised. How do you form a concept of something so volatile? This desirous, entrepreneurial, eternally driven creature is born of a social order in which system and transgression are becoming hard to tell apart. There is now a form of productivity abroad which is potentially endless, an unstaunchable energy or 'bad' sublimity which is the enemy of all symmetry and proportion, and which threatens to rebuff all stable representation.[14] The entrepreneurial subject needs certain settled forms – of law, politics, culture and so on – if it is to thrive. The problem is that its own restless dynamism threatens constantly to overturn them. Civilisation is thus pitched into a crisis from which Idealist thought seeks to rescue it.

It is Hegel, above all, who attempts this task. In his view, Spirit can be captured and contained in a complete system, one furnished with the stoutest of foundations. There is, as we have seen, something at the very heart of conceptual systems – subjectivity – which offers to give them the slip. They are threatened with dissolution by the very principle they seek to explicate. The triumph of Hegel and some of his colleagues is to discover an absolute foundation in (of all things!) this most mercurial of phenomena – to find in the immediate presence of the subject to itself, the absolute identity of subject and object, or the fact that subjectivity is a ground beneath which we cannot delve, the axis on which the whole world can be seen to turn.

\* \* \*

If the subject resists the concept, then it might always lend itself to the image instead. Perhaps it is only with the advent of Romanticism ('spilt religion', as the neo-classicist T.E. Hulme scornfully dubbed it) that the treasure house of imagery known as art truly begins to rival religious faith.[15] Even so, Idealism prepares the way. Hegel may rank art lower than philosophy, but Schelling hails it as the 'exemplary public form of philosophical consciousness'.[16] In his view, art blends the will with spontaneity, the conscious mind with the unconscious. As such, it offers a precious insight into the very ground of our being, namely the unconscious process of self-productivity which is Nature as a whole. The human subject is a form of self-conscious production; but this self-fashioning is also its way of participating in the world's perpetual conjuring of itself into existence, in accordance with its own mighty laws. Subject and object, culture and Nature, freedom and necessity, can thus be harmonised. It is the function of the work of art to cast Nature's self-productivity in palpable form, and in doing so to permit us a rare insight into the intelligibility of that process. 'The objective world,' Schelling writes, 'is simply . . . the unconscious poetry of the spirit; the universal organon of philosophy – and the keystone of its entire arch – is *the philosophy of art*.'[17] It is art that gives us access to the inner workings of reality, providing us with knowledge of the Absolute in a way that the concept, at least in Schelling's view, cannot. Art, he remarks in his *System of Transcendental Idealism*, represents an intuition that has become objective. An eternal idea of Reason manifests itself in this humble piece of matter, rather as the spiritual Father is incarnate in the corporeal Son.

We need not, then, abandon all attempts to take this shy creature, the subject, into captivity. For Schelling, art is our privileged mode of access to the slippery non-thing known as subjectivity. For Fichte, too, the subject can be known, but only if one conceives of it as a practice rather than an object. Many a philosophical problem starts to dissolve once one begins from the subject as an agent, rather than as a source of contemplation or passive receptacle of sense data. The subject for Fichte is that peculiar creature that knows itself in the act of positing itself. Its being and self-knowledge are thus identical.

So sovereign is the Fichtean subject that the material world, being secretly its own creation, can put up no genuine resistance to its designs. The self's infinite striving, a desire which knows no inherent closure, is the condition of possibility of any reality whatsoever. 'No striving, no object' is Fichte's slogan. 'Only to the extent that anything is related to the practical faculty of the self,' he writes,' does [it] have an independent existence.'[18] In an infantile fantasy of omnipotence, there can be no authentic otherness. Even so, this all-privileged subject must stoop to conquer. Only by setting limits to itself, falling into finitude by conjuring up this or that entity to square off against, does this pure, untrammelled freedom become determinate enough to be conscious of itself. It is as though in perverse style this supremely self-assured entrepreneur fashions stumbling blocks to its own freedom, simply in order to flex its muscles against them and relish its own powers. Perhaps there is a remote parallel here to the way that desire, for Freud, fearful of losing itself in achieving its object, thrives on blockages which it throws up itself. Fichte's so-called absolute ego, another locum tenens for the Almighty, is infinite, self-grounding, self-causing, spontaneous, unconscious, unconditioned and undetermined. It can intuit itself only in the act of self-positing, in which self as infinite and self as finite – Father and Son, so to speak – are spontaneously at one.[19]

Though Fichte is not especially deep in aesthetics, this subject has more than a resonance of the work of art. Like the aesthetic artefact, it is self-founding and self-determining; like an artefact, too, it presents as objective what is secretly its own creation, constituting what it cognises. The self is that 'whose being or essence consists simply in the fact that it posits itself as existing', and as such 'exists for itself'.[20] If art in Schelling's eyes is the key to the inner stuff of the cosmos, human activity for Fichte is always in some sense artistic, since by imposing a form on reality it freely determines the world to exist in a certain way.

In one sense, however, all this brave talk of aesthetics was to no avail. Art may be more palpable than philosophy, the image more cogent than the concept, but it tends to leave the populace almost as cold. It is too minor a matter to replace religious faith, which links the daily conduct of countless ordinary men and women to the most sublime of truths. No symbolic system in history has ever remotely rivalled it in this respect. In the end, Idealism proved too cerebral a doctrine, as some Romantic authors were to protest. It may have replaced the Reason of the *philosophes* with a somewhat less sanitised Spirit, but it found it hard to translate its truths into an everyday idiom. For all their mystifications, this was not a mistake that the churches were prone to make.

\* \* \*

If there can be no graven image of freedom – if the age of bourgeois liberty is an iconoclastic one – then some unsettling political consequences would seem to follow. Power, to be effective, must inscribe itself on the senses. The churches, and Roman Catholicism par excellence, had little to learn about how the numinous is sensuously incarnate in gesture and performance, in the odour of incense, the colour of a chasuble or the crook of a knee. Ideology is the place where abstract propositions infiltrate sensory life, absolute values unfold in historical time, the contingent is imbued with an air of necessity and obligation is alchemised into a feeling of self-fulfilment.

We have seen already how this neglect of culture or lived experience risked diminishing the force of Enlightenment Reason. It is a mistake that the Idealists and Romantics will try not to repeat. So much is apparent from *The Oldest Systematic Programme of German Idealism*, an anonymous document in Hegel's handwriting which is probably the work of Schelling. 'Unless we make ideas aesthetic, i.e. mythological,' the author insists, 'they will have no interest for the people.'[21] If philosophy is to hold sway over the multitude, there must be a 'religion of the senses', in which the poet will become 'the teacher of humanity'. Philosophy stands in need of such palpable presence in any case, but the need is all the more pressing if it is to become a force in the streets and taverns. To do so, it must give birth to a 'mythology of reason', reconciling concrete and abstract, sense and rationality. The case represents a compromise between the elitist double truth thesis and the radical Enlightenment view that the masses can be illuminated. The populace can indeed come to share in truth and reason, but in fictional, affective, figurative form.

'Mythology must become philosophical to make people rational,' proposes the *Systematic Programme*, 'and philosophy must become mythological to make philosophers sensuous.'[22] Art, as Jürgen Habermas puts it, 'was to reacquire its public character in the form of a new mythology'.[23] Hölderlin insists time and again on the need for a shared mythology to forge a fragmented society into unity. Like a number of others, he finds this desirable condition in ancient Greece, marked as it is by a fusion of high culture and unspoilt Nature, spontaneity and civilised self-awareness. Friedrich Schlegel remarks in his 'Discourse on Mythology' that his nation has no mythology at present, but is close to obtaining one. Germany would indeed manufacture a full-blown mythology a century or so later, though not of the kind that Schlegel himself would have found particularly palatable.

Myth, then, is to serve as a new form of religion, folding populace and intellectuals into a single project. In this sense, the marriage of philosophy and mythology is a form of class collaboration. To blend the two is to lend ideas the tangible force of image and fable, and thus to bring reason within the ambit of the common people. Art and myth both dismantle the opposition between the sensible and the intelligible, as indeed (so Schleiermacher points out) does language itself. If so many of the German Romantics idolised Spinoza, it was largely because they saw his thought as reconciling cerebration and the senses in just this way.[24] Even the austerely iconoclastic Kant held that the understanding depends upon the productive imagination.

'All the wealth of human knowledge and happiness consists in images,' remarks Johann Georg Hamann, whose rejection of rational theology powerfully impressed Kierkegaard.[25] The poetic Muse, Hamann goes on to argue, will 'purify the natural use of the senses from the unnatural use of abstractions, by which our concepts of things are as maimed as the name of the Creator is suppressed and blasphemed'.[26] Such anaemic concepts must be returned to the life of the body, a return that Hamann's fervid literary style performs as well as proposes. The discursive must be alchemised into the intuitive. If Schelling, along with so many of his confrères, contemptuously writes off allegory, it is among other things because the allegorical signifier, unlike the much-revered symbol, drives a wedge between the sensible and intelligible. Non-sensible ideas are offensive on several counts, not least because they are thought to be uncongenial to the masses. The people would see a sign, a craving which the Enlightenment spurns as so much superstition. The good and the true must accordingly be translated into the beautiful, so that philosophy and the masses may be brought together. Keats's 'Beauty is truth, truth beauty' celebrates such a wedding of the rational and the sensory. In proclaiming the death of art, Hegel anticipated that one of the several obstacles to this project would be that as modernity moved into its later phases, art itself would grow increasingly abstract.

Schelling's mythology of Reason is not of the kind that Max Horkheimer and Theodor Adorno find in the Enlightenment. For them, the phrase suggests not that Reason must be converted into myth, but that this is what it has secretly been all along. Reason and myth are really stages of the same narrative, variations on the same attempt to subjugate Nature to some semblance of order. 'Just as myths already entail enlightenment,' Horkheimer and Adorno comment, 'with every step enlightenment entangles itself more deeply in mythology.'[27] For Dialectic of Enlightenment, both myth and Reason involve the mastery of Nature, the erasure of the unclassifiable, the principle of abstract equivalence and the subsuming of the material world to sign or scientific formula. 'All mythology,' Marx writes, 'overcomes and dominates and shapes the forces of nature in the imagination.'[28] For some of its critics, abstract rationalism is simply a more sophisticated version of Claude Lévi-Strauss's pensée sauvage, with its meticulous, well-nigh obsessional taxonomies of the natural world.

As the familiar insists on returning, on each occasion in faintly different guise, time in this mythical or rationalist world appears folded on itself, so that nothing truly unpredictable can break upon the scene. Everything that takes place has taken place in some form already, since myth is cyclical and Reason reveals a world that is everywhere the same. What myth knows as fate, scientific rationalism knows as the necessity of natural laws. Neither form of cognition is able to curve back upon itself, grasping the conditions which put it in place. Moreover, just as knowledge for the Enlightenment is partly an instrument of power, so the same can be claimed of myth. By and large, both modes reject the severance of knowledge and power which is the condition of critique. So it is that Enlightenment 'regresses to the mythology it has never been able to escape'.[29] Commodity fetishism is one such species of primitive magic. It is one of a myriad ways in which superstition and idolatry survive the clear-headedness of an Age of Reason.

* * *

Enlightenment Reason may seep into myth, but it can also enlist it in its own cause. Pointing up the affinities between Christianity and pagan mythology, for example, could be an oblique way of trying to discredit the former. For Schelling and his colleagues, however, the point is not to unmask myth as illusion, as some apologists for enlightenment sought to do, but to harness it to rational ends. A new mythology, broadly disseminated among the masses, would by no means prove the enemy of Reason. On the contrary, it would lend it a much-needed material body. The fractured bonds between citizens, as well as the threatened alliance between Nature and humanity, might be restored by a communality of image and belief. Coterie ideas and common opinions, high theory and popular practice, would no longer be at daggers drawn. Myth would serve as a mode of displaced religion, uniting the mystical and the mundane, priest (or philosopher) and laity (or common people) in a shared symbolic order. The abyss opened up by the Enlightenment between a coterie who lived by the idea and a populace who lived by the image might accordingly be bridged.

The two chief meanings of the term 'culture' would thus be fruitfully coupled. Culture in the sense of certain cherished icons and insights would be steadily diffused throughout culture in the sense of a whole form of life. The poet or philosopher would be invested with the status of secular priest, and art or mythology converted into a set of quasi-sacred rites. The damage to the human spirit inflicted by individualism, as well as by a withered rationality for which Nature was so much dead matter, might thus be repaired. A more organic ideology of everyday life would evolve, one which reunited the cognitive, ethical and aesthetic domains that Kant's thought had helped to split asunder.

That popular mythologies can be legislated into existence by philosophical fiat is itself, ironically, a rationalist assumption. It is rather like imagining that one could dream to order. Schelling speaks rather more realistically, though still with a touch of pathos, of waiting upon history 'to return mythology to us as a universally valid form'.[30] Mythology, like everything else, has its material conditions. If Marx sees mythical thought as an early attempt to impose an order upon Nature, he also points out that it tends to disappear when this mastery has been achieved by modern technological means. 'Is the view of nature and of social relations that underlies the Greek imagination, and also therefore Greek mythology,' he inquires in a celebrated passage, 'possible with automatic machines, railways, locomotives and telegraphs? What chance has Vulcan against Roberts and Co., Jupiter against the lightning conductor, and Hermes against the *credit mobiliser*?'[31] In Nazi Germany, the historical conditions for mythology were to emerge with a vengeance. If the ruins of mythology are to be found anywhere, it is in the rubble of the Third Reich. It was Walter Benjamin who declared that myth would survive as long as the last beggar. In any case, how is the self-reflective pursuit of philosophy to translate itself into a symbolic mode which is not generally seen as self-aware? Are not myths, as Frank Kermode has claimed, fictions that have forgotten that they are such?[32]

All the same, there was a need to rehabilitate the symbolic dimension of social existence. One of the embarrassments of the industrial middle class, as we have seen already, is that its native styles of thought (rationalism, pragmatism, secularism, materialism, utilitarianism and the like) tend to undermine the very symbolic resources necessary for its own social reproduction.[33] It is hard to generate any very edifying world-view from such drably prosaic materials. Liberalism and Utilitarianism do not fare well as symbolic forms. Besides, individualism is a divisive doctrine, and as such inhospitable to the idea of a corporate identity. Industrial capitalism accordingly finds it hard to generate an 'organic' ideology of its own, and so must have recourse to one imported from elsewhere. Coleridge's clerisy-ruled countryside, Thomas Carlyle's feudal England and the secularised religion of Comte and Saint-Simon are cases in point. So, too, is John Stuart Mill's attempt to supplement the imaginative deficiencies of Jeremy Bentham with a dash of Coleridgean Idealism.[34] In a curious time warp, a hard-headed market society dreams romantically of dashing young aristocratic leaders and paternalist medieval abbots.[35] The humdrum prose of the present is forced to derive its poetry from the past. It is worth noting the contrast with Marx, who in *The Eighteenth Brumaire of Louis Bonaparte* rejects all such historical graftings and recyclings.

It is not easy, then, for an industrial capitalist order to come up with a vision that will seize the hearts and minds of the people. It needs an admixture of more traditional values – faith, loyalty, reverence, organic bonds, transcendent truth, metaphysical sanctions, hierarchical order – if it is to make up for a certain emotional and symbolic deficit in its world-view. From Burke and Carlyle to Pugin and Ruskin, the radical-Romantic legacy in England serves among other things to fulfil this task. One of its most prominent twentieth-century inheritors is D.H. Lawrence. The more rationalised social life grows, the more vital the strategy becomes, but by the same token the more implausible it tends to appear. Textile manufacturers do not generally make convincing epic heroes, and industrial Manchester is hard to recast as a medieval monastery. At the root of the problem lies the fact that economic life under capitalism is less dependent on extra-economic values than previous modes of production. One does not hammer steel for the sake of God, honour, Fatherland or paternalist lord. Since economic activity is without much built-in spiritual purpose, that meaning has to be imported from elsewhere, and the join is awkwardly apparent.

The irony of the situation is plain. The very system which discredits religion in its spontaneously secular dealings is also the one most urgently in need of the symbolic unity that religion can provide. If traditional faith no longer offers such cohesion, new forms of it will have to be invented, all the way from mythology to the Religion of Humanity, Culture to Hellenism, high Victorian medievalism to F.H. Bradley's neo-Hegelianism or Durkheim's hypostasised Society. You may ditch religious belief à la Nietzsche, demythologise it in the manner of the Feuerbachians, Saint-Simonians or Positivists, seek to transform the conditions which give birth to it in the style of Marx, treat it with F.D. Maurice as social critique rather than ruling ideology, or, as with Kierkegaard, greet the whole notion of social consensus with a certain radical-Protestant scepticism. Yet it is hard not to feel that while religion in its classical forms is rapidly losing ground, the various regents and understudies for it on offer are for the most part too esoteric, rationalistic or downright implausible to merit much credence. It is unlikely that those who have turned their faces from the Pope in Rome will flock instead to the High Priest of Humanity in Paris, Auguste Comte.

It is this symbolic deficit of middle-class society that the recourse to mythology seeks to set right.[36] It is in this spirit that Herder, despite his Enlightenment belief in 'the operation of *one principle*, namely *human reason*' in the vast diversity of human affairs,[37] inveighs against the rationalist misconception that enlightenment can ever be simply a question of the understanding. Instead, it must touch the mainsprings of social action, which is to say the pieties and affections of ordinary men and women. Reason for Herder is a historical faculty, one which realises its inexorable purposes in a prodigal variety of cultural forms; and it must sink its taproot into the life of the senses if it is to prove effective. In taking issue with his great mentor Kant, he even has recourse to a kind of materialism, protesting not only that Kantian philosophy sets aside language, of which Herder himself is one of the first great modern theorists, but that Kant's categories of time and space depend on both language and the body. David Hume anticipates something of his case in this respect, insisting as he does that philosophy, if it is to deliver a plausible account of the deity, 'must find some method of affecting the senses and imagination.'[38]

The Enlightenment's disdain for popular experience, Herder insists, has alienated the common people from the sources of their own culture.[39] It is in protest against this that he himself turns from Weimar classicism to folk art. To compound their odious elitism, the *Aufklärer* have betrayed their mission to illuminate the people by their scandalous support of princes and despots. If they have not done this, then they have beaten a craven retreat into a purely intellectual enclave. The Enlightenment, Herder charges, has served to justify colonial oppression, and in doing so has proved itself an anti-poetic power, stifling the folk from whom the truest poetry wells up. Weimar classicism is aloof and purist, divorced from the commonplace and icily indifferent to foreign cultures. Literature must become more earthy and *engagé*. History is the work not of politicians but of poets, prophets and visionaries. It is the narrative of nations, not of states.

As a precursor of cultural studies, as well as an ardent apologist for the civilisations of the non-Western world, Herder calls for a more demotic conception of culture, one that will encompass folklore, national literatures and the customs of the masses. In this, he is at one with the German Romantic Ludwig Tieck, an author who draws deeply on folklore and popular culture in much of his fiction.[40] Like Marx and Engels in his wake, Herder also startlingly prefigures modern environmental politics. 'Let it not be imagined,' he declares, 'that human art can with despotic power convert at once a foreign region into another Europe by cutting down its forests and cultivating its soil . . .'[41] The author of these sentiments, one should recall, is an apostle of the Enlightenment himself: a liberal, universalist egalitarian who preaches a gospel of Reason, progress, perfectibility and the innate goodness of humanity. His shafts against the movement thus spring from that most discomforting of all critiques, an insider's one.[42] As an apologist for cultural pluralism and the key role of language in human affairs, as well as a critic of pure Reason, Herder is in some ways a more enlightened version of Hamann, shorn of his febrile mysticism.[43]

In similarly popularising vein, Fichte remarks in the Foreword to his *Vocation of Man* that the work aims for a readership beyond professional philosophers, and 'ought to be intelligible to all readers who are able to understand a book at all'.[44] Yet few of Fichte's other works are readily intelligible even to professional philosophers, least of all anglophone ones, and even then they are scarcely as esoteric as, say, Schelling's *System of Transcendental Idealism*. The first sentence of Fichte's *Science of Knowledge* declares that the book is not intended for the general public, a warning that the briefest glance at its pages renders instantly superfluous. It was the fate of some of these thinkers to appeal to the common people in the content of their work while frightening them off by its form. The anti-clerical diatribes of the Enlightenment, which were not generally aimed at a popular audience, can prove more accessible to the non-philosopher than many an Idealist or Romantic work that makes a play for the common man.

The idea of a new mythology would descend from Herder, Schelling and their colleagues to Friedrich Nietzsche, and from there to Georges Sorel, modernism and fascism. Yet it did not go uncontested. The mature Hegel was no great enthusiast for a mythology of Reason, even though Georg Lukács would later brand him as a mythologiser. Hegel's idea of Reason, Lukács protested, was 'the projection into myth of the failure to understand reality concretely as a historical process'.[45] Yet if poetry for some Romantics is destined to replace philosophy, the opposite is the case in Hegel's view. He writes dismissively in *The Phenomenology of Mind* of 'the habit of always thinking in figurative ideas', a cast of mind which finds the incursions of abstract thought troublesome and distasteful.[46] Reason is affronted by such synthetic creations, which he rejects as neither fish nor fowl, poetry nor philosophy. Perry Anderson points out that there is no real concept of culture in Hegel's work, a term which never occurs in it.[47] Social reality has grown too intricate and self-aware to be captured in an image, which is why art as a mode of cognition must now yield pride of place to philosophy. Truth must vanquish the sensory. Art could provide an image of social reality for the ancient Greeks, but only because their world lacked the theoretical self-consciousness of modernity, art for Hegel being a largely unconscious affair. In such conditions, the artist was able to articulate the world-view of an entire culture. Now, however, the work of art is resonant of little beyond itself. That this is so is a sign of its emancipation, but also of its evisceration. It is restricted by its very nature to a specific content, and so is unable to provide the age with an image of totality – a totality which has become as sublimely unrepresentable as the Almighty himself, and which only the concept can now hope to yield us. As David Roberts writes, 'art now finds its full comprehension and justification only in theory'.[48]

Hegel was not to know that art would live on partly for the reasons that he considered its death knell had been tolled. It would gain a formidable new lease of life from the very crisis into which modernity had plunged it. The more problematic it seemed, the more it could reap fresh resources from confronting the conundrum of its own near-unthinkable existence, as Romanticism gave way to symbolism, symbolism to aestheticism, aestheticism to modernism and modernism to postmodernism. Nor was Hegel to know that art would eventually find a new role for itself by being required – of all impossible tasks! –to act as a stand-in for religion in an agnostic age.

Kant, who famously forbids the fashioning of graven images, regards the moral law as sublimely exceeding all sensory icons of itself. We are not to submit to its sway because of the allure of 'images and childish devices', a conformity which would constitute no virtue at all. He recognises, to be sure, the perils of this position. If moral truth is divested of everything that might commend it to the senses, he inquires in the *Critique of Judgement*, can it evoke more than 'a cold and lifeless approbation', rather than any truly motivating sentiment? Indeed so, he replies – for when nothing any longer 'meets the eye of sense', the idea of morality imposes itself on us all the more insistently, unhampered as it is by material media. Does not the sublime move us at least as much as beauty?[49]

As a Christian, Kant might have reflected that there is indeed for those of his persuasion a sensible image of the sublimely ineffable, namely the tortured body of a reviled political criminal. It is graven images, not human ones, that the Mosaic Law forbids, setting its face against idolatry and reification. If there can be no humanly fashioned icons of Yahweh, it is because the only authentic image of him is humanity itself, and one human individual in particular. Sensible images of the ineffable are generally known as symbols, another shamefaced piece of theology.[50] The model of how a lowly piece of matter comes to smack of the infinite is how the parcel of flesh known as Jesus is the incarnate Son of God.

'Sensuous representation,' argues Friedrich Schiller, 'is, viewed in one aspect, *rich* ... But viewed in another aspect it is *limited and poor*, because it confines itself only to a single individual and a single case which ought to be understood as a whole sphere. It therefore curtails the understanding in the same proportion that it grants preponderance to the imagination ... '[51] Here, *in nuce*, is the nub of the dilemma. In modern societies, understanding and imagination are likely to move in different domains. What we can grasp intellectually gives the slip to concrete representation, such is its intricacy and impalpability. The more abstract social existence grows, the more it drives a wedge between human faculties which (so the story goes) once consorted harmoniously with each other. Yet the increasingly abstract condition of social life is also bound up with its alienated, fragmented nature; so that in such fissiparous circumstances, the state feels a particular need to forge its citizens into a corporate body. And this in turn generates the need for tangible icons and sensory images. The hope of some Idealists and Romantics is that Reason and the imagination might once more fruitfully coexist. A mythology of Reason is one such attempt to unite them.

\* \* \*

To bring its truths to bear on everyday experience, religion has always exploited the resources of image, ritual and narrative. Reason must now strive to do the same, either through a new mythology or through that curious new discourse, bred in Germany in the mid-eighteenth century, known as the aesthetic. This latter project is outlined in Friedrich Schiller's *On the Aesthetic Education of Man*, behind which looms the spectre of Kant's austere Protestant iconoclasm. Schiller is certainly a Kantian of sorts, but what inspires his great treatise is the fear that his mentor's moral theory can never be effectively translated into social ideology. Reason in Kant is too aloof from the life of the senses, too much at war with the flesh to take root in everyday life. It has something of the Freudian superego's sadistic disregard for the needs and natures of those it subjugates. In Schiller's view, the faculty of Reason needs to infiltrate the sphere of the senses as a kind of fifth columnist, tempering and refining it from within so as to make it spontaneously receptive to the decrees of the moral law. Reason, in short, must cease to conduct itself like a paranoid absolutist prince, placing too little trust in the masses' good-hearted readiness to conform to its ukases. Like the champions of mythology, then, Schiller is anxious to bridge the gap between philosophy and people, as Reason stretches out a hand to sensory life. Both projects – the new mythology and the aesthetic – try to reinvent the Janus-faced nature of religion, which looks to certain sublime truths on the one hand and to everyday existence on the other.

Linking reason and the senses is the role of the aesthetic – a concept which originally has nothing to do with art. As the etymology of the term would suggest, it concerns sensation and perception. The aesthetic in the modern sense of the word is a science born at the heart of the Enlightenment – one which, as a kind of prosthesis or humble handmaiden of Reason, seeks to bring the life of the senses under its sway, reducing this disorderly domain to some species of logic.[52] As such, it is an extension of Enlightenment rationality, rather than, as with Romanticism, an attempt to transform it. Without such a project, one courts the danger of a sovereign form of Reason that is blind to all that makes its subjects living, feeling, desiring creatures.

For Reason to become hegemonic rather than coercive (Schiller is writing with the sound of the French revolutionary Terror in his ears), it must be aestheticised, conjoined with beauty and pleasure, so that obligation and inclination are at one. A hegemonic power is one that fuses the political with the aesthetic. Edmund Burke, whose great theme from beginning to end is hegemony, argues much the same case.[53] Citizens are unlikely to bend the knee to a moral or political law for which they feel no affection. As Schiller suggests in his essay 'On Grace and Dignity', moral beauty is a question of the grace with which we conform to the moral law.[54] In Freudian parlance, the point is to introject the law's decrees so that they become spontaneous inclination. It is on our bodies that the law must go to work, not only on our minds. Reason must govern in collusion with the senses it subdues, rather as an astute sovereign rules in a way that allows each citizen to feel that he is doing no more than obeying the diktats of his own desires. Reason must be a form of enlightened absolutism, not a despotism of the concept. The aesthetic accordingly plays a kind of propaedeutic or mediatory role, refining and defusing the raw stuff of sensation for its eventual subjugation at the hands of Reason. Otherwise, as creatures sunk degenerately in our desires, we are likely to experience the imperatives of the moral law as unpleasantly arbitrary and absolutist, and thus fail to comply with them. In their natural condition, the senses have much in common with the mob, with what Schiller calls its 'crude, lawless instincts, unleashed with the loosening of the bonds of civil order, and hastening with ungovernable fury to [its] animal satisfactions'.[55] It is an analogy as old as Plato. The *canaille* will listen to reason only if reason addresses those of its instincts that already incline it to the good. Schiller's vision, so to speak, is Catholic rather than Protestant in this respect, trusting as it does to those redemptive capacities in men and women which have not been entirely corrupted by their depravity, and which is where divine or aesthetic grace can find a foothold.

Schiller's great text is thus a political allegory. Its reflections on the relations between Reason and sense are never very far from a view of the relations between ruling class and populace. Indeed, Schiller makes the point himself, drawing a homology between the relations of Reason to Nature on the one hand, and the relations of state to society on the other. Rather as Reason must work with the grain of human nature, so the state, whose demand for cohesion is absolute, must nonetheless respect the 'subjective and specific character' of its materials (the common people), welding them into unity without detriment to their diversity. The aesthetic, as we have seen, is thus code for a kind of liberal absolutism. Yet the work of art itself is more akin to a republic. Indeed, it is possible to see the ideal republic as a kind of work of art writ large. The aesthetic artefact is governed by a general law, but one which allows each of its constitutive parts to be self-determining. Indeed, its general law is nothing but the interrelations of its various self-determining parts. 'Poetry,' writes Friedrich Schlegel, 'is republican speech: a speech which is its own law and end unto itself, one in which all the parts are free citizens and have the right to vote.'[56]

There is, as one might expect, a gendered aspect to the relations between Reason and Nature. The two may be cajoled into wedlock, but this does not abolish their inequality. If Reason has to work as a secret agent within sensory existence, it is because that existence is its antagonist as well as its ally. It is the place where Reason and the moral law must bed themselves down if they are to inspire citizens to virtue, but it is also a domain in which these exalted abstractions will never feel entirely at ease. This is because their true home is in eternity. Schiller speaks revealingly at one point in his essay of 'our degrading kinship with matter'.[57] It requires no great imaginative leap to see matter and Nature here as feminine, as Schiller's text deploys an idealised version of woman as beauty as a defence against woman as sensuality. Reason, needless to say, is masculine. Yet it lives in intimate relation with its degenerate sexual partner, rather as for Edmund Burke's great essay on the sublime and beautiful, the severely masculine law must become a cross-dresser, tart itself up in alluring feminine drapery, if it is to soften its rigours to the point where it can win our affections and cajole us into consent. We should not, all the same, be allowed to lose sight of the ugly bulge of its phallus through its diaphanous vestments. Beauty may be essential, given that we are sensory creatures, but it must not be permitted to obscure altogether the sublime terrors of authority. A 'stiffening' of the sublime, Burke comments, remains necessary.

In another essay, Schiller contrasts what he calls the 'body' or stylistic dimension of a discourse, where the imagination can be allowed a certain licence, with its conceptual content, and warns against the rhetorical signifier coming to usurp the conceptual signified. Such a move would assign too high a status to the feminine, women being preoccupied with the 'matter' or external embellishments of language rather than with the truths it conveys. Men and women consort together as harmoniously as signifier and signified, but Woman must nevertheless know her semiotic place, which unlike the Saussurean signifier is certainly not on top.[58]

We have seen that the aesthetic – or culture, as one might also call it – provides us with the form of the ideal political republic. 'Taste alone brings harmony into society,' Schiller writes, 'because it fosters harmony in the individual . . . only the aesthetic mode of communication unites society, because it relates to what is common to all.'[59] Because the community of taste is in Kantian style one of freedom, autonomy, equality, universality, disinterestedness, fellow feeling and unconstrained consensus, it is possible to find in aesthetic judgement, of all marginal activities, a model of social unity, one which sets its face against anarchy, privilege, autocracy, self-interest and elitism. In a social order accustomed to neither freedom nor equality, the aesthetic constitutes an enclave of free and equal individuals, a kind of public sphere in miniature. It is a shadowy utopia at the heart of the unregenerate present. The vision is as audacious as it is absurd. If we are to rely for our political unity on a faculty as wayward and rarefied as aesthetic judgement, our condition must be dire indeed.

Even so, the aesthetic figures here as a whole alternative politics. Perhaps it might better be called a non-political kind of politics, as in the lineage of *Kulturkritik* which stems from Schiller and his colleagues. Culture or the aesthetic is now acting as a displacement of politics, as it is of theology. This is surely one reason why aesthetic theory plays such a key role in the thought of a civilisation notorious for its philistinism. In an age more concerned with trading in works of art than with appreciating them, the aesthetic crops up as a vital topic in one major European philosopher after another. If it assumes such centrality, it is among other things because it represents the missing mediation between a self-interested civil society and a flourishing political republic. It is what educates desire into disinterestedness. As for the work of art itself, it offers nothing less than a new model of subjectivity appropriate to such a politics. Like the ideal citizen, it is autonomous, free-standing and self-determining, obedient to no law that it has not fashioned itself.

Schiller seeks to approach politics indirectly, by way of culture. The cultural is in his view the matrix of the political, rather as Antonio Gramsci is sometimes misread as arguing that the working class must amass cultural capital before it can seize political power.[60] If revolution is to be repelled, culture or the aesthetic must be summoned to edify and enlighten the people. There will be a gradual spiritual reshaping rather than a sudden political rupture. Art takes the place of insurrection. *Bildung* is the solution to social disaffection. If this is so, however, it can only be because culture has already been defined in counter-revolutionary terms. It is really a synonym for moderation and many-sidedness. Not all appeals to culture need be of this kind, of course, rather as not all appeals to Reason are invitations to cool down. For the French revolutionaries, to be reasonable meant to throw up barricades rather than dismantle them.

There is, however, a chicken-and-egg problem here. Schiller may see culture as the precondition of an enlightened politics, but Kant holds that culture itself is dependent on political freedom. Only in a republic can it truly flourish. The early Novalis concurs with this opinion. Besides, the shift from the cultural to the political is not a simple one, since the former is understood in a way which pitches it into conflict with the latter. For Schiller, culture is a realm brimful of all conceivable possibilities. It harbours a plenitude of human powers, all of them awaiting their harmonious expression; and as such it does not take kindly to being restricted to a determinate goal, any more than it looks favourably on sectarian points of view. Culture is marked by an absence of determination, or, if one prefers, by a kind of unlimited determinability. It is a fantasy of absolute freedom, a sort of nirvanic suspension of everything determinate (and thus finite). Like the Almighty himself, it is both everything and nothing, transcendent of all particulars, the ground of all possibility. As Nicholas Halmi remarks of the Romantic symbol, 'it is supposed to be at once meaningful and incapable of being reduced to any particular meaning'.[61]

Put more prosaically, the man of culture can turn his hand to anything he chooses, bringing to bear on any specific task a sense of unbounded possibility. It is as though while bent on a particular project, he is always silently signalling that he could just as easily be doing something different, and doing it every bit as proficiently. As a general activating capacity, culture or the aesthetic would seem to be the opposite of any definite activity, which hardly seems to equip it for a political function. It has no inherent inclination to this mode of action rather than that, since any such bias would be detrimental to its disinterestedness. 'Because it takes under its protection no single one of man's faculties to the exclusion of the others,' Schiller writes, 'it favours each and all of them without distinction; and it favours no single one more than another for the simple reason that it is the ground of possibility of them all.'[62] Rather as God loves us all alike, so culture loves all our faculties alike. It looks benignly upon the whole of Creation, admirably free of invidious preferences. Whether culture really does predispose us to genocide as much as to altruism, at least in Schiller's sense of the term, is perhaps to be doubted. The point, however, is the self-contradictory nature of this curious phenomenon, as a kind of nothingness pregnant with the entire universe. Unable to say one thing without saying everything, culture risks being so boundlessly eloquent as to be speechless. It is the negation of all concrete commitments in the name of totality – a totality which is purely void because it is no more than a totalisation of negated moments. It is what we need in order to act creatively, yet there is a sense in which any particular action represents a falling off from it. As an infinity of human powers, it would seem to be ruined as soon as realised. Here, then, is another ground of possibility which cannot be represented in what it brings into being. Culture is a secular name for God.

If it is to prove socially redemptive, culture must pass over into determinate deeds. Yet how is it to become a political force without betraying its own amplitude of spirit? Can disinterestedness survive a descent into actions which are inevitably partial and partisan? If it is to be preserved as an ideal, culture must be insulated from the infections of actual existence. Only thus will it preserve its powers intact. Yet this distance from the real is exactly what disables those powers. In one sense, the aesthetic is socially useless, exactly as its philistine critics maintain. It is just that in Schiller's eyes it is gloriously rather than disreputably so. 'Beauty,' he insists, 'produces no particular result whatsoever, neither for the understanding nor for the will. It accomplishes no particular purpose, neither intellectual nor moral; it discovers no individual truth, helps us to perform no individual duty and is, in short, as unfitted to provide a firm basis for character as to enlighten the understanding.'[63] Yet it is this sublime incapability that must fly to the aid of a divided, disenchanted world. Self-interest has grown so tenacious that only a completely impartial faculty is capable of countering it. Yet this is the last thing that can bring it low.

One way of squaring this circle is to find in the very autonomy of the aesthetic, its disdain for programmes and practical measures, the foretaste of a future in which men and women might themselves be autonomous – might become, in fact, as freely self-determining as the work of art is thought to be at present. Where art was, there shall humanity be. By virtue of political transformation, we, too, shall eventually be able to flourish as ends in ourselves, not for any determinate goal. An aesthetic rationality is an anti-instrumental one, withdrawing the self from the sphere of exchange-value and utility. The anti-pragmatic nature of the aesthetic thus becomes a politics in itself, as the writings of Shelley, Marx, Morris and Wilde all testify. In an ingenious irony, the pointlessness of present-day art, its socially dysfunctional status, can be alchemised into a sign of utopia. Indeed, Friedrich Schlegel holds that the playfulness of art imitates the pointless play of the world, and is thus referential in its very autonomy.

What is perhaps most memorable about Schiller's treatise on aesthetics is less its utopian features than its eloquent polemic against the present. 'In the very bosom of the most exquisitely developed social life,' Schiller laments, 'egoism has founded its system.'[64] The result is endemic conflict, social fragmentation, the triumph of the machine, a crippling division of labour and the stunting of human capabilities. Society as it stands is the very ruin of culture – of that totality of powers, exercised purely for their own self-delight, which stands in judgement on the paucity of the industrial capitalist present. It is these aspects of Schiller's work which will descend as a fruitful legacy to Marx, whose critique of capitalism is always at some level an aesthetic one. Politically, then, the idea of culture faces two ways at once. If it springs from an emergent middle-class order, it also represents a searching critique of some of its most abhorrent features. The robustly self-realising human subject, with its well-balanced fullness of powers, is an idealised version of the common-or-garden bourgeois. It is also a deadly indictment of him.

An all-round fullness of powers may sound a noble enough goal. Like most edifying ideals, however, it has its odious corollaries. By the time of Huysmans and Walter Pater, it is becoming hard to distinguish it from a promiscuous openness to all experience. The Hellenic can slide easily enough into the satanic. If art must take incest and necrophilia on board, the aesthetic is at war with the moral. Truth is ugliness, not beauty. If the artist is to redeem the whole of reality, whether as naturalistic novelist or demonic post-Baudelairean poet, he must undergo what Yeats calls the baptism of the gutter, refusing orthodox moral distinctions so as to become imaginatively at one with the slime and refuse of human existence. Only in this way will he be able to gather the excremental into the eternal. It is an aesthetic version of crucifixion and resurrection, one which invests the poet with a certain aura of sanctity. Yet he is also sacred in the ancient sense of being both blessed and cursed. To live by imaginative empathy is to be bereft of a self; to be without a self is to exist as a kind of nothingness; and nothingness is unnervingly close to evil.

By the time of Schiller, Schelling and their colleagues, a social order in which God's presence could be felt in workaday pieties and practices was on the wane; but this did not mean that his immanence in everyday life was any less desirable. For this purpose, a rational theology simply would not serve. Instead, myth, art and culture (and the greatest of these is culture) sought to become ersatz forms of religion. They were the means by which transcendent truths might be converted into the currency of common experience. As it turned out, this was not where culture and religion were to prove most akin. It was rather that while culture helped to legitimise the ruling powers, it also provided a source of protest against them. As such, it inherited something of the political ambivalence of religious faith. It is common knowledge that Marx regarded religion as the opium of the people, as well as the holy water with which the priest sprinkled the bad conscience of the bourgeoisie. It is less widely bruited that he also saw it as the heart of a heartless world. There are worse ways, incidentally, of summing up Romanticism.

\* \* \*

'We must be men,' writes Samuel Taylor Coleridge, 'in order to be citizens.'[65] It is a Schillerian sort of claim. To become an effective political organ, the state must first be a cultural one, educating its more rough-and-ready members in the habits of civility. Something similar is true for Fichte, for whom a state-organised educational system will allow individuals to make the transition from the raw appetite of civil society to the sweetness and light of the sphere of culture. In his view, the liberal state creates the external, material conditions for freedom, while the culture-state nourishes such liberty spiritually and internally.[66] There is no doubt that the masses can be apostles of culture, since in Fichte's eyes culture is first of all the way of life of a distinctive *Volk* rather than the values of an urbane minority.[67]

The later Coleridge held a similar view of the culture-state. A clerisy, or network of cultural commissars, dispersed like so many secular parsons throughout the nation, would foster the moral and physical welfare of the people. Culture would take the Church as its model. In its mission to diffuse civility and legality, the clerisy, as the learned caste of a National Church, would introduce 'habits of sobriety, industry and obedience in the lower orders', breeding in the countryside a 'healthful, callous-handed but high-and-warm-hearted tenantry ... ready to march off at the first call of their country with a Son of the House at their head'.[68]

Reared in the Christian faith by his Anglican vicar father, Coleridge moved in radical materialist circles (Hartley, Priestley, Godwin), then gravitated to German Idealism and metaphysical obscurantism, and finally found solace in Tory high Anglicanism. In short, having immersed himself after his youthful revolutionism in various secularised forms of religion, he recircled to the genuine article. What was the point of this excursus? There are several reasons for Coleridge's return to religious orthodoxy, but one in particular is worth singling out. As popular discontent erupted throughout early industrial England, and the poet himself shifted sharply to the political right, he felt the need for a religious faith more lucid and dogmatic in its zeal for political authority than anything to be found in Kant or Spinoza. The Idealism which had enthused him proved in the end too cerebral, and camouflaged a faith, confined, as it was, almost entirely to the intelligentsia. Lord Liverpool, the recipient of a letter from Coleridge on the subject of social distress, speaks of him as trying to 'rescue speculative philos- ophy from false reasoning, and make it suited to the interests of religion' (though he adds, unsurprisingly for a recipient of a missive from Coleridge, that 'at least, I believe this is Mr. Coleridge's meaning, but I cannot well understand him').[69] Religion knows how to engage the populace, as German philosophy does not.

In his first *Lay Sermon*, Coleridge laments the fact that the educated classes have abandoned their role of political leadership, subverted by the scepticism, materialism and agnosticism of Enlightenment thought. They are scarcely likely to restore their failing hegemony by disseminating the writings of Hegel or Schelling among the ranks of the warm-hearted, calloued-handed tenantry. Instead, they must have recourse once more to religion, espousing a more sophisticated version of the masses' own beliefs. In this way, social hierarchy may be maintained within a common culture. The signal virtue of Christianity is that there is a version of it for the learned (theology) and one for the common people (devotional practice); and though the two may find themselves in occasional contention, they are bound together within the ecclesiastical institution itself. It is harder to come up with a popular version of Hegel's *Phenomenology of Mind* or Schelling's *System of Transcendental Idealism*.

'Coleridge is very desirous to be a refined and sensible philosopher and metaphysician,' commented Henry Cross Robinson, 'and at the same time conform with the people in its religion.'[70] The comment neatly encapsulates the dilemma in question. In the end, popular faith and recondite philosophy were to prove incompatible, and Coleridge returned to the Anglicanism of his childhood. Though there were several reasons for this reversion, the political motive was surely a forceful one. His adventures among the Idealists had generated some vital ideas for his prose, as well as providing abundant material for his poetry. Yet there is a sense in which, as far as the question of faith went, he might as well have remained where he was.

For Schiller, Fichte and Coleridge, the task of the state is the ethical formation of humanity. In this project, culture or *Bildung* forms the mediation between the brutish creature of civil society and the moderate, civilised, sweetly reasonable citizen. In civil society, individuals live in a state of chronic mutual antagonism; the state, by contrast, is the transcendent sphere in which these divisions are harmoniously reconciled. Culture is a form of ethical pedagogy which grooms us for political citizenship by liberating the collective self buried within each breast. It is this ideal self which finds supreme expression in the universal sphere of the state. By retrieving our shared humanity from our sectarian selves, culture rescues the spirit from the senses, salvages unity from conflict and plucks the changeless from the temporal. The rift between state and society – between how the average bourgeois citizen would wish to represent himself, and how he actually is – is accordingly healed. Friedrich Schlegel believes in 'exalting all politicians and managers into artists', a version of the culture-state with a vengeance.[71] Culture and the state, as David Lloyd and Paul Thomas point out, 'are both sites in which division is supposed to be transcended'.[72] Both present themselves as profoundly impartial agencies, setting aside distinctions of birth, class, gender, rank, property, privilege and the like in order to form the fundamental ground on which citizens can converge simply by virtue of their shared humanity. If the state itself is a somewhat remote image of this communality, art and a national culture bring it forcefully home to lived experience. It is a generous-hearted vision, for all its political illusions.

Disinterestedness, to be sure, requires a solid material basis. Shaftesbury, like many another civic humanist, believed that to be absolved from prejudice and partisanship involved being free from greed, want, envy, possessiveness and a capacity to be bribed, all of which were likely to corrupt one's political judgement. The political state needs citizens who can rise above their endemic egoism to achieve a dispassionate view of the common good, which means among other things men who are prosperous enough not to bend public affairs to their own advantage. To know the truth, you need to be well-heeled. In a choice irony, disinterestedness is founded on property, which in turn is the fruit of self-interest. Only by possessing a reasonable portion of the world's goods can one place the world judiciously at arm's length. The aesthetic may have seen itself as remote from the world of property, appetite and privilege, but this is one of several ways in which it is the product of it.

* * *

Idealism had a hand in producing one of the most successful of all modern surrogates for religious faith: nationalism.[73] It is a movement which Romanticism was to bring to fruition. It is in nationalism that the concept of culture first assumes its current depth and resonance, long before the advent of professional anthropology or the rise of the culture industry. The idea of culture itself dates back to the Enlightenment, but the rise of nationalism lends it new importance. Nationalism, needless to say, is a secular movement in its own right, and should be treated as such. All the same, there are aspects of it which owe a heavy debt to religious thought and feeling. For a certain vein of Romantic nationalism, the nation, like the Almighty himself, is sacred, autonomous, indivisible, without end or origin, the ground of being, the source of identity, the principle of human unity, a champion of the dispossessed and a cause worth dying for. It is an ideal to be honoured by solemn rites, and gives birth to a pantheon of saints, martyrs, venerable patriarchs and totemic heroes. The nation is incomparably greater than any individual, rather as God transcends his own Creation; yet it also lies at the core of personal identity, which is also true of the Christian deity.

By the mid-twentieth century, nationalism had come to seem every bit as ubiquitous as the Supreme Being, having spread from one end of the earth to the other. It was even possible to see it not only as religious but as specifically Roman Catholic. 'Like a divine religion,' writes the Irish nationalist leader Padraic Pearse, 'national freedom bears the marks of unity, of sanctity, of catholicity, of apostolic succession.'[74] It is surprising that he does not include a ban on contraception among its distinctive features. Romantic nationalism – in the case of Ireland, Pearse, the Young Irelanders and the Celtic Revival, in contrast to Tone, O'Connell, Parnell, Larkin and Connolly – is also much given to veneration – though since the object of worship is the nation, and therefore in a sense oneself, it tends to betray a certain narcissistic strain.

Like culture and the aesthetic, Romantic nationalism is an anti-political brand of politics. It maintains a certain fastidious distance from the workaday world of power and administration. It is hard to imagine Pearse or Sibelius chairing a sanitation committee. If it brings divinity down to earth, it also raises politics to a more ethereal plane. 'Nation state' signifies a secular set-up (state) infused with the spiritual wisdom of the common folk (nation). Conversely, as the nation is sublimed to the state, the everyday culture of the people is endowed with official status. As such, it achieves a dignity and recognition it has rarely enjoyed before. Politics becomes a less pedestrian pursuit, charged as it is with a visionary ardour rarely witnessed in the corridors of power. The rational and the Romantic are intertwined. Legal and political order, along with certain imperishable moral truths, are linked to the everyday affections and aversions of the masses. Ancient myth and modern progress, popular customs and military strategy, are yoked together. So, indeed, are past, present and future, which nationalism seeks to gather into organic unity. The secular, fragmented time of the modern is countered by the sacred, unruptured narrative of the nation. It is not easy to envisage a more potent coupling of culture and politics. The cultural politics of postmodernity cannot hold a candle to it. Reason, in the sense of certain universal truths, could finally cross the gap that divided it from the masses. Despite the fears of the *Kulturkritikers*, whose views we shall be examining later, culture could now be a political force with no detriment to its spiritual status.

Nationalism is a primary source of the notion of culture as totality – as the whole way of life of a people or ethnic group. At the same time, however, it promotes an idea of culture as partisan. This is a strikingly rare combination. For Schiller, as we have seen, culture and partisanship are sworn antagonists. The same is true for Matthew Arnold, whose views on the question we shall be considering later. Nationalism, by contrast, takes a stand, but does so in the name of culture. The nation's way of life may constitute a unity, but it is also a source of ferocious dissent. The common culture known as the nation is pitched into conflict with the colonial powers. For *Kulturkritik*, culture is about harmony; for identity politics, it is a matter of militancy. For nationalism, it is a question of both.

In common with some Idealist thinkers, the Romantic artist dreams of an organic bond with the common people. So much is evident from Wordsworth and Coleridge's *Lyrical Ballads*, which was greeted with accusations of Jacobinism.[75] The poet is the unacknowledged legislator of mankind, a role nowadays inherited by the banks and transnational corporations. W.H. Auden once remarked that it sounded more like the secret police. 'We have been called upon to educate the earth,' writes Novalis with becoming modesty.[76] With nationalism, this fantasy becomes reality, as artists, scholars and intellectuals are assigned prominent roles in a popular political movement. For a precious moment, the intellectual can become a public activist in the manner of a Yeats or Senghor, proclaiming his solidarity with the lowlier members of the nation. The scholar, remarks Fichte in *The Vocation of the Scholar*, is the guide of the human race. It is an unlikely claim in normal conditions; but as nationalist politics gather pace, hitherto obscure archivists, archaeologists, genealogists, philologists and antiquarians find themselves thrust into the political limelight.

Nationalism is the most poetic form of politics in the modern age – 'the invention of literary men', as Elie Kedourie remarks.[77] A number of its iconic figures have been more preoccupied with the spirit of the nation than with agrarian reform. As a British army officer observed when his soldiers shot Pearse and his comrades dead in 1916, 'We have done Ireland a service: we have rid it of some second-rate poets.' There was indeed a plethora of indifferent versifiers among the Republican dead. Like the poet, the nationalist rebel helps to ease into the world a magnificently autonomous artefact. Nations, like works of art, are self-creating, and nationalist politics are especially hospitable to the creative imagination. They tend to give rise to some distinguished works of art, as neo-liberalism and social democracy do not. It is thus that nationalism provides a link between the two chief senses of culture – as a body of artistic and intellectual work, and as a whole way of life. Culture in the former sense may seem an improbable saviour of humanity, but to place art at the service of the nation is to lend it a function in an age when it appears to lack one. One of nationalism's more modest achievements is to offer a practical solution to the problem of art's dysfunctionality in the modern era. Culture in the sense of a national form of life is a far less unlikely redeemer. Indeed, it has furnished modernity with one of its most potent political conceptions. For all its demonic variants and Romantic delusions, nationalism has proved by far the most successful revolutionary current of the modern epoch. In its coupling of ardent idealism and everyday existence, it is a match for religion itself; the only problem in this respect is that it is also a strictly transient phenomenon. Once it has achieved political independence, nationalism can be allowed to wither away. This is also why seeing Marxism as a replacement for religion involves a kind of category mistake. Christians hope still to believe on their deathbed, whereas political radicals trust that they will be free to abandon their efforts long before that point.

Like several of his German colleagues, Herder, a pre-eminent theorist of nationalism, sees the world itself as a prodigious work of art, self-originating and self-sustaining, combining unity and diversity. The diversity consists in a galaxy of distinctive nations, all of which contribute in their own unique way to the unfolding totality of human powers (Herder's *Humanität*). Indeed, the early Herder is easily read as a cultural relativist, holding as he does that all these different cultures are mutually incommensurable. They are to be judged only by their own internal standards. His vision of a universal history of humanity is a later evolution. He refuses to rank one civilisation over another, or to reject the so-called primitive in the name of the civilised. He also combines his nationalism with an ardent internationalism, much as he disdains a shallow Enlightenment cult of cosmopolitanism. In his view, the Eurocentrism of the Enlightenment, with its monochrome history of humanity, must be vigorously contested. The linguistic turn in philosophy, in which Herder plays a decisive role, is closely bound up with a nationalist sensitivity to the variety of languages and cultures. (Language, Hamann insists, is 'the first and last organ and criterion of reason.')[78] If religion is of supreme value, it is largely because it lies at the heart of each nation's popular culture, so that a reversion to faith is a return to the folk. In this sense, Herder discerns a link between the scepticism of the Enlightenment and its elitism. Ideas may be the province of the intelligentsia, but religion constitutes a kind of emotional democracy, a treasure house of instincts and affections accessible to all. He also insists that if the people are to come into their own, the state, in Marxist style, must wither away.

Fichte, who was denounced as a Jacobin, preaches a somewhat sinister gospel of self-sacrifice for the national good in his *Address to the German Nation*. Only by such immersion in the corporate being is the individual able to thrive. The nation, in a famous flourish, is the work of God. It is culture, not politics, that endows it with a unique identity. Yet he, too, proclaims an internationalist vision of a kind, claiming that each nation should find its own peculiar path to autonomy. In fact, few political currents are more international than nationalism. Fichte also insists that national unity should be achieved through equality and individual rights, *pace* those who have glimpsed in him a forerunner of fascism.

The other world-changing movement influenced by Idealist thought is Marxism. It was here, astonishingly, that the abstruse speculations of the philosophers took on a guise which was to transfigure the lives of innumerable men and women. Is Marxism, like Romantic nationalism, a substitute form of religion? The kernel of Marx's thought – the materialist theory of history, with its doctrines of class struggle, the primacy of the economic, the succession of modes of production, the conflict between the forces and relations of production and so on – owes nothing to religious conceptions. Nor is there any very obvious continuity between the Holy Trinity and the labour theory of value, or the Virgin Birth and the ratio of fixed to variable capital. In this sense, at least, Marxism is a thoroughly secular form of politics.

In a broader sense, however, there are clear affinities between religious thought and Marx's vision of history. Justice, emancipation, the day of reckoning, the struggle against oppression, the coming to power of the dispossessed, the future reign of peace and plenty: Marx shares these and other motifs with the Judaeo-Christian heritage, however coy some of his epigones may be about confessing the fact. There are votaries of Marx who will readily confess his debt to the most arcane Hegelian ideas, yet who jib at the proposition that he might also have paid his dues to religious thought. Marxism should feel enriched by this legacy, not embarrassed by it. He himself was an enthusiastic reader of the Old Testament prophets.

Marx also learnt something from the Judaeo-Christian rejection of fetishism and idolatry, as well as from its tragic insistence that dissolution is the prelude to new life. There is no need to conclude from this, in the crudely reductive manner of the philosopher John Gray, that modern revolution is simply a continuation of religion by other means.[79] Fredric Jameson is right to observe in his *Marxism and Form* that the claim that Marxism has a religious provenance has been among other things 'one of the principal arguments in the anti-Communist arsenal';[80] but he adopts a more affirmative attitude elsewhere in his work, remarking in *The Political Unconscious* that Marx's doctrine is not necessarily discredited by its debt to this legacy.[81] 'I certainly hope that Marxism projects a salvational history,' he observes in *Valences of the Dialectic*. He blots his copybook a little, however, in assuming that salvation for Christianity is a purely individual affair.[82] On the contrary, both Jewish and Christian Scripture conceive of salvation in terms of an entire people, while Marx, who is often pilloried for thinking only in collective terms, is much preoccupied with the emancipation of individual powers.

* * *

Idealism did not succeed in replacing an orthodox version of Christianity with a secularised one. Among other things, it was too esoteric an affair for that, even if it was always far more than a handful of learned works. Karl Korsch speaks in his *Marxism and Philosophy* of how 'German idealism had tended, even on the theoretical level, to be more than just a theory or philosophy'.[83] Yet much of its thought was as remote from the common people as Leibnizian monadology or Newtonian physics. There is, to be sure, no reason why philosophy should define its goal as enlightening the masses; but we have already seen that such an aim was close to the heart of some Idealist thinkers. In this respect, their success is to be measured by their own aspirations.

Besides, Idealist thought was too dewy-eyed about humanity, in the manner of young, ebullient social movements, to match Christianity's bleak moral realism. It was too callow to acknowledge how much in human nature stood in need of repair. Some strains of Romanticism shared this illusion. Theologically speaking, most Idealist thinkers were Pelagians. There was evil, to be sure, but it sprang for the most part from the repression, division or estrangement of powers which were benign in themselves. That these powers might be inherently flawed, even pathologically so, was not a typical tenet of Idealism, though it is to be found among the Romantics. The difference between these two versions of human nature is an aspect of the difference between Marx and Freud. The latter is a devout believer in Original Sin, while the former is not.

Powers which are still in the ascendant are more likely to idealise human capabilities than those which have passed their prime, as the distance between Shelley and Hardy might suggest. They are likely to regard the doctrine of Original Sin as offensively demeaning. Yet that doctrine, at least in its mainstream versions, does not regard men and women as utterly corrupt. On the contrary, it holds that they have a capacity for redemption which can never be suppressed, but only if they repent – which is to say, only if they take soberly realistic account of the tenacity of human egoism, the persistence of violence and self-delusion, the arrogance of power, the compulsive recurrence of conflict, the fragility of virtue and the eternal dissatisfaction of desire. Otherwise, it is a case of buying one's cheerfulness on the cheap. By and large, the Idealists do not imagine any more than did the Enlightenment *philosophes* that a

radical self-dispossession is a necessary condition of human flourishing. It is one of their less well chronicled blind spots.

For all its suggestive reflections on the idea of tragedy, Idealist
thought is essentially anti-tragic. The same is true in a more
qualified sense of Romanticism. It is no accident that the
English Romantics produced only a meagre amount of tragic drama
worth reading, let alone performing. Both currents of thought
come up with theodicies or justifications of evil, a sure index of
moral callowness. Discord and affliction in the present will be
shown in the fullness of time to have played their part in the flourishing of humanity as a whole. Suffering can be justified by being
cast in narrative form. In a nationalist variant of Social Darwinism,
Fichte held that strife between nation states would promote the
general welfare of the species, as superior powers vanquished
weaker ones and in doing so spread the gospel of civilisation. Fables
of a past Fall from paradise, a current state of division and disaffection, and a future kingdom of peace and unity weave their way
through the fabric of Idealist and Romantic thought like an
unbroken thread.

Idealist thought is one of the last great attempts to confront
orthodox religion with a vision of the world as spiritual and as
systematic as its own. In its concern with foundations and absolute
grounds, its striving for unity and totality, it looks back in some
respects to the great rationalist syntheses of the Enlightenment.
Indeed, the frontier between the two phases of thought is often
uncertain: into which category, for example, is Herder to be slotted?
The distance between the Enlightenment's a priori axioms and
the absolute spiritual principles of the Idealists is hardly great.
At the same time, in its reflections on the unfathomable depths of

the subject, Idealism looks towards Romanticism, from which, once more, it can often be distinguished only by the slimmest of borders. There are plenty of occasions when the distinction has little force. Schelling is as much a Romantic as Shelley is an Idealist.

If Enlightenment rationalism placed its faith in concept and system, a good deal of Idealism retains that trust, but brings this intellectual armoury to bear on the world of Spirit. It was never very likely, however, that something as quicksilver as Spirit would rest easy with anything as arthritic as a system of concepts. For Hegel, a new style of thought, one of a dialectical kind, was needed to cope with a world whose truth is its perpetual becoming, of which common-or-garden Reason can give us only a snapshot or evanescent image. Generally speaking, Spirit for Idealism could still be contained within system, even if one can feel it straining at the leash. In some Romantic thought, by contrast, it breaks loose from that system, thus testifying to its own sublimely creative power, but also to the loss of its ability to hold the whole of reality in a single thought. It is to this topic that we can now turn.

# CHAPTER 3

# ROMANTICS

IF ROMANTICISM TURNS for the most part from system to Spirit, it would seem more a question of religion than theology, more a matter of faith than knowledge.[1] Concepts can no longer contain the human subject, which is testimony to its energy and exuberance, but which also suggests that it is drifting free of any knowable foundation. In order to be valid, any system of ideas must contain its own antithesis. As Friedrich Schlegel wryly observes, 'it is equally fatal for the mind to have a system and to have none. It will simply have to decide to combine the two.'[2] 'All searching for a single principle,' declares Novalis in his joust with Fichte, 'would be like an attempt to square the circle.'[3] Whereas Fichte perceives a kind of absolute in the infinitely aspiring self, Novalis detects just the opposite. To spurn the absolute is in his view the very precondition of striving. 'Unending free activity in us,' he writes, 'arises through the free renunciation of the absolute – the only possible absolute that can be given us and that we only find through our inability to attain and know an absolute.' The drive to philosophise is consequently an activity without end, 'and without end because there would be an eternal urge for an absolute ground that can be satisfied only relatively, and that would therefore never cease.[4] 'We seek the absolute everywhere,' Novalis writes, 'and only ever find finite things.'[5] Hölderlin similarly repudiates absolute foundations. For the Idealists, the Absolute served among other things as a form of secularised divinity. Now, even that is proving elusive. An essentially religious striving for the infinite remains, but the object of this desire is impenetrable and obscure. For some Romantic artists, what is left of God is simply the yearning to be at one with him. In this respect they prefigure psychoanalysis, an atheism which deals in a quasi-religious desire for an impossible fulfilment.

Generally speaking, Romanticism is a darker, more troubled affair than Idealism, even if in another of its moods it shares its zest and buoyancy. What evades the grasp of philosophy is desire, in all its sublime infinity. If desire is infinite then it is also eternally unsatisfied, shuttling from one sterile object to another in pursuit of a paradise that is always lost, and coming in the end to rest only in itself. Like Goethe's Faust, it must content itself with this endless process of becoming, not with any assured end product. 'Hölderlin's poetics,' writes David Constantine, 'are a theory of perpetual onward movement.'[6] Striving, wandering and uprootedness are key motifs of his poetry. If Enlightenment Reason signifies a kind of perfection, a faculty which in Swiftian phrase is always true and just, art for the Romantics is in quest of a completion it can never attain, and would cease to exist were it to do so. In this respect, it is a model of the humanity which produces it, whose very essence is to have a history. The human subject is now present only in so far as it is absent, knowable only in its perpetual lack. 'We seek everywhere the unconditional,' Novalis comments, 'and find only the conditional.'[7]

It is thus the adventure of poetry, not the closure of philosophy, that most truly reflects the human condition. 'Whereas idealism embodies the fulfilment of the Subject in the labour of the concept,' write Philip Barnard and Cheryl Leser, 'the Jena romantics ... envisage the production of the Subject (the Subject's auto-production) in the work of art ... one might say that faced with a subject frozen in Kantian antinomies, like Frankenstein in the polar ice, idealism invents the speculative dialectic while romanticism invents literature.'[8] Once thought is pulled up short by a yearning that can only be known existentially, it is inevitable that conceptual discourse should give way to the birth of Literature, an event which Philippe Lacoue-Labarthe and Jean-Luc Nancy's *The Literary Absolute* regards as first breaking upon the world in the writings of the Jena Romantics.

Hegel's solution to desire is love. Instead of seeking fulfilment in an object, the subject must acknowledge that it can flourish only through another of its kind. It is when two free, equal individuals engage in an act of mutual recognition that desire can transcend itself into something rather more edifying. Schopenhauer's response to human longing is to annihilate it, a condition of nirvana-like indifference best exemplified by the aesthetic. Art is the death of desire.[9] For Friedrich Schlegel, desire comes to rest in beauty, which in turn finds its epitome in the work of art. Art is a refinement or sublimation of desire, raising it to universal status while defusing its disruptiveness. Its role is to convert passion into the dispassionate. There may come a point at which to persist in our desire means jeopardising the harmony of our impulses as a whole, a harmony which beauty is taken to signify. A balance must therefore be struck between the fullest possible degree of self-expression and the requirements of aesthetic symmetry. One must realise one's powers in a way compatible with a certain all-roundedness. This moral equipoise is best exemplified by art, and in Schlegel's judgement achieves supreme consummation in the culture of classical Greece.

There is a sense in which Schelling and Fichte, unlike Kant or Hegel, are as wary of the cold touch of the concept as any Romantic artist. The Absolute is to be grasped not discursively but intuitively, aesthetically or in the very act of self-reflection. Yet both thinkers are confident that it can still be known with certainty, whereas a Romantic like Novalis holds in his *Fichte Studies* that the Absolute, like the self, can be apprehended only negatively, in a kind of incessant homesickness or nostalgia.[10] We feel its presence in the very failure of our efforts to attain it, as infinity for Kant can be glimpsed for a fleeting moment in that straining at the frontiers of the finite which is the sublime. The Absolute can be shown but not said. Perhaps it is simply a regulative idea or convenient fiction, essential but out of reach. In this respect, Romanticism is a species of negative theology, stranded somewhere between an assured faith on the one hand and the death of God on the other.

'Our first task,' announces Fichte in his *Science of Knowledge*, 'is to discover the primordial, absolute self.'[11] Novalis, by contrast, holds that to aim directly for the Absolute in this fashion is a dangerous fantasy, an intoxication of the spirit which can drive men mad. It would be like staring straight at the sun. Friedrich Schlegel is also a convinced anti-foundationalist, holding as he does that any attempt to identify a first principle is bound to lead to an infinite regression.[12] Art can speak of God only allegorically. Our imperfect knowledge of the Absolute involves a form of irony, as any specific viewpoint is overshadowed by the possibility of an infinity of others. Irony for Romanticism is as fathomless as desire. Jacobi likewise rejects all efforts to ground humankind in itself, rather than in its Creator. The conditions of possibility of knowledge, he insists against Kant, cannot themselves be an object of knowledge. If the transcendent is off-bounds, so is the transcendental.

Schleiermacher shares this suspicion of solid grounds. For him, too, there can be no unimpeachable foundations. Knowledge is always imperfect, agreement purely provisional, and no total scheme of philosophy is possible. If we need an image of how our existence resists being totalised, we have only to turn to the discursive nature of language, prime medium of our humanity, which can never be brought to a close. Meaning for the founder of modern hermeneutics is always an unstable affair. For Schleiermacher as for Kierkegaard, the individual is irreducible to any sort of system. Neither can there be any final reconciliation between the individual and the universal. Existence is prior to reflection, and manifests a density that eludes the grip of the concept. Being is irreducible to thought. Philosophy must be alert to its embeddedness in the material world, rather than (as with Idealism) absorbing the world into its own innards. In any case, it is feeling, not thought, that constitutes our primary relation to reality. The affections which for some Enlightenment thinkers posed an obstacle to our knowledge of things are for the Romantics a vital mode of access to them. 'Feeling's a kind of knowledge,' as George Eliot's Adam Bede remarks.[13]

An abstract view of objects, for Schleiermacher as much as for Hamann, rests on a fundamental conviction of their reality, one which cannot itself be theorised.[14] Faith is thus the foundation of knowledge. Acts of cognition presuppose a backdrop of belief which is irreducible to reason. Such faith can thus do service for a rational foundation, since a foundation in reason alone would seem to be self-undoing. The language in which one described such a ground could always be further explicated, so that the ground in question would cease to figure as absolute. To describe is to displace. As Wittgenstein once remarked, it is hard to conceive of a foundation without feeling the urge to slip another one beneath it, just as it is hard to imagine an origin without feeling that you can go back beyond it. Yet a foundation which can only be intuited, or which is merely a matter of faith, would seem to buy its solidity at the price of a certain opacity. It is as mysterious as it is unassailable. It cannot be gainsaid, but neither can it be demonstrated.

In general, as we have seen, the Romantics share the theodicy of the Idealists. Humanity has fallen into strife and dissension, but only as an essential prelude to a future state of harmony, one that will prove superior to the primitive unity from which we have lapsed. The Fall is a *felix culpa*. Some Romantic thinkers, however, are unconvinced that this paradise can ever be regained. Civilisation and consciousness have severed humanity from Nature, and it is hard to see how these things, by some homeopathic miracle, can heal the very wounds they have inflicted. Perhaps we must accept that the lost object of desire can never be retrieved – that its absence is absolute, and that our fruitless pursuit of it at least has the virtue of launching that endless voyage into consciousness we call history. A fissure has opened up between subject and object, and one of its several names is desire. What allows us to act and speak, including what allows us to mourn the lost object, is the very trauma of its removal. Otherwise, our blissful union with it would strike us dumb. Poetry stems from a primal rent in our being which it also seeks to repair, and as such is both sickness and cure.

There is a similar ambiguity about the Romantic imagination. In Wordsworth's case, so M.H. Abrams observes, this revered faculty 'plays a role equivalent to that of the Redeemer in Milton's providential plot'.[15] It is a Christ-like capacity of redemption and reconciliation, one which mimes God's own creative power. Like one who receives the Holy Spirit, the artist, inspired by this divine capability in his breast, feels a sacred charge to communicate it to his fellow creatures. It is by virtue of this power that we can project ourselves into the emotional interior of others, so that the imagination is deeply bound up with love.[16] It is the ruin of the Kantian distinction between the moral and aesthetic, since virtuous conduct is founded on fellow feeling, and fellow feeling flows from imaginative sympathy. For the Shelley of *A Defence of Poetry*, the imagination is a form of sacrificial self-dispossession, and as such a riposte to possessive egoism. This is one of several senses in which it figures as a political force. There is a centrifugal motion about it which carries us out of our own purblind existence and allows us to recreate the experience of being something or someone else. If it lies at the core of the self, it is also a decentring of it. It is this empathetic faculty, not some bland Olympian *apatheia*, which is the true meaning of disinterestedness, for Romantics like William Hazlitt as much as for eighteenth-century benevolists like Goldsmith and Hutcheson. To be disinterested is to promote others' interests above one's own. It is the enemy of egoism, not of partisanship.

It is through this imaginative force that individuals become most intensely alive; yet in doing so they also become conscious of sharing in some larger, more corporate form of existence, aware that the roots of the self sink down to infinity. What makes a thing uniquely itself is the way it participates in some greater whole, rather as for Christianity it is through a dependence on God's grace that we can be most unreservedly ourselves. The imagination is a secular form of grace, one which seizes upon the self from some unfathomable depth beyond it, but which in doing so allows it to flourish in its own inimitable way. Men and women can subdue the earth and transform their conditions without the sin of hubris, since the power which allows them to do so springs from a region beyond themselves. The subject does not fundamentally belong to itself.

To speak against the imagination would thus seem something of a blasphemy, not least in literary circles. For Coleridge, it is what reconciles opposites and resolves contradictions. For Fichte, it is the infinitely productive spirit that brings reality into being in the first place. Schleiermacher regards the imagination as the key human faculty. Novalis sees all our powers and faculties as deducible from it. For William Blake, it is the only authentic mode of human existence. It is the vital link between the I and the Not-I, subject and object, spiritual and material, time and eternity, inner and outer, self and world. It is also a transformative force, reshaping the stuff of reality into the translucent medium of human desire. As a redemptive power, it brings the dead to life by de-reifying the world around us. Objects in their natural state are relatively unreal, mere snapshots of a process in perpetual motion. It is the imagination which restores them to their full splendour, setting them in their contexts and recreating them in the image of their eternal essences. As the poetry of Hölderlin would suggest, Romantic art seeks to disclose the divinity implicit in things, re-enchanting a world gone stale and sour.

Rarely have such fulsome claims been made for a human faculty. However, this life-giving spirit can be cursed as well as blessed, demonic as well as angelic. That it brings the world so magnificently alive bears witness to its formidable power; yet it also suggests that without its animating force, things in their natural condition would be brute and unregenerate. Coleridge's 'in ourselves alone doth Nature live' may be heard either as a cry of triumph or a lament. What if reality were to lapse into inertia once the creative mind is withdrawn from it, as objects in some Berkeleian fantasy might vanish if God were to take his eye off them?

It is true that this faculty is the key to resolving contradictions; but this means that contradictions are resolved in imaginary terms rather than in actual ones. Besides, if the imagination enhances the life of things, it can also show them up as trifling against the backdrop of its own resplendent glory. The more perishable time appears in contrast to this immortal power, the more exquisitely precious each moment becomes, yet the more each of them is haunted by the sickening prospect of its own demise. The more insistently present things appear, the more poignantly they remind you of their potential absence. In intimating that there are untold worlds beyond the present, the imagination also makes the subjunctive seem inherently superior to the indicative. To this extent, it is an implicit comment on the paucity of the present.

The imagination can be a revolutionary force, but it also holds out some spiritual solace for revolutions that have gone awry. It must distance itself from reality if it is to perform its transformative work on it, yet this distance can easily slide into divorce. The power which binds us to the world can also estrange us from it. Goethe regarded the imagination as a split faculty, a source of terror and delirium as well as a fount of creative energy.[17] There was something of the arbitrary and anarchic about it. It could be wayward, narcissistic and unruly. As a classicist in love with order and equipoise, he found in this much-vaunted faculty an alarmingly indeterminate power. He thus felt the need to distinguish between benign acts of imagining and morbid ones, a distinction embarrassingly easy to dismantle. If the imagination can give rise to deception as well as redemption, it is because a capacity to err is built into it. This most exalted of capabilities is never very far from idle fantasy. John Keats is especially alert to its snares and seductions. Yeats uses the word 'dream' to mean delusion about as often as he uses it to mean poetic vision. As some Romantic authors would come to acknowledge, the imagination can never be unequivocally affirmed. One must confront the alarming possibility that the sources of creativity are tainted at source. The doctrine of Original Sin is by no means unfamiliar to this style of thought.

Wordsworth's poetry, as Geoffrey Hartman has superbly shown, is troubled by the half-suppressed suspicion that the imagination is far from the curative power the poet himself would wish it to be.[18] On the contrary, it manifests itself in certain apocalyptic moments as death-dealing and disruptive, a sublimely unfathomable force which rears up abruptly to blot out the world of sense and plunge us headlong into the frightful abyss of the self. There is something of Freud's Thanatos about it, as well as a smack of the Lacanian Real.[19] Far from reconciling us to reality, the Wordsworthian imagination pitches us out of our abode in Nature and leaves us traumatised and bereft. In opening up an unsettling gap between the natural and the transcendent, it dissolves the everyday world into so much meretricious show and reminds us that our true home is in eternity, not in any sublunary spot. As such, it is as much a divisive capacity as a unifying one. It has the terror of the divine as well as its beneficence. For Wordsworth, part of the task of poetry is to naturalise and domesticate this turbulent power.

Nature was not always looked on affably by Romantic thinkers. Schiller regarded it as destructive, amoral and indifferent, while Fichte abhorred the idea of natural necessity. Both saw this too-solid stuff as a threat to human freedom. The not-I might prove a necessary springboard for the I, but it cannot help reminding us there is more to the world than the almighty subject. Other thinkers were eager to dismantle the opposition between Nature and culture. Nature was itself a magnificent work of art, while culture constituted an organic whole. Like an accomplished aesthetic artefact, the natural world combined the true, the good and the beautiful. For Spinoza, it was God's own body. The human and natural spheres were both governed by certain great evolutionary laws, which we violated at our peril. Schelling detected a primal creative force or *natura naturans* at work in Nature, one with all the protean, shape-changing power of the artist. Some Romantic artists found in both Nature and the imagination a blessed respite from history. Both could serve as secular modes of transcendence. Yet as peaceable, harmonious and commonly shared, the natural world could also signify a form of politics. 'Nature is the enemy of eternal possessions,' writes Novalis.[20]

Nature gives voice to a universal spirit, yet lends it a local habitation and a name. It is as timeless and self-moving as the deity, the transcendent source of all life and an unfailing means of grace. There is an immensity about it which chastens men and women and recalls them to their humble place in the cosmos; yet it is also a partner in dialogue and a vital seat of the affections, inspiring its acolytes to love and loyalty. It is both intimate and anonymous, beautiful and sublime, mutable and monumental, combining the sternness of a patriarch with the tenderness of a mother. It is a union commended by Edmund Burke in his aesthetic treatise as the most effective form of sovereignty. In a bathetic moment in that essay, Burke casts around for a human example of such a blend of qualities, and comes up with (of all things) the grandfather.

\* \* \*

Nature, however, was not the only available image of organic unity. Few themes have run more consistently throughout modern European culture, from the eighteenth century to the late Victorians, as a veneration for ancient Greece. Peter Gay draws attention to the classical roots of the Enlightenment, an age which cast a fond backward glance to the rational humanism of classical antiquity rather than to what it saw as the barbarism of a more recent past.[21] Marilyn Butler speaks of Greek revivalism as the 'lingua franca of the international Enlightenment'.[22] Ancient Rome was equally in vogue. Shaftesbury was much taken with what he saw as the virtue and liberty of the classical world, describing ancient Greece as the 'sole polite, most civilised, and accomplished nation',[23] while Edward Gibbon celebrated the gravitas, simplicity, public spirit, humanism, individualism and spirit of liberty of the Roman Republic.[24] The French revolutionaries were to redouble the compliment. Frank M. Turner argues that at some point in the late eighteenth century a passion for classical antiquity, hitherto a fairly minor phenomenon, suddenly becomes central. 'The search for new cultural roots and alternative cultural patterns,' he writes, 'developed out of the need to understand and articulate the disruptive political, social, and intellectual experience that Europeans confronted in the wake of the Enlightenment and [French] revolution.'[25] It was a Graecomania that lasted at least until Heidegger's idyllic vision of the pre-Socratics.

The turn to the classical world was of prodigious cultural importance. It represented a vein of humanism of quasi-religious intensity, one which in intellectual circles offered a formidable challenge to the faith of the churches. For some enthusiasts of Plato and Aeschylus, the kinship between Greek myths and Christian doctrines could serve as a covert critique of the latter. Less polemical authors regarded Greek antiquity as exemplary of 'how, in a word, religion may be combined with Culture.'[26] Goethe thought the cult of Greek classical antiquity, whatever its undoubted defects, far preferable to Christianity. Schelling wrote with a flourish that 'all possibilities within the realm of ideas as constituted by philosophy are completely exhausted by Greek mythology.'[27] To his mind, such myths were not only the foundation of all philosophy; they also drew science, art and religion in their wake. Schiller and Schlegel hero-worshipped the classical Greek artists. Since they appeared to blend rational virtue with sensuous pleasure, they could stand as a living refutation of the ethics of Immanuel Kant. Matthew Arnold described ancient Greece as 'a country hardly less important to mankind than Judaea.'[28] The Hellenic was religion naturalised and aestheticised, stripped of its more unlovely aspects (duty, self-sacrifice, eternal punishment, the moral law) and rendered fit for gentlemen. Like religion, too, it was culture as a way of life in common, not simply as personal refinement or high-minded ideal.

The Romantics, then, turned back to a lost paradise in order to fare forward, as some of their modernist inheritors were to do as well. Ancient Greece stood for a childhood that was also a maturity. It was elusive because it was gone, but also because it was still to come. Hölderlin, one of the most passionate of Hellenists, taught that the spirit of Athens must flourish again in Germanic form.[29] It was hard for these zealots to acknowledge that Hellenism itself was simply another myth, one to set beside the rich store of antiquity's own.

'To no small extent,' Turner argues, 'knowledge of the classical world and acquaintance with the values communicated through the vehicle of classical education informed the mind and provided much of the intellectual confidence of the ruling political classes of Europe.'[30] This potent cultural resource acted as a password or badge of recognition among gentlemen across a range of places and periods. 'They are the writings of men of culture like ourselves,' Oscar Wilde's Classics tutor J.P. Mahaffy observed with charming self-deprecation of the works of the ancient Greeks. In the organic life-forms of antiquity, one meaning of culture – the way of life of a people – was infused with the vital energy of culture in the aesthetic sense.

The so-called Hellenic virtues – equipoise, erotic joy, wholeness, symmetry, serenity, harmony, stability, self-restraint, the life of the senses, blitheness of spirit, many-sidedness, a trust in spontaneous instinct and the like – were easy enough to contrast with the ugliness, disproportion, frenetic energy and leaden moral earnestness of modern bourgeois life. 'The poetry of the ancients,' writes Friedrich Schlegel, 'was the poetry of enjoyment, and ours is that of desire.'[31] It was not hard to contrast them either with the intemperate ardour of the mob. In the manner of much patrician ideology, Hellenic values were moral and aesthetic together. Their apologists were in quest of a cultural form that was brimful of boundless energy, yet which contained it within an organic mould. Such a form would radiate harmony and serenity while remaining fluid, mobile and ceaselessly dynamic. As such, it would offer a refuge from the restless exertions of the modern without danger of inertia. A finitude of form would be reconciled with an infinity of content. Content in the Romantic image, an image of which Hellenic *sanitas* is one example, is always on the point of exuberantly overflowing its formal limits, but is always just reined back by some inner reticence. In this sense, the Romantic image is both still and mutable, dead and alive, achieved yet open-ended. It arrests itself in an achieved form without detriment to its vitality. Motion is caught up in perpetual stasis, eternally curving back on itself like a fountain.[32] Infinity is converted into eternity, as the work of art stands free of the ravages of time while remaining fluid and alive. For Walter Pater, it is gem-like yet flaming with vitality, organic and inorganic at the same time. It is yet another micro-model of the Almighty. Yet the image is political as well as theological. Desire is contained rather than annulled, so that it no longer represents a 'bad' infinity of endless, fruitless yearning. Modern dynamism can thus be reconciled with traditional order. Or, to put the point more prosaically, the middle classes can surge forward without threat to political stability.

It is an ideal that haunts Romanticism from one end to another, from Coleridge's idiosyncratic observation about waterfalls – that they combine an unchanging form with an ever-changing content – to Yeats's dancer, fountain, spinning top and chestnut tree. Yeats was also to find this ideal in the Anglo-Irish Big House, where passion and precision, the spirited and the ceremonious, are as much in accord as they are in the verses which celebrate them. The image crops up again as the still point of the turning world of Eliot's *Four Quartets*, the form of motion that is also abstention from motion,[33] and the Chinese vase that seems to move perpetually in its stillness. It can even be glimpsed in Keats's rather curious reference to 'full-grown lambs' in his *Autumn* Ode. Perhaps this is a species of oxymoron, since lambs are by definition not full-grown. Full-grown lambs are sheep. Yet lambs can be fully grown as lambs go. The phrase suggests the mystery by which something can be self-identical yet still capable of growth; kinetic yet self-contained.

\* \* \*

Politically speaking, ancient Greece could provide an image of stability in a revolutionary epoch. For the most part, however, the idealisation of antiquity came with a republican inflection. '[Ancient] Greece,' comments Nicholas Boyle of the champions of revolutionary France, 'was [for them] a forerunner of the world's first fully enlightened, cosmopolitan, and rational state.'[34] 'Hellenism,' writes David Constantine, 'has revolutionary potential: it deduced from ancient Greece, especially from Periclean Athens, the model of a just society.'[35]

The political ambiguity of Hellenism ranks among the extraordinary contradictions of Romanticism in general. In a literary tour de force, Isaiah Berlin encapsulates a range of them in two or three dashing pages of *The Roots of Romanticism*. Romanticism is both youthful and decadent, exotic and everyday, dynamic yet tranquil, life-affirming but death-loving, individualist and communitarian, in love with the concrete yet shrouded in spiritual vagueness, primitive and dandyish, simple and sophisticated, inspired by the past but enthused by originality, devoted to unity yet rejoicing in diversity, committed to art as an end in itself yet also as an instrument of social regeneration.[36] In similar vein, Carl Schmitt remarks that there is 'a romanticism of energy and a romanticism of decadence, romanticism as the immediate actuality of life and romanticism as a flight into the past and tradition'.[37] If the movement includes some of the most fervent advocates of the French Revolution, it also contains some of its most rabid antagonists.[38] In a classic essay, A.O. Lovejoy wryly notes that Romanticism is supposed to have begotten both the French Revolution and the Oxford Movement.[39] Rarely has a trend of thought so enraptured by unity displayed so little. What sense can one make of a cultural current which includes both Percy Bysshe Shelley and Joseph de Maistre, a thinker who believed that irrational social institutions were more valid and enduring than rational ones, held that critical thought should be forcibly suppressed by a despotic state, and regarded scientists, democrats, atheists, intellectuals and Jews as among the enemies of civilisation?

All the same, there is no cause to surrender to a nominalism of the concept. For one thing, some of these apparent discrepancies can be accounted for in terms of chronology. From around the turn of the eighteenth century in Germany, a number of erstwhile radical-republican *Frühromantiker* (Novalis, the Schlegel brothers, Hölderlin, Schleiermacher) begin to strike more reactionary postures. Thinkers like Novalis and Friedrich Schlegel, who started out as zealots of anti-absolutism, sexual freedom and liberal reform, end up in the arms of monarchism, mysticism, aristocratism, medievalism and the Roman Catholic Church. It is now religion rather than art which will redeem the social order. It is this vein of German Romanticism that some of the Nazis were to acclaim. In England, the political apostasy of Wordsworth, Coleridge and Southey, or (as many a Romanticist would have it) their reversion to sanity after a regrettable spell of revolutionary infatuation, has been well enough mapped.

Romanticism, then, altered with the political times. Once revolutionary idealism faded in the light of realpolitik, it could shift readily enough into a more retrograde brand of idealism, one which dreamed fondly of feudalism or absolutism as a solution to contemporary ills. Yet this was rarely a complete volte-face. The *Frühromantiker*, for example, may have evolved from extolling the French Revolution to a politics not far removed from those of the Oxford Movement,[40] but they were never democrats, let alone full-blooded insurrectionists, to begin with. Their liberalism was mixed with a communitarianism that could shift over the course of time from left to right. Most of them advocated some form of elitist rule even in their more radical days. They were certainly deeply suspicious of the masses.

The contradictions of Romanticism are more than symptoms of incoherence. If the movement is divided against itself, it is largely because it is both a product of middle-class society and a protest against it. Its flamboyant individualism is among other things an idealised version of the entrepreneur; yet it is also a rebuke to the faceless civilisation he is busy fashioning, one in which men and women are reduced to so many cogs and ciphers. Spiritual individualism is to be prized, but its more possessive variety must be countered by some more corporate form of existence, whether in the form of Nature, *Geist*, art, culture, world-spirit, political love, medieval guilds, ancient Greece, utopian communities or the Kantian consensus of taste.

There is a similar ambiguity about the creative mind. Men and women are to be seen as self-determining agents, capable of transforming themselves and their conditions, and history thus comes to assume a value it never had for Newton or Locke. The problem is how to rescue the human subject from mechanical materialism in this way without falling prey to hubris. Human creativity must be defended against the determinists, but in doing so a civilisation with the world freshly at its feet must guard against an impious overreaching. The Fichtean fantasy of conjuring up objects simply in order to square off against them is a case in point. Carl Schmitt's *Political Romanticism* castigates the Romantics for reducing the world to an occasion for subjective fantasy, mere grist to the mill of the all-powerful ego.

There was, however, a solution of kinds to this dilemma. There is a 'bad' kind of passivity, which treats individuals as mere receptacles of sense data or functions of their environment, and it is this which the doctrine of the creative mind seeks to counter. Yet there is also a form of wise passiveness, a state of *Gelassenheit* in which human beings can be patiently, reverently open to the creaturely life around them. Keats's negative capability is one such suspension of the meddling will. A balance between activity and passivity may accordingly be struck. One instance of this equipoise is the inspired poet, whose mastery of his art springs from his dependence on a power which is not himself.

Other ambiguities abound. To champion feeling rather than reason is to challenge the bloodless rationality of the merchant and the clerk. Yet it may also be to prize the customary and instinctive over rigorous inquiry, and thus to insulate the social order from rational critique. The Romantic aversion to analytic thought was to breed some ominous effects in the later phases of the movement. 'The light is in my heart,' protests Jacobi, 'and as soon as I try to carry it to my intellect, it goes out.'[41] Those who have struggled to read him will know exactly what he means. Since affections are for the most part local, the turn from reason to feeling may mean exchanging an abstract universalism for a stiff-necked parochialism. The Romantic cult of the sensuous particular can have much the same consequences. Burke's little platoon is not always to be preferred to a global perspective. Feeling can be rallied to the standard of reaction as easily as it can be pressed into the service of revolt. The seat of the affections is commonly the family, which is scarcely a subversive force.

The notion of the organic can offer a welcome alternative to mechanistic reason. It is also a rebuff to a social order in which individuals seem to have lost all vital connection with one other. Yet to model social life on an organism is perfectly compatible with the idea of hierarchy, the head being palpably more important than the toenails. It also tends to favour gradual evolution over radical change. For an evolutionist like Edmund Burke, the mere fact that an institution has been long in the making is generally enough to justify it. Longevity is a kind of legitimacy. History is a conservative argument in itself, considerably more cogent than some abstract proposition. David Hume thought much the same.

There are other respects in which Romanticism is at odds with itself. Nature, art and the imagination are all precious resources for social renewal. Yet they can also offer an Olympian refuge from history when political hopes begin to fade. So it is that Wordsworth turns from the Jacobins to the mountains. The idea of a living universe challenges the inert matter of the rationalists, as well as upbraiding a crassly instrumental stance towards Nature. Yet it can equally serve as a mystification. Nature may not be dead matter, but neither is it exactly a subject. In any case, to regard Nature, art or humanity as an end in itself may be to forget that instrumental reason has its place in human affairs. There can certainly be no social change without it. Such a rationality was the stock-in-trade of the Romantics' sworn enemy, Utilitarianism; yet as the nineteenth century wore on, that doctrine was to result in some admirable social reforms. Dickens's crowd-pleasing contempt for it in *Hard Times* is typically brash and un-nuanced.

An art which is its own *raison d'être* is an eloquent riposte to exchange-value, but it is not easy to see how it can redeem the world. For the radical Romantics, art represents the values we live for, but it is not for art that we live. Autonomy is a political as well as aesthetic value, so that the self-dependence of the work of art speaks of more than itself. Somewhere between Shelley and Tennyson, this insight is mislaid. The imagination gradually ceases to be a political force. As the era of industrial capitalism unfolds, the autonomy of the artwork begins to speak only of itself. Radical Romanticism melts into *fin-de-siècle* aestheticism. Art itself comes to stand in for the *promesse de bonheur* it once held out.

There are further contradictions in Romantic thought, which can be touched on only briefly. For one thing, the idea of infinity can be a gesture of dissent, defying a rationalism for which what is real is what can be calculated. Yet it also tends to belittle the finite, and in doing so, ironically, can come to reflect the way in which rationalism itself devalues the world. For another thing, regarding humanity as en route to perfection may be a smack at the petty-bourgeois puritans, with their dour creed of human depravity; but it also fits well enough with the middle class's faith in its own unfathomable powers. Finally, it is worth noting that self-determination, so vital an idea to the Romantics, is politically double-edged. It can mean republicanism, anti-colonialism and popular democracy, to be sure; but it is also the creed of the captains of industry.

\* \* \*

Romanticism placed its indelible stamp on the modern age. From art to sexuality, ecology to subjectivity, it forms a major part of its cultural unconscious. The fiction of Charles Dickens is testimony to how swiftly and pervasively it transformed the common sensibility. Modern thinkers are inescapably post-Romantics, rather as they are ineluctable post-Darwinists or unwitting post-Freudians. It would be harder to claim that they are spontaneous post-Fichteans. Moreover, Romanticism fared especially well as a stopgap for religion, stepping from priest to poet, sacrament to symbol, holiness to wholeness, paradise to political utopia, grace to inspiration, God to Nature and Original Sin to the nameless crime of existing.

In general, however, it was the fate of the movement not to supplant the ruling powers but to supplement them. From Blake to Lawrence, some of its artists and thinkers offered a magnificent denunciation of industrial capitalism, one memorably recorded in Raymond Williams's *Culture and Society 1780–1950*.[42] As with the *Kulturkritiker* at whom we shall be glancing later, it was a critique which sprang largely from the radical right. Blake himself is a signal exception. It emerged, in other words, from the world-view which informed some of the most eminent literary art of the early twentieth century. Yet if it raised its voice against the spiritual devastation which industrial capitalism brought in its wake, it did so for the most part while consecrating the rights of capital. There were, to be sure, some honourable exceptions. In *fin-de-siècle* England, William Morris was to harness this tradition to a political current – the working-class movement –to produce a cultural critique that stood unrivalled in the annals of socialism until the advent of the Frankfurt School.

A Romantic homesickness for the pre-modern past – for the primitive, archaic, atavistic, barbaric or mythological – was to bear poisonous fruit in modern times. It was a legacy inherited by some modernism. Yet it was precisely because of its fondness for feudalism, hierarchy, Tradition, Lancelot Andrewes, classical China, ancient Mexico, pagan fertility cults or the imaginary organic society of seventeenth-century England that modernism could also act as a scourge of materialism, the cash nexus, possessive individualism, the despoiling of Nature, the debasement of popular culture and the dominative exercise of human powers. In this respect, its political ambiguities were not far from those of its Romantic precursors.

In the trek from the era of Hölderlin to the age of Hofmannsthal, Romanticism was to suffer something of the fate of the religion whose mantle it sought to inherit. As the unbelieving nineteenth century unfolded, it grew increasingly defensive and besieged, as did the churches. In the movement from the *Frühromantiker* and radical English Romantics to the Symbolists, Pre-Raphaelites and *fin-de-siècle* aesthetes, the drive to change the world was gradually overtaken by an impulse to disown it. A Romanticism which had once assumed an embattled stance in the public sphere became steadily privatised. It was, to be sure, a conflict which had been evident all along. There is a tension in Romantic thought between an urge to spurn the world and a desire to transform it. So is there in religion.

If art and religion were being thrust simultaneously out of the social mainstream, it seemed logical for them to end up in each other's arms. It was in this spirit that Matthew Arnold sought to press poetry into the service of religion, as we shall see in the next chapter. The truth, however, is that like the hapless Babes in the Wood, neither party was in good enough shape to come to the aid of the other.

# CHAPTER 4

# THE CRISIS OF CULTURE

IT IS REMARKABLE HOW long it took modernity to achieve an authentic atheism. Even when it did so, it was by no means by disproving or dispelling religious faith. Not believing in God is a far more arduous affair than is generally imagined. Whenever the Almighty seems safely despatched, he is always liable to stage a reappearance in one disguise or another. As Bruce Robbins writes, one needs to present the history of secularisation 'as real and significant, even if God-terms [i.e. God-substitutes] always invite further suspicion and further secularisation.'[1] Secular concepts, Robbins points out, themselves 'contain so much religious baggage' that religious faith is not easily consigned to a benighted past.

If the Enlightenment failed to dislodge religion, it was among other things because it did not entirely suit its political purposes to do so. Even had it done so, its species of rationality was both too critical and too cerebral to win the hearts and minds of the populace, who were more likely to be enthused by the Immaculate Conception than by some bloodless Supreme Being. The attempt to supplement this brand of Reason with a feel for everyday experience – aesthetics, in a word – could never be more than a coterie affair, rather as the

Idealist and Romantic project to reach the masses through mythology was never able to escape a certain sterile intellectualism. Only with the advent of the twentieth-century culture industry could the dreams and desires of the populace be brought en masse under the aegis of power, though never without resistance. There is a sense in which the mass mythology of which some earlier philosophers had dreamed was finally to arrive in the shape of cinema, television, advertising and the popular press.

What, then, of the idea of culture? If this had always been the most plausible candidate to inherit the sceptre of religion, it was because it involves foundational values, transcendent truths, authoritative traditions, ritual practices, sensuous symbolism, spiritual inwardness, moral growth, corporate identity and a social mission. Religion is both vision and institution, felt experience and universal project, and culture at its most self-assured sought to lay claim to all these features. The question was whether it could also rival the churches in bridging the gap between the values of a minority and the life of the common people that some Enlightenment scholars, Idealist sages and Romantic artists had found so disquieting. Could culture in the sense of minority values be linked with culture as a whole way of life? The Church had sealed the rift between them in its own fashion, enfolding clergy and laity in a single institution; and though the simple faithful may not be exactly on all fours with cardinals and theologians, this matters less than the faith they share. Within this social order, hierarchy and communality are fully compatible. A Swabian peasant will not grasp the doctrine of Original Sin in quite the same manner as a Tübingen theologian, but there are affinities between the two forms of understanding.

In 'The Idea of a Christian Society' and *Notes towards the Definition of Culture*, T.S. Eliot turns to the question of how religion might mean theology for the elite and mythology for the masses, yet be free of any conflict between the two. There is a distinction at work here between the conscious and the unconscious, as the truths articulated by the intelligentsia are lived out as spontaneous habit and unreflective custom by the common people. The same values are shared by both groups, but at different levels of awareness. Spiritual hierarchy can thus be reconciled with a common culture. Socialist equality is spurned, but so is liberal individualism. A similar theory lurks behind Eliot's drama, which is meant to stratify both characters and audiences into distinct levels of comprehension. The protagonist of *Murder in the Cathedral* is fully conscious of his tragic situation, whereas the Women of Canterbury, like many an Eliotic theatre audience, have for the most part only a dim sense of what is afoot. There are befuddled characters in *The Family Reunion* and *The Cocktail Party*, as there will be spiritually mediocre men and women in the circle and stalls, who are only vaguely aware that something momentous is taking place, and who cannot be expected to rise to any more incisive insight. Human kind cannot bear very much reality, not least its more menial members. Culture is the most complex form of self-awareness, but also the most richly unreflective. For Eliot as for Burke, it signifies a kind of social unconscious. It is the shadowy underside of the calculative and theoretical, revealing itself less in articulate belief than in taken-for-granted behaviour.[2]

Might culture succeed in becoming the sacred discourse of a post-religious age, binding people and intelligentsia in spiritual communion? Could it bring the most occult of truths to bear on everyday conduct, in the manner of religious faith? If it could, culture as normative idea would be at one with culture as descriptive category. Both senses of the idea – roughly speaking, the aesthetic and the anthropological – were involved in the dream of an organic society, in which everyday life would be invested with something of the creative elan of art. Could these two conceptions of culture now converge once more in the heartlands of industrial capitalism, so that culture might step into religion's shoes as a guarantor of social order and moral conduct?

The answer, in a word, was that they could not. No symbolic form in history has matched religion's ability to link the most exalted of truths to the daily existence of countless men and women. It is no wonder that the governing powers of Europe greeted the prospect of its demise with such alarm. Yet if the Enlightenment had failed to oust religious faith, and the Idealists and Romantics had failed to secularise it, the concept of culture proved too fraught and elusive to serve as a stopgap. It was clear that there could be no salvation in aesthetic culture alone. It was too minority a pursuit for that. Yet neither could one place any great hope of redemption in the idea of culture as a whole form of life. There are no whole forms of life. Human societies are manifold and contentious. Culture is more likely to reflect social divisions than to reconcile them. Once those contentions begin to infiltrate the concept of culture itself – once value, language, symbol, kinship, heritage, identity and community become politically charged – culture ceases to be part of the solution and instead becomes part of the problem. It can no longer present itself as a corporate alternative to one-sided interests. Instead, it shifts from a bogus transcendence to a militant particularism. This, in effect, has been the fate of culture under postmodernism.

\* \* \*

Edmund Burke did not have the term 'culture' at his disposal, but he was aware that the thing itself is a potent antidote to revolution. Indeed, there is a sense in which it is the very opposite of the political. Or at least, like the aesthetic, it is politics in non-political guise. The concept of culture has many sources in the modern age (nationalism, localism, the migration of peoples, imperialist anthropology, anti-capitalist critique, the decline of religious faith, identity politics and so on), but one could do worse than name the French Revolution as one of its chief progenitors. It is in reaction to that cataclysm that the notion of culture gathers a certain urgency. For Burke, culture is a question of organic intricacy, immemorial custom, sedimented habits of feeling, spontaneous allegiances, taken-for-granted pieties, time-hallowed institutions, instinctive affections and aversions, the subtly coercive force of tradition, the treasure house of a language, the veneration of ancestors and the love of country, landscape and kins-folk. As such, it inhabits a kind of geologically slow time, one which will strenuously resist the sudden transformation that is afoot across the Channel. The idea of cultural revolution on this view is some-thing of an oxymoron. A people refined by the grace that culture can bestow is one which sets aside unruly passion and clamorous parti-sanship in the name of concord and civility. To agitate against the status quo is political, whereas to defend it against such unmannerly behaviour is not. Culture speaks in moderate, even-tempered tones, whereas the voice of politics is rough and raucous. Agitating for women's rights would not count in Matthew Arnold's view as culture, whereas a courteous plea for patriarchy might well make the grade. All-roundedness turns out to be curiously one-sided.

True to this inheritance, the title of Arnold's best-known work, *Culture and Anarchy* (1869) really means Culture or Anarchy, rather as his *Literature and Dogma* really means Literature or Dogma. The anarchy in question is among other things that of the very mercantile classes extolled as apostles of culture by the eighteenth-century commercial humanists. By Arnold's time, however, culture in the sense of individual cultivation is no longer politically resilient enough. The point is not to staff the ranks of society with men of culture, but to deploy culture as a bulwark against social unrest. *Culture and Anarchy* thus seeks to bring the aesthetic version of culture to bear on the sociological one, at a moment when the class struggle in Victorian England is sharpening. The work's historical context is that of the Second Reform Bill, which hoped to secure the political incorporation of the working class into parliamentary democracy. The point of Arnold's book is to assimilate them spiritually as well.

Yet these two senses of culture are at strife throughout the text, as the argument slides continually from the one to the other. Culture is both temporal and eternal, social policy and personal cultivation, the process of attaining perfection and the condition of perfection itself. It is to be understood not primarily as a practical mode of life but as an 'inward operation' or contemplative state of mind. It 'places human perfection in an internal condition'.[3] In a series of anodyne formulas for which the work quickly became the butt of satiric parody, culture is a question of 'sweetness and light', 'our best self', 'the study of perfection', the power to 'make reason and the will of God prevail', 'seeing the object as it really is' and 'the best which has been thought and said in the world'. Because none of these resonant abstractions has much exact meaning, perhaps intentionally so, each of them can be evoked to reinforce the others, in a circular motion which anticipates the astonishingly repetitive prose of Arnold's later *Literature and Dogma*. In the light of these high-minded vacuities, one is not inclined to doubt that Arnold is seeing the object as it really is when he accuses himself (though it is secretly a self-compliment) of not being a philosopher. He may not have a philosophy, but he most certainly has an ideology.

The nullity of this concept of culture is more than the result of shoddy thinking. On the contrary, there is a certain necessity to its nebulousness. Culture cannot be precisely defined because its essence lies in its transcendence of the specific. Its vacuity is thus in direct proportion to its authority. Because it cannot be pinned down, it cannot be criticised either. Frederic Harrison was not slow to spot this portentous vacancy in a mischievous parody of Arnold's argument. Arnoldian culture meant 'everlasting movement, and nothing acquiesced in; perpetual opening of all questions, and answering of none; infinite possibilities of everything; the becoming all things, the being nothing'.[4] For Harrison himself, a disciple of Auguste Comte and Fellow of a notably progressive Oxford college (Wadham), culture meant in the first place not a condition of mind but the more palpable business of social reform. So it did for Arnold, in another of his personae.

Culture in Arnold's view is not in itself a question of action. It is rather the source from which fruitful action may spring. As with Schiller's aesthetic state, it signifies that supremely disinterested totality or many-sidedness from which all specific activity or social interest is bound to appear as a falling away – 'mere machinery', in Arnold's own loftily dismissive phrase. As such, it subtly devalues the very condition it seeks to repair. Arnold is at pains to insist in the teeth of his critics that it is only 'rough and coarse action' (the class epithets are noteworthy) that he wishes to forestall; but it is hard to avoid the suspicion that he regards action as simply externalising what has already been inwardly determined, rather than as a condition of such inwardness. Action may give expression to states of mind, but it is not constitutive of them.

As with Schiller, an impartial view of the whole means acting with a sense of the relativity of one's conduct in the great scheme of things. Culture is thus a formula for living ironically. One must be engaged and dispassionate at the same time. Arnold himself is a self-confessed philistine or member of the middle class; yet since he is also something of a maverick among his venal, coarse-minded confrères, he is able to pass judgement on the way of life to which he belongs as though from the outside. A certain playful detachment from one's own convictions is a mark of the man of culture; but it is also a kind of politics, since 'culture is the eternal opponent of the two things that are the signal marks of Jacobinism – its fierceness, and its addiction to an abstract system'.[5] Culture tempers the stridency of the political with an appeal to equipoise, keeping the mind serenely untainted by whatever is tendentious or sectarian. It is a classic Oxfordian case. Unlike the cerebral, excitable French, the English are notable both for their sangfroid and their incapacity for systematic thought. They are not the dupes of their own opinions. Arnold's prose style, with its urbane, eirenic quality, its occasional sense of the author smirking behind his hand, is itself an attempt to defuse such vehemence. It also serves to dissemble the fact that this self-composed sage is considerably more rattled by political circumstance than his bland, mildly self-satisfied style of writing would suggest. Thomas Carlyle's wrathful, apocalyptic prose provides an instructive contrast.

The opposite of Arnold's blithe self-irony, which refuses in patrician spirit to take anything too seriously, is the grim fanaticism of both middle-class moralist and plebeian tribune. In their stubborn one-sidedness, both are fatally bereft of a Hellenic suppleness of mind. Each is inclined in Hebraic fashion to pass absolute judgements, whereas the man of culture, with his eye fixed steadily on the whole, regards all such verdicts as myopic. Culture may figure as a critique of industrial capitalism, but it is just as disdainful of the forces that challenge it. Radical politics may denounce the profit motive or the privileges of the gentry, but culture grasps their role in the diverse totality of human existence. It is, in short, a kind of high-minded fatalism, serene in its conviction that everything has its place. As such, it is also a form of theodicy.

Arnold has a high regard for whatever belongs to the historical highway (the Church of England, for example), and a somewhat low estimate of whatever is marginal or heterodox (such as Methodism). It is not, to be sure, that he considers Anglicanism to possess more of the truth than Methodism. Neither of them in his view have much truth at all. It is simply that what matters is to float with the mainstream. It is as though being incorporated into the whole constitutes a virtue in itself. The case is purely formalistic. It is a curious view for a thinker who regards himself as a middle-class heretic, a lonely avatar of civility marooned in an ocean of barbarism. If belonging to the mainstream is a virtue in itself, one-sidedness is *ipso facto* a vice. To be committed is to be uncultivated. Culture is a question of symmetry. Equipped with this prejudice, Arnold is able to strike some highly specific political postures without appearing to do so. He is not, he would seem to suggest, opposed to this or that case on substantive grounds, simply on formal ones. It is the fact that an opinion offends against symmetry, proportion, equanimity and many-sidedness that inspires him to reject it, even when it is plain enough to the tolerably disinterested reader that he finds it thoroughly objectionable in any case.

Yet culture cannot settle for such neutrality at all. In an age of class struggle, creeping secularism, market anarchy, moral disorder and a patriciate incapable of spiritual leadership, culture clearly has no future as mere inner cultivation. Instead, it must become practical, corporate and reformative. If it is to replace religion, which is really Arnold's goal, it must descend from its ethereal heights to become a militant social mission. It must encompass 'the love of our neighbour, the impulses towards action, help, and beneficence, the desire for removing human error, clearing human confusion, and diminishing human misery, the noble aspiration to leave the world better and happier than we found it'.[6] Yet how is this not to prove the ruin of culture as the view from Mount Olympus? How is Arnold the Oxford aesthete to be reconciled with Arnold the industrious inspector of state schools? How are symmetry and totality not to be fatally compromised the instant they seek to realise themselves? If they fail to enter upon material existence, however, it is hard to see how culture can be more than a beautiful, ineffectual angel beating its wings in a luminous void, to steal Arnold's own words about Shelley.[7] The more *engagé* culture becomes, the less it can act as a conciliator; but the more it seeks to conciliate, the less effective it is likely to prove.

How can the culture of the privileged be more widely disseminated? If it is not, then those minority values are themselves likely to come under siege. Only by being diffused can they ultimately be preserved. Yet to propagate these values among the masses may spell their demise. It is hard to extend cultural values to new social groups without seeing them change in the process; but Arnold does not anticipate that those who are invited to share his own beliefs might take a hand in reshaping them. Culture, if it is to survive, must not be confined to the cloister, but neither is it open to being fundamentally remade. It may be a practical, collective, perpetually open-ended process, but it also smacks of an immovable ideal. It sets its face against utility, but must now be harnessed to some urgent social ends. If it does not prevail, political anarchy may ensue. Since the power of religion is on the wane, culture would seem the only means by which middle-class rapacity and working-class rancour can be moderated. It is worth noting, incidentally, that Arnold's notion of anarchy includes both middle-class individualism and proletarian revolt, even though the working-class militancy of his age was directed *against* the laissez-faire doctrine of the philistines. It represented a demand for more social control rather than less.

Culture, then, must assimilate these unlovely social strata into the social whole. If it does not – if, in Arnold's phrase, it fails to bring the East End of London along with it – it may find itself in ruins. The strategy is more self-interested than generous-hearted. Extending culture to the masses is a moral obligation, but it is a notably self-serving one as well, rather as tending the sick of the East End of London in Dickens's *Bleak House* is among other things a way of preventing their potentially lethal infections from migrating to the wholesome suburbia of those who nurse them. 'Culture,' Arnold writes, 'knows the sweetness and light of the few must be imperfect until the raw and unkindled masses of humanity are touched with sweetness and light.'[8] In fact, so he claims, culture 'seeks to do away with classes', and the men of culture are in this

129

sense the true apostles of equality. What Arnold is really seeking to do away with, however, is not classes but class struggle. Like many an ardent liberal, he finds strife and dissension offensive. Culture, he declares, is the enemy of hatred and discord. He does not seem to recognise that a degree of contention might be involved in the process of making it prevail.

Despite his distaste for conflict, Arnold is eager to see the might of the state unleashed against working-class demonstrators. Since the state is 'the nation in its collective and corporate character', such repression is purely disinterested. Carting working men off to prison for voicing their political opinions is an attempt to subdue sectarian interests in the name of a certain well-trimmed totality. We need, Arnold observes, to 'suppress the London rough on behalf of the best self both of themselves and of all of us in the future'.[9] The so-called best self, which is incarnate in the state, must forcibly quell 'whatever brings risk of tumult and disorder, multitudinous processions in the streets of our crowded cities'.[10] Our higher selves, so to speak, must take our inferior ones into custody. Sweetness and light are by no means incompatible with manacles and leg-irons. As with most calls for peace and harmony, it is only certain forms of violence that are under censure.

It is surprising, then, how determinate culture can become when confronted with a spot of political resistance. In itself, it is no more than a free motion of thought, without prejudices or presumptions; yet it manages all the same to bring to light what Arnold calls 'the intelligible law of things', and despite its meticulous vagueness feels able to inform men and women that they 'have no rights at all, only duties'.[11] Though culture has no vulgarly partisan opinions, it succeeds in convincing us that feudal privileges should be abolished 'gradually and gently' rather than passionately or abruptly. Despite its lack of definitive content, as well as its disdain for 'mere machinery', it manages to persuade Arnold himself to oppose the Real Estate Intestacy Bill (of 1866).

As a liberal who champions strong government, Arnold marks the point at which laissez-faire capitalism is in transit to some more corporate version of itself. Middle-class economic anarchy, he maintains, has now dissolved 'the strong feudal habits of subordination and deference' of the working class,[12] infecting them with something of the middle class's own disruptive cult of liberty; so that a new, state-centred ideology known as culture must restore these declining values. The middle classes are in danger of destabilising with their unruly market forces the very stratified political order which legitimises their form of life. They thus stand in need of a more powerful state for political purposes, as well as a more corporate ideology for moral ones. In the idea of the culture-state, the two requirements may be conveniently coupled.

To call for a stronger state is to confess that a free play of mind has its limits. One must not be so disastrously open-ended as to bring political order itself into question. Hellenism is essential if that order is to be sweetened and refined, rendered palatable to the masses; yet this sinuousness of thought is also at risk of undermining it. Liberalism of the spirit must not pose a threat to liberalism of the political or economic kind. The mind can play freely only in certain social conditions, and there may be a need for illiberal measures to preserve those conditions intact. Violence and prejudice, in a word, lie at the root of tolerance.

Culture, then, is both problem and solution. If it is the answer to anarchy, it also betrays something of that tendency itself when pressed to an extreme. Hellenism must not be so magnificently many-sided as to undermine Hebraism. By Hebraism, Arnold means obedience, conscience, self-discipline and the fear of God, all of which may be contrasted with what he calls 'rowdyism'. Knowing must not be allowed to deal a death blow to doing. Recklessly diffusing one's powers is no advance on fanatically narrowing them. What if the ironic detachment of aesthetic culture is at odds with culture in the moral and political sense?

Hellenism, then, is too deficient in the superegoic virtues to be entirely acceptable at times of political peril. Indeed, Arnold's Hellenic desire to combine all possibilities results in the rather odd strategy of seeking to unite Hellenism itself with Hebraism. Since the former is patrician and the latter bourgeois, their unity reflects something of the fusion of social classes which was actually afoot in Victorian England. If the upper classes need stiffening, the middle classes need softening. A judicious coupling of culture and conscience is thus in order, as a laid-back aristocratic leadership is infused with Hebraic zeal without loss to its serenity of spirit. At the same time, the leaden-spirited captains of industry must be exposed to Homer and Goethe without detriment to their dynamism. Like much of Arnold's political thought, the solution is entirely cerebral.

Only a few years after the publication of *Culture and Anarchy*, another work much preoccupied with the mutinous working class made its appearance. Nietzsche's *The Birth of Tragedy* (1872), with its reflections on the Dionysian and Apollonian, hardly seems a tract for the political times in the manner of Arnold's essay. Yet if Nietzsche clamours for the rebirth of myth and tragic wisdom, it is not least because of what he sees as the sullen stirrings of a 'slave class' in society, the fruit of what he disparagingly terms an 'Alexandrian' or scientific-rationalist culture. 'There is nothing more terrible,' he writes, 'than a class of barbaric slaves who have learned to regard their existence as an injustice, and now prepare to avenge, not only themselves, but all generations.'[13] What looms here is nothing less than 'a disaster slumbering in the womb of theoretical culture'.[14] In the face of such impending storms, Nietzsche asks, who dares to appeal with any confidence to our 'pale and exhausted' religions? What is needed instead is a recrudescence of myth, which will put paid to the secular spirit of progress and optimism currently beguiling the masses. If Nietzsche calls for a renewal of the tragic vision, it is for reasons rather more urgent than aesthetic ones.

* * *

In *Literature and Dogma*, Arnold recasts his whole argument in religious terms. With commendable candour, he begins the work by declaring that the chief political problem of the age is 'the lapsed masses'. 'Many of the common people,' he remarks in a companion work, *God and the Bible*, 'have embraced a kind of revolutionary Deism, hostile to all which is old, traditional, established and secure; favourable to a clean sweep and a new stage, with the classes now in the background for chief actors.'[15] What is bringing religion into discredit is the labour movement. 'Many of the most successful, energetic, and ingenious of the Artisan class, who are steady and rise,' Arnold informs us in *Literature and Dogma*, 'are now found ... rejecting the Bible altogether, and following teachers who tell them the Bible is an exploded superstition.'[16] He fails to mention that he holds just the same view of the Bible himself.

What is at stake here, in fact, is a version of the Enlightenment's so-called double truth doctrine. There is no harm in civilised gentlefolk like Voltaire or Arnold casting doubt on the divinity of Christ, but it is a different matter when it comes to trade-union militants. 'One is not always to attack people's illusions about religion,' Arnold warns, 'because illusions they are.'[17] Many an *Aufklärer* would have heartily agreed. There is no harm in a spot of illusion if it keeps the workers from laying their hands on private property. What has altered since the Enlightenment, however, is that religious doubt has now seeped into the ranks of the masses themselves, and is never very far from socialism. In Arnold's situation, in contrast to Voltaire's, it is the scepticism of the people, not their superstition, which is most disquieting. The progressive-minded infidels are now embattled working men, not middle-class philosophers. If the rationality of the Enlightenment was too remote from the religion of the people, religion is now too secluded from the increasingly agnostic masses. In seeking to rectify this situation, Arnold saw himself as continuing the work of his Broad Church father.[18] The fact that he did not believe in the Broad Church, or in any other church for that matter, seemed to him not the slightest impediment to the achievement of this worthy goal.

The solution to the problem is not to reconstruct the populace, purging them of their freshly acquired scepticism, but to reconstruct the Bible. One cannot do with Christianity as it is, but one cannot do without it either. Culture, Arnold declares, is essential if the Bible is to 'reach the people'. He means by this that if orthodox religion is failing to impress the lower orders, a suitably poeticised

Christianity might do so instead.[19] The masses must come to appreciate that 'the language of the Bible is fluid, passing, and literary, not rigid, fixed and scientific',[20] which is to say that it is the discourse of poetry and culture rather than of moral absolutism or metaphysical doctrine. Literary critics like Arnold himself thus find themselves invested with a vital new function. It is the task of the literati, with their flexible, non-dogmatic spirit, to insist on the figurative nature of what, taken as gospel truth, might well seem grossly improbable to a rationalist age, and a rejection of which might shake the foundations of political authority.

The need, Arnold declares, is to 'recast' religion, so that a degutted, demythologised version of Scripture, shorn of its supernaturalism, may claim the allegiance of the common people and continue to exert a restraining moral influence upon them. In fact, there is a sense in which this was the aim of much of the intellectual history we have been investigating. From the theism or agnosticism of the Enlightenment to the mythologising of the Romantics and demythologising of the Victorians, there is a pressing concern that the common people should believe – whether in the sense of being abandoned to their barbarous superstitions for reasons of political prudence, introduced to a more rational religion, subjected to secular mythologies, incorporated into some *soi-disant* culture state or, as with Arnold, sold a gentrified form of Christianity that has been poeticised away for more convenient mass consumption.

Culture, then, is in the service of religion, which, in turn, is in the service of politics. Or as Arnold himself puts the point, 'If conduct is, as it is, inextricably bound up with the Bible and the right interpretation of it, then the importance of culture becomes unspeakable.'[21] The task of culture is to extract the moral kernel of religion from its dogmatic shell in order to refurbish religion as a form of ideological authority. It must preserve the numinous aura, emotive rhetoric and high moral tone of religious belief, while discreetly emptying it of its improbable content. Dogma involves reasoning, for which, as Arnold comments, 'so many people have not much aptitude'. The populace cannot be expected to engage in rational debate on religious questions;[22] but they feel an instinct for reverence and submissiveness, which is rather more to the point. 'The metaphysical method,' Arnold complains, 'lacks power for laying hold on people.'[23] If religion does not lose metaphysics, it is likely to lose the masses.

The Jesus of Arnold's imagining would hardly be out of place at an Oxbridge High Table. His 'uncontentious, winning, inward modes of working'[24] exemplify the 'mildness and sweet reasonableness' that typifies culture. This, one should note, is asserted of the Jewish prophet who declared that he came to bring not peace but a sword, spoke of breaking up families and casting fire on the earth, antagonised the religious authorities of his day by consorting with crooks and whores, threw the merchants and money-changers out of the Temple, called down the most frightful curses on the heads of the ultra-pious pharisees, and warned his comrades that if they were to be true to his word they, too, would be done to death by the state. It is the sour unreasonableness of a document that admonishes us to yield up our lives for the sake of strangers that is most striking, not its diffusion of sweetness and light. There is nothing moderate or middle-of-the-road about the scandalous extremity of its demands, as a theologian like Kierkegaard was aware. Moreover, there is a sense in which Christianity, a creed which turns on a tortured body, is as anti-aesthetic as it is unreasonable. For all his supposed suppleness of mind, Arnold fails to consider the possibility that the relevance of religion to the masses might lie not in the need for political stability, but in the fact that the Jewish Bible presents Yahweh as a champion of the poor and powerless, a non-deity who spurns religious cult, rails against fetishism and idolatry, refuses a title and image and sets his people free from slavery.

Arnold's assumption that Old Testament religion is a formalistic affair, a matter of law and ritual observance in contrast to the spiritual inwardness of the Gospel, is a standard piece of Christian anti-Semitism. Religion in the New Testament is in Arnold's view 'mainly a personal affair', a modern-day liberal platitude that would have come as something of a surprise to St Paul.[25] No doubt the victims of the Inquisition would have rejoiced to hear it. Like the Jewish Bible, the Christian Scriptures concern the destiny of a whole people. They are remote from any conception of the sovereign individual subject. Even so, by adding the two texts together, one may arrive at yet another judicious balance between culture and conduct, being and doing, Hellenism and Hebraism. The Old Testament concerns itself with conduct, while its Christian counterpart instructs us to 'attend to the feelings and dispositions whence conduct proceeds'.[26] The only defect of this claim is that it is palpably false, rather as it is untrue that, as Arnold imagines, Jesus advanced a 'new religious ideal'. He was a Jew, not a Christian.

Religion, then, is to be reconstituted as a mode of morality tinged with transcendence, or an 'ethics heightened, enkindled, lit up by feeling'.[27] The Bible in Arnold's opinion is the most crucial piece of writing in the world, but only, it would appear, if it is thoroughly sanitised. A text which speaks of salvation in terms of feeding the hungry and visiting the sick is accordingly reduced to a question of sentiment. Not any old sentiment, to be sure. Arnold informs us in *God and the Bible* that the religious feelings are those of 'love, reverence, gratitude, hope, pity, and awe',[28] emotions which are not exactly politically innocent. Christian righteousness, he believes, is essentially a matter of 'inwardness, mildness, and self-renouncement'. It is not hard to see the appeal of these virtues to a ruling power confronted with popular discontent. The Gospel is reduced to a question of tone, in the detection of which literary types are thought to be peculiarly proficient. Hence, so Arnold informs us, a statement like 'We all want to live honestly, but cannot' is moral, whereas 'Blessed are the poor in heart, for they shall see God' is religious. Religion is essentially a matter of resonance. It is because it is a question of tone, metaphor, edifying sentiment and rhetorical effect that the literary critic must oust the philosopher and theologian in the field of religious inquiry.

It is important to recognise that Arnold himself does not believe in God at all, though in selfless spirit he is eager that others should. This, however, should not confront them with too arduous a task, provided it is Arnold's own deity they take on board, since this, like his notion of culture, is no more than an empty transcendence. God is 'the power, not ourselves, that makes for righteousness', or alternatively 'the stream of tendency by which all things fulfil the law of their being'.[29] It is a far cry from the Yahweh who tells the Jews that their incense stinks in his nostrils. If Arnold's notion of culture is a stand-in for God, so is his God. Religious faith, he insists, is a matter of experience rather than reason, yet his own arid formulations are quite as abstract as the most scholastic dogma. When Marx insists in a letter to Arnold Ruge that religion is 'without content', he is guilty of being a vulgar Marxist. As an account of the religious thought of Matthew Arnold, however, the comment is entirely accurate.

To redefine God as the 'not ourselves', as Arnold is anxious to do, is to seek to restore some hazy sense of otherness to a society in which self-interest has run riot. Unless men and women are persuaded to look beyond their own petty affairs to society as a whole, the stability of the social order is clearly at risk. The later George Eliot preaches much the same gospel, as do the Positivists with whom she was closely allied. From the Comtists to the neo-Hegelians, altruism is much in vogue. All citizens must be martyrs, immolating their selfish instincts on the altar of the communal good. As Mrs Humphry Ward puts it in her novel *Robert Elsmere* (1888), society has need of a new social bond, and will find it in an idea of culture that makes for selflessness. In this way, 'the rich devote themselves to the poor and the poor bear with the rich'.[30] It seems an equitable enough exchange. Liberal capitalism is evolving beyond doctrinaire individualism towards a more unified system, one which involves a more thorough integration of a potentially seditious working class. Something of this evolution can be traced in the distance between Dickens's early fiction and the later novels. Yet this growing corporatism has yet to attain its full ideological expression, and Arnold's work is among other things an attempt to accomplish this task.

As the political crisis deepens, conduct for Arnold comes to take precedence over culture, Hebraism to gain an edge over Hellenism. Ancient Israel – 'this petty, unsuccessful, unamiable people, without politics, without science, without charm'[31] – evokes from the author of *Literature and Dogma* a well-bred shudder of distaste. It is hardly the kind of nation you would invite to lunch at your club. Yet its paucity of culture matters less than the fact that it offers a paradigm of righteous conduct. There is a growing feeling, Arnold declares in *God and the Bible*, that modern liberalism, by which he means the doctrine of human rights, is no substitute for the old religious faith. Liberalism is an insufficiently vigorous creed with which to confront political turmoil, and must be supplemented by some more absolutist species of faith. 'The barrenness and insufficiency of the revolutionary formulas' may be contrasted in this respect with the compelling moral poetry of Scripture. 'All men are born naturally free and equal' is less likely to be revered as a doctrine than 'the fear of the Lord is the beginning of wisdom',[32] even though Arnold himself does not believe in the Lord and has not the faintest fear of him. The unwitting intellectual dishonesty of his writings on culture and religion, the artless way in which they give away the ideological game, is among their most intriguing features.

There is something Machiavellian about Arnold's case. Machiavelli, too, urged respect for religion while remaining entirely indifferent to it himself. Some such cult, he considered, was essential to the maintenance of civic order, even though he felt a proto-Nietzschean distaste for the lily-livered sort of virtues it supposedly commended. 'Religion,' writes Quentin Skinner of Machiavelli, 'can be used to inspire – and if necessary to terrorise – the ordinary populace in such a way as to induce them to prefer the god of the community to all other goods.'[33] It is a political strategy at least as old as ancient Rome.

It is ironic that Arnold's wrath was aroused by the sight of others casting doubt on the God in whom he himself no longer believed.

In a deeply discreditable act of bad faith, he refused to support an authentic demythologiser of his day, Bishop John William Colenso, who had run into trouble with the guardians of religious orthodoxy for his liberal-rationalist interpretation of Scripture. Despite the fact that Arnold himself shared much the same view of the Bible as Colenso, he was quick to rebuke him for the ideological damage his work might wreak. 'The great mass of the human race,' he writes, 'have to be softened and humanised through their heart and imagination, before any soil can be found in them where knowledge may strike living roots ... only when [ideas] reach them in this manner do they adjust themselves to their practice without convulsing it.'[34] It is as though Arnold had taken to heart the lesson ignored by so many of the *philosophes* and driven home by Schiller. It was just that his insistence that abstract reason would fail to inspire the populace involved callously abandoning a courageous fellow liberal to his fate.

As Lionel Trilling observes, Arnold held that 'the factory operatives whom Colenso had in mind could not possibly be edified – that is, their spirits could not be raised, their moral sense heightened nor their religious faith strengthened – by this work.'[35] Accordingly, the thinker who placed his faith in disinterested inquiry, striving to see the object as it really was, unscrupulously sacrificed the claims of reason to the cause of ideology. The people were not to be infected with doubt, a state of mind subversive of authority. If he was ready to silence Colenso on this score, Arnold was prepared with equal fervour to censor himself. He rejected his verse drama 'Empedocles on Etna' from an edition of his poetry on the grounds that it seemed calculated to depress rather than edify the reader.[36] Gloom is ideologically disabling. Thomas Hardy, confronted with the outraged cries of the reviewers, was to discover this truth not long afterwards. The purpose of art is to cheer you up.

\* \* \*

If culture will not quite serve as a stopgap for God, one can always try humanity instead. The task of the modern age, according to Ludwig Feuerbach's *Foundations of the Philosophy of the Future*, is to convert theology into anthropology, dislodging the Almighty from his throne and hoisting Man into his place. As with Arnold, the point is not to eradicate religious sentiments but to reconstruct them. It is futile to waste time on worshipping an invisible God when we could be engaged on the rather more gratifying task of worshipping ourselves. 'To become God, to be human, to cultivate oneself,' writes Friedrich Schlegel, 'are all expressions that mean the same thing.'[37] Even Marx, who was wary enough of hubristic humanism, not least when it came to the plundering of Nature, observes that 'religion is only the illusory sun which revolves around man as long as he does not revolve around himself'.[38] The final phrase reflects the collective narcissism of Feuerbach's Religion of Humanity.[39] Nineteenth-century rationalists like Herbert Spencer, George Eliot and G.H. Lewes are similarly anxious to divert our feelings of awe, reverence and obligation from the deity to humanity itself. Science for these thinkers is a quasi-religious pursuit, evoking as it does a sense of unfathomable mystery. In this sense, what can sabotage religious faith can also reinforce it, or at least provide a convincing alternative.

It is easier to deify Man if he happens to be feeling reasonably satisfied with himself. The Religion of Humanity belongs to the more buoyant years of the European bourgeoisie, when there seemed good reason to engage in some agreeable self-flattery. Indeed, the creed is witness to the middle class's absurdly inflated opinion of itself. Man in Feuerbach's eyes is marked by a boundless strength, as well as by a complete lack of sin. His infinitude knows no limits. As Charles Taylor remarks, 'modern humanism tends to develop a notion of flourishing that has no place for death'.[40] Christianity, by contrast, a faith which turns on an executed body, places death at the centre of its vision, in the belief that there can be no flourishing without confronting it.

Where God was once absolute monarch, Man for the Feuerbachians will now wear the crown in his stead. Theologically speaking, this is to misunderstand the nature of divine authority. It is theological orthodoxy to hold that the sovereignty of God is not that of a despot, however benevolent, but a power which allows the world to be itself. It is thus a critique of human sovereignty, not a prototype of it. To claim that God transcends the world is to say that he has no need of it, and thus betrays no neurotic possessiveness about it. It is his in the sense that it is free-standing like himself, subsisting in its own autonomy. This is one reason why science is possible. Creation is the opposite of ownership, and divine power the antithesis of dominion. These, however, are not questions that detained the ideologues of Humanity. As usual, it proved easier to dispose of a caricature of the opposition rather than the real thing.

The Religion of Humanity first saw the light of day in the throes of the French Revolution, with its panoply of saints, martyrs and feast days, its Festival of Reason and adoration of the Fatherland. A decree of 1793 abolishing the worship of God was followed the next year by one authorising the worship of the Supreme Being.

The reign of atheism had turned out to be somewhat short-lived. The latter decree declared that the people acknowledged the existence of this sublime entity, along with the immortality of the soul.

It is ironic in this respect that Auguste Comte was to establish his Positivist Religion of Humanity largely as a counterblast to Jacobin rationalism. Comte, a heterodox disciple of Saint-Simon, viewed religion as a matter of sentiments rather than doctrines, social cohesion rather than supernaturalism. In both respects, he is a French cousin of Matthew Arnold, though of a more rationalist, relentlessly systematising kind. His Church was to encompass the whole of society, entrusting the moral welfare of the people to the ministrations of a secular clergy. A *dirigiste* state would preside over an economy still largely in private hands. Banks, of all grossly improbable institutions, were to serve the function of medieval guilds and corporations. The masses would be incorporated into a new religion of fraternal love, one which drew upon Christianity but also aspired beyond it. Artists would be enlisted in the service of social reconstruction, inspiring the masses to action in accordance with the new scientific vision.

The latter point is of some significance. Comte was thought by the votaries of Saint-Simon to be too deeply under the sway of scientific rationalism to mould public opinion. 'How can the artists,' they scoffed, 'become impassioned with the icy demonstrations of science?'[41] In the Positivist scheme of things, they protested, 'the scientists transmit to the artists the coldly contrived plan of the social future in order to have it accepted by the masses'.[42] In their own view, however, it was impossible to translate scientific reason into sensory terms. To this extent, the legacy of Schiller and the Romantic mythologisers rested on a false assumption. There could be no such passage from theory to ideology. Only if social science were itself based on a religious vision, as Saint-Simon himself advocated against Comte, could it find a seat in the affections of the people.

In essence, Saint-Simonism is a melange of modern rationalism and French Catholic-Restorationist reaction.[43] 'The words "order", "religion", "association", and "devotion" ', write the Saint-Simonians, 'are a sequence of hypotheses corresponding to the sequence "disorder", "atheism", "individualism", and "egoism" ', meaning their opposites.[44] This, too, was the creed of the Positivists, who also set up their own places of profane worship, instituted priests and sacraments and engaged in thrice-daily private prayer to some indeterminate addressee. Comte, their founder, was designated High Priest of Humanity, the veritable Pope of the human species. A new, anarchic industrial order had uprooted the old religious faith but put nothing in its place; and if socialism were not to fill this vacuum, the Religion of Humanity must do so instead. Whereas religion had once served to legitimise the status quo, post-religious religion now stood ready to receive the baton. The symbolic forms of Catholicism were appropriated, having first been drained in Arnoldian fashion of their supernatural content. It was, as one commentator remarked, a kind of Catholicism without Christianity, a phenomenon not unfamiliar in the history of the Roman Catholic Church.

Like Arnold, Comte saw orthodox religion as obsolete; but the enlightened talk of the Rights of Man which had helped to discredit it was too critical and negative a foundation on which to build a new social order. As we have seen already, the industrial-capitalist system, unable to breed an 'organic' ideology of its own, and powerless to translate its market logic into affective terms, was to be supplemented with an alien graft. As Andrew Wernick comments, Comte 'saw that the heart and not only the head has to be engaged if the saving grace of the spirit was to unite the scattered elements of a divided and fragmented society'.[45] In a bizarre mixture of sacerdotalism and scientific rationalism, metaphysics was banished through the back door only to be readmitted in heavily muffled guise through the front.

Emile Durkheim is another who saw religion primarily as the symbolic cement of social existence. In *The Elementary Forms of the Religious Life*, it represents the social dimension of human existence, which an individualist culture urgently needs to restore. Like Comte and Arnold before him, Durkheim sees history as in transition from an increasingly outmoded order to a world as yet powerless to be born. With the decay of religious faith has gone the loss of transcendence; but 'because he participates in society, the individual naturally transcends himself when he thinks and acts'.[46] Society itself, somewhat in the manner of Jacques Lacan's *L'Autre*, can therefore step into the breach from which the deity has disappeared and figure as a secularised form of otherness. It is the sociologist, not the priest, poet or philosopher, who now holds the key to the sacred rites of social solidarity. In a reversal of Schelling and his colleagues, the sociologist must replace myth with rational discourse, rather than translate reason into mythological terms.

The idea of religion as a source of social cohesion receives scant support from the Christian Gospel. By and large, the teaching of Jesus is presented by that document as disruptive rather than conciliatory. He has come to tear father from son in the name of his mission. Ethnic, social and domestic bonds take second place to the demands of justice. The solidarity of faith stands askew to the priorities of the powers-that-be. To belong to this community is to be marked out for death by those authorities. All existing institutions are finished, washed up, subject to the judgement of a future of justice and comradeship that is even now breaking violently into the present. The form of life Jesus offers his followers is not one of social integration but a scandal to the priestly and political establishment. It is a question of being homeless, propertyless, peripatetic, celibate, socially marginal, disdainful of kinsfolk, averse to material possessions, a friend of outcasts and pariahs, a thorn in the side of the Establishment and a scourge of the rich and powerful. Indeed, Pierre Bayle points to this fact as an argument against the political necessity of religious faith. Christianity, he remarks, is no basis for civil order, since Jesus proclaims that he has come to pitch society into turmoil.[47]

Durkheim does not consider religion and science mutually commensurate. It is true that the latter in his view grows out of the former, meaning that reason has its roots in religious faith. In this sense, the Enlightenment's war against superstition is unmasked as a form of Oedipal conflict, in which the rationalist offspring strives to disown its pious progenitor. Rather as the Oedipal child disavows its disreputable parentage in the belief that it was self-born, so the Reason of the *Aufklärer* likes to imagine itself as sprung from its own loins, thereby repressing the history which went into its making. As contemporary phenomena, however, reason and religious faith occupy separate spheres. Religion for Durkheim is not a rational affair. He is a secular fideist on this score. It is a question of human needs and desires, and the cultic practices with which they are bound up have more in common with Nietzschean mythology than they do with the discourse of the laboratory.

The role of religion, rather like that of art for the Victorians, is to edify men and women, raising them above their imperfect condition and rendering them capable of finer achievements. In this respect, faith has more in common with the American Dream than it does with a sense of guilt or a hunger for justice. As Durkheim observes, it is 'warmth, life, enthusiasm, the exaltation of all mental activity, the transport of the individual beyond himself'.[48] Romantic sentiments are accordingly harnessed to corporate ends. The dream of some Enlightenment and Victorian thinkers – that science might finally usurp religion – is exposed as baseless. Indeed, it involves in Durkheim's eyes a kind of category mistake. Religion is not primarily a set of theoretical claims about the world, which might then find themselves in competition with the scientific outlook. As a set of social practices, it moves us to action in ways in which Reason alone is incapable. From a scientific viewpoint, religious doctrines may well be false, but this is scarcely the point. It would be like claiming that the death of Cordelia is incapable of moving us to tears because there never was such a woman. Ludwig Wittgenstein held a similar view of religious faith. The opposite case – that religion is a set of erroneous propositions or species of bogus science – has been advanced in our own time by such old-fashioned nineteenth-century rationalists as Richard Dawkins, who dismisses religious belief without grasping the kind of phenomenon that it is meant to be.[49]

The Marxist philosopher Louis Althusser, who began life as a devout Roman Catholic, inherits this outlook in a different form.[50] Ideology in his view is a form of subjectivity embedded in a set of social practices, not a set of propositions. As the mode in which men and women live out their relations to political society, it offers no rivalry to theoretical knowledge, which in Althusser's view is a practice without a subject. Whereas theory is conscious that society and the human subject lack all unity, ideology invests both with a degree of coherence, enough for men and women to take purposive action in the world. Ideology, in short, plays something of the role for Althusser which myth performed for some earlier thinkers. It is a symbolic perfomance, an orientation to reality, an existential medium, a mode of organising our everyday experience. As such, it is no more capable of being judged true or false than a greeting or a curse. Georges Sorel treats myth in much the same pragmatic style in his *Reflections on Violence*. Myth and ideology are both heuristic fictions. As indispensable Apollonian illusions, they carve enough sense out of the Dionysian chaos of reality to furnish us with some sense of purpose and identity.

Althusser's reflections on theory and ideology thus represent a belated version of a problem we have been examining all along. How is reason to be translated into lived experience? By what devices might philosophy set up home in the desires and affections of the people? Reason must stoop to the realm of myth and image if is to address the masses, but how is this not to be the ruin of it? Althusser's solution to the question is ideology, seen as the medium in which the science of historical materialism can be converted into political action. Ideology, in a non-pejorative sense of the term, provides the vital nexus between theory and practice. For some earlier philosophers, a similar mediation was to be found in myth or the aesthetic.

As naturally amphibious creatures, we are able in Althusser's view to live simultaneously in the divided worlds of science and ideology. To write a materialist treatise on the monarchy is a matter

149

of science, whereas to glance up from one's computer to shudder at the sight of the sovereign on television is a question of ideology. The difference between the two spheres, then, is not quite a recycling of the Enlightenment double truth doctrine. It does not follow that middle-class philosophers breathe the pure air of theory while the masses are left to wallow in the mire of ideology. For one thing, ideology in Althusser's lexicon is by no means an inherently pejorative term. A march against racism is a question of social practice and lived experience, and is thus in Althusserian terms as much an ideological affair as sporting a swastika. For another thing, everyone, intelligentsia and populace alike, crosses constantly from one of these domains to the other.

Moreover, there is no reason why a plumber should not be a theorist and a philosopher an ideologue. The distinction in question is epistemological rather than sociological. Reason, or theory, need not be confined to a coterie, and myth or ideology is by no means the monopoly of the masses. What Althusser's left-rationalism fails to acknowledge is that theory itself grows out of lived experience – that in this sense at least, the two worlds are not entirely distinct. Reason has its roots in the human body. It is easier to see how theory might be brought home to everyday existence if one recognises that this, after all, was its birthplace. In any case, there is no special philosophical problem about how ideas are lived out in practice. It happens every day. If there is a problem, it is one that Althusser has created himself, by defining theory in ways that put it at odds with action and experience from the outset. Exactly the same was true of some Enlightenment philosophers.

# CHAPTER 5

# THE DEATH OF GOD

FOR SOME ENLIGHTENMENT savants, religion is an error, if an occasionally fruitful one; for Romanticism, there is some profound truth to be extracted from its mystical shell; for Marx, Nietzsche and Freud, it is a syndrome which demands vigilant interpretation. Perhaps it is with Nietzsche that the decisive break comes. He has a strong claim to being the first real atheist. Of course there had been unbelievers in abundance before him, but it is Nietzsche above all who confronts the terrifying, exhilarating consequences of the death of God. As long as God's shoes have been filled by Reason, art, culture, *Geist*, imagination, the nation, humanity, the state, the people, society, morality or some other such specious surrogate, the Supreme Being is not quite dead. He may be mortally sick, but he has delegated his affairs to one envoy or another, part of whose task is to convince men and women that there is no cause for alarm, that business will be conducted as usual despite the absence of the proprietor, and that the acting director is perfectly capable of handling all inquiries. When it comes to humanity doing service for divinity, we have the curious situation of Man, panic-stricken at his own act of deicide, plugging the resultant gap with the nearest thing to hand, namely his own species. Man is a fetish filling the frightful abyss which is himself. He is a true image of the God he denies, so that only with his own disappearance from the earth can the Almighty truly be laid to rest. Only then can timorous, idolatrous Man pass beyond himself into that avatar of the future which is the *Übermensch*. Only somewhere on the other side of Man can authentic humanity be born.

Nietzsche himself awarded the accolade of first atheist to Arthur Schopenhauer. Yet though it is true that the only form of religion which attracted this gloomiest of philosophers was an atheistic one (Buddhism), there is a sense in which his infamous Will is a grisly parody of the Almighty, and thus remains secretly theological. Like God, this baleful power is the essence of all phenomena; like God, too, it is closer to human beings than they are to themselves. In this latter respect, it is a forerunner of the Freudian unconscious, as well as a malevolent version of Augustine and Aquinas's godhead. The malign twist that the Schopenhauer of *The World as Will and Representation* adds to the traditional vision of God is that this power which constitutes the very pith of my being, which I can feel from the inside of my body with incomparably greater immediacy than I can know anything else, is as blankly unfeeling and anonymous as the force that stirs the waves. There is indeed a kind of transcendence at the heart of humanity, but it is one which is implacably alien to it. Subjectivity is what we can least call our own. Who says consciousness says false consciousness. We bear a dead weight of meaninglessness at the very core of our being, as though permanently pregnant with monsters. It is as though Schopenhauer's macabre world-view derides the idea of God at the same time as it mocks the post-metaphysical progressivists who imagine they can get on without it.

The futility which Schopenhauer finds in human existence manifests itself in exactly the places which the Romantics and sentimentalists thought most precious – in our instincts and affections, in the stirrings of desire and the motions of the spirit. Desire is no longer a positive capacity. For Freud, who like Ludwig Wittgenstein was much influenced by Schopenhauer, it can no longer be seen as unequivocally on the side of human liberation. We have seen that human longing for Idealist thought achieves its fulfilment in the Absolute, while the Romantics, though somewhat more sceptical of this goal, see value in the process of striving to attain it. For Schopenhauer, by contrast, desire is pathological. What is now irreparably flawed in his view is nothing less than the whole category of subjectivity itself, as the bright-eyed vision of those writing in the exuberant aftermath of revolution darkens into a view of humanity as one enormous marketplace. For this fervent pessimist, there is no grand *telos* to 'this battle-ground of tormented and agonised beings, [with] constant struggle, *bellum omnium*, everything a hunter and everything hunted.... this world of constantly needy creatures who continue for a time merely by devouring one another, pass their existence in anxiety and want, and often endure terrible afflictions, until they fall at last into the arms of death'.[1]

Formally speaking, Schopenhauer's Will plays something of the same role as the Hegelian Idea or Romantic life force. But it has absolutely nothing of their value, and it does not evolve toward a benign end. In fact, it does not evolve at all. It is little more than the uncouth rapacity of the average bourgeois raised to metaphysical status. If there is a God, then he is a satanic one, and the last thing one would dream of doing is to pray to this gratuitously vindictive being. His Creation is entirely worthless. It is plain common sense that the vainglorious bunch of egoists known as human beings would have been better off never existing. To imagine that the achievements of the human enterprise might outweigh its afflictions is in Schopenhauer's eyes sheer madness. Piously convinced of their own supreme value, these self-deluded wretches spend their time scrambling over one another in pursuit of some paltry prize that will turn instantly to ashes in their mouths. As with Samuel Beckett's depleted figures, they are not even capable of rising to the dignity of tragedy.

Schopenhauer remains a full-blooded metaphysician, a nightmarish version of the Hegel he envied so deeply, as well as a sort of religious heretic. His bleak universe may be bereft of meaning, but there is a sense in which the idea of the Will imbues that meaninglessness with a certain overall shape. A lack of purpose and value is to be found everywhere you look. It is remarkable how formally coherent utter futility can be made to appear. Besides, though the Will has neither goal nor meaning, it may serve as a cosmic explanation quite as cogently as the Supreme Being. The totalising forms of Idealist thought are preserved, but their content is now meagre and debased. What can transcend this forlorn condition is no longer political action, religious faith or the creative imagination. It is through aesthetic contemplation alone, in the form of a pure, self-oblivious empathy with our fellow victims, that we can see into the heart of things and experience a momentary release from the imperious whims of the ego and the cruel clutches of the Will. In the wake of the death of God, only the death of desire can save us. The task of art is to abolish desire rather than re-educate it. If it once held out a promise of communal redemption, it is now a form

of spiritual self-extinction. The self is not to be realised but annihi-
lated, and the aesthetic is one place where, like Keats before the
nightingale, it can be allowed to dissolve ecstatically away.

What Nietzsche recognises is that you can get rid of God
only if you also do away with innate meaning. The Almighty can
survive tragedy, but not absurdity. As long as there appears to be
some immanent sense to things, one can always inquire after the
source from which it springs. Abolishing given meanings involves
destroying the idea of depth, which in turn means rooting out
beings like God who take shelter there. Like Wilde in his wake,
Nietzsche is out to replace what he sees as a vacuous depth with a
profundity of the surface. Max Weber comments in his essay
'Science as a Vocation' that every theology presupposes that the
world has meaning, and that only a plucky few can acknowledge
that it does not. The true *Übermensch* in his view is the social scien-
tist, who can confront the blankness of the universe and live
without religious consolation. For those who cannot attain this
dangerous truth, Weber remarks, 'the doors of the old churches are
open widely and compassionately'.[2] It is a modern-day version of
the double truth thesis: the average citizen may be allowed to live in
salutary illusion, while the intelligentsia gaze unflinchingly into the
void. One might add that in Weber's view the epitome of life's
senselessness is death, which for Christianity is where it is most
charged with meaning. The political philosopher Leo Strauss,
father of American neoconservatism, presses Weber's case to a
Machiavellian extreme. Political rulers must deceive the common
people for their own good, keeping from their ears the subversive
truth that the moral values by which they live have no unimpeachable basis.[3] They must conceal this lack of foundation from the

credulous gaze of the masses, drawing a veil over it as over some unspeakable indecency.

Nietzsche sees that civilisation is in the process of ditching divinity while still clinging to religious values, and that this egregious act of bad faith must not go uncontested. You cannot kick away the foundations and expect the building still to stand. The death of God, he argues in *The Joyful Wisdom*, is the most momentous event of human history, yet men and women are behaving as though it were no more than a minor readjustment. The time has come, then, to renounce the consoling fantasy that you can do away with God without also putting paid to Man. As Gilles Deleuze comments in *Difference and Repetition*, 'God is retained so long as the Self is preserved'.[4] In Nietzsche's eyes, all such essences involve some hint of celestial design or metaphysical substratum. Unless these, too, are rooted out, men and women will continue to languish in the shadow of the Almighty.

Of the various artificial respirators on which God has been kept alive, one of the most effective is morality. 'It does not follow,' Feuerbach anxiously insists, 'that goodness, justice and wisdom are chimaeras because the existence of God is a chimaera.'[5] Perhaps not; but in Nietzsche's view it does not follow either that we can dispense with divine authority and continue to conduct our moral business as usual. Our conceptions of truth, virtue, identity and autonomy, our sense of history as shapely and coherent, all have deep-seated theological roots. It is idle to imagine that they could be torn from these origins and remain intact. Morality, for example, must therefore either rethink itself from the ground up, or live on in the chronic bad faith of appealing to sources it knows to be spurious. In the wake of the death of God, there are those who continue to hold that morality is about duty, conscience and obligation, but who now find themselves bemused about the source of such beliefs. This is not a problem for Christianity – not only because it has faith in such a source, but because it does not believe that morality is primarily about duty, conscience or obligation in the first place.

Nietzsche speaks scornfully of French freethinkers from Voltaire to Comte as trying to 'out-Christian' Christianity with a craven cult of altruism and philanthropy, virtues which are as distasteful to him as pity, compassion, benevolence and suchlike humanitarian clap-trap.[6] He can find nothing in such values but weakness cunningly tricked out as power. These, too, are ways of disavowing God's disappearance. God is indeed dead, and it is we who are his assassins, yet our true crime is less deicide than hypocrisy. Having murdered the Creator in the most spectacular of all Oedipal revolts, we have hidden the body, repressed all memory of the traumatic event, tidied up the scene of the crime and, like Norman Bates in *Psycho*, behave as though we are innocent of the act. We have also dissembled our deicide with various shamefaced forms of pseudo-religion, as though in expiation of our unconscious guilt. Modern secular societies, in other words, have effectively disposed of God but find it morally and politically convenient – even imperative – to behave as though they have not. They do not actually believe in him, but it is still necessary for them to imagine that they do. God is too vital a piece of ideology to be written off, even if it is one that their own profane activities render less and less plausible. There is a performative contradiction between what such civilisations do and what they proclaim that they do. To look at the beliefs embodied in their behaviour, rather than at what they piously profess, is to recognise that they have no faith in God at all, but it is as though the fact has not yet been brought to their attention. One of Nietzsche's self-appointed tasks is to do precisely that.

If God has been shouldered aside for a repressive morality, there is a sense in which the middle-class atheist continues to believe in divinity, and in a satanic God to boot. In this sense, the double truth thesis is in need of adjustment. 'Privately, I don't happen to believe myself, but it's prudent that the masses should' is rewritten as 'I acknowledge that faith makes no sense, but even so I carry on spontaneously believing.' Like an unquiet ghost, one can go on living because one does not know one is dead, and this is the situation of religion. Or, as Slavoj Žižek puts it, *we* know that God is dead, but does he?[7] If God really has expired, however, this is by no means unqualified good news. If he is dead, then, as Lacan claims contra Dostoevsky, nothing is permitted, since for one thing there is no one to grant permission. We now have nobody to assume the burden of responsibility but ourselves, whereas having a signed and certified warranty to act as we do is a great assuager of guilt. We may expect, then, that our moral unease will intensify in the wake of God's demise, as angst and *mauvaise foi* tighten their hold on humanity.

Nietzsche's struggle, as Andrew Wernick notes, was not just one of Dionysus against the Crucified, to adopt his own words, but one against Christianity's 'enlightened afterlife', a tale we have been tracing in this study.[8] As Bruce Robbins puts it, 'God had in fact gone into hiding and now had to be smoked out of various secular phenomena, from morality and Nature to history, humanity and even grammar.'[9] For Nietzsche, these specious forms of religion were simply ways of dissembling our deicide, and had to be swept away with the corpse. There were to be no such opiates for the stout of heart. The Overman or post-human animal is he who has freed himself from those forms of sham religion known as Nature, Reason, Man and morality. Only this audacious animal can peer into the abyss of the Real and find in the death of God the birth of a new species of humanity. As with Christian faith, the only place to begin is with a confession that our hands are steeped in the blood of divinity. Man, too, must be dismantled, in so far as he is modelled on the unity and infinity of the godhead. He is defined so completely by his dependence on his Creator that the two must fall together. There can be no obsequies for the Almighty without a funeral ceremony for humanity as well. The death of God must herald the death of Man, in the sense of the craven, guilt-ridden, dependent creature who bears that name at present. What will replace him is the Overman. Yet in his sovereignty over Nature and lordly self-dependence, the Overman has more than a smack of divinity about him, which means, ironically, that God is not dead after all. What will replace him continues to be an image of him.

That the death of God involves the death of Man, along with the birth of a new form of humanity, is orthodox Christian doctrine, a fact of which Nietzsche seems not to have been aware. The Incarnation is the place where both God and Man undergo a kind of kenosis or self-humbling, symbolised by the self-dispossession of Christ. Only through this tragic self-emptying can a new humanity hope to emerge. In its solidarity with the outcast and afflicted, the crucifixion is a critique of all hubristic humanism. Only through a confession of loss and failure can the very meaning of power be transfigured in the miracle of resurrection. The death of God is the life of the iconoclast Jesus, who shatters the idolatrous view of Yahweh as irascible despot and shows him up him instead as vulnerable flesh and blood.

The absence of God may be occluded by the fetish of Man, but the God who has been disposed of would seem little more than a fetish in the first place.[10] As with William Blake's Urizen or Nobodaddy, he was a convenient way of shielding a humanity eager to be chastised from the intolerable truth that the God of Christianity is friend, lover and fellow accused, not judge, patriarch and superego. He is counsel for the defence, not for the prosecution. Moreover, his apparent absence is part of his meaning. The superstitious would see a sign, but the sign of the Father that counts is a crucified body. For Christian faith, the death of God is not a question of his disappearance. On the contrary, it is one of the places where he is most fully present. Jesus is not Man standing in for God. He is a sign that God is incarnate in human frailty and futility. Only by living this reality to the full, experiencing one's death to the very end, can there be a path beyond the tragic. It is not a claim that fits well with the Religion of Humanity.

There is a sense in which Marx, too, regards the death of God as involving the end of Man. God is the product of a self-alienated humanity, and will wither away only when this condition has been repaired. In so far as 'Man' can be taken to signify the falsely unified subject of bourgeois humanism, the impending demise of this puffed-up creature is as welcome to Marx as it is to Nietzsche. In another sense, however, Marx remains a Romantic humanist of a familiar kind, which is to suggest that his atheism remains incomplete. It is now humanity, not its divine architect, which lies at the source of all being. He writes at one point of Man as lying at the root of historical reality, a root that Nietzsche is intent on digging out and casting away. It is true that the forces of production make a less plausible substitute for the deity than the Will to Power or the

*Übermensch.* Even so, we have seen already that Marx's thought, not least in its earlier forms, is deeply informed by Judaeo-Christian thought. It is not here, then, that an authentic atheism is to be found.

Marx's vision of the future remains an anthropological one, as Nietzsche's does not. By and large, he is an essentialist when it comes to the human animal, which is not the case with Nietzsche. It would be hard to imagine the latter speaking of the self-realisation of human species-being. It is also true, as we have seen already, that Marx falls victim to Feuerbachian fantasies from time to time. In all these ways, then, Nietzsche would appear the more full-blooded unbeliever. Yet his atheism also remains incomplete. Since built-in meanings must yield in his view to humanly manufactured ones, it is hard to see how this does not turn the *Übermensch* who performs this task into a mini-Creator. Like the Almighty, he rests upon nothing but himself. There can be no talk of autonomy or self-generation without a backward glance at theology. Man can displace God only if he is self-creating, hence abolishing his dependency and contingency; yet for him to become self-creating is to perpetuate the deity in a different form. It is to pay homage to religion in an attempt to abolish it. In what Christian theology would see as a naive opposition, human autonomy and a dependence on God can only be seen as opposites. It is true that this magnificently civilised beast of an *Übermensch* is the product of a history or genealogy, but it is one which brings him to birth as superbly self-fashioning. You cannot peer behind the Man of the Future to see what puts him in place, any more than you can in the case of God. When it comes to his view of the self as a fiction, Nietzsche is at his most staunchly atheistic. The autonomous, self-determining Superman, by contrast, is yet another piece of counterfeit theology. Besides, though Man in Nietzsche's view is not the principle on which everything else turns, and thus a form of surrogate deity, there is indeed such a principle, namely the Will to Power. The decisive break does not come with Nietzsche after all.

For Marx, the self-fashioning subject is not a foundation beneath which we are unable to dig. On the contrary, it is the product of Nature, labour, power, history, culture, kinship and the like. If Marx's materialism is atheistic, it is not because it refuses spirit in the name of matter, but because it acknowledges the material preconditions which put men and women in place, and which will still be present in the realm of freedom. The sovereignty of Man, which for Nietzsche is triumphantly consummated in the *Übermensch*, is thus severely qualified. In this sense at least, humanity for Marx is not a self-determining absolute, and so cannot scramble on to the empty throne of its Creator. If Marx is more religious than Nietzsche in some ways, he is less so in others.

\* \* \*

If Nietzsche is free to preach atheism, it is among other reasons because he has no concern with the corporate sense of culture, and so is indifferent to the question of finding supernatural rationales for it. In fact, he has scant interest in any form of social cohesion, the very idea of which is an affront to his flamboyant individualism. Kierkegaard's very different brand of individualism involves much the same aversion. Culture and Protestantism make uneasy bedfellows. The idea that two individuals might be in some way commensurable is an offence to Nietzsche's patrician hauteur, as it is to Kierkegaard's radical-Protestant sensibility. There can be no exchange-value in the realm of the spirit. The phrase 'common standards' for Nietzsche is a crass oxymoron. Social bonding means mediocrity, herd-like uniformity, the ruin of the noble spirit and the ascendancy of the masses. He dismisses conventional virtue in *The Twilight of the Idols* as little more than social mimicry, and in *Beyond Good and Evil* scoffs at the concept of the common good. Not only is he unconcerned to retain religious belief for socially utilitarian reasons, but he regards such a project as self-contradictory. How can selfless values serve self-interested social ends? Social order can be left to the police and politicians. Here, at least, is one thinker with a drastic solution to the dilemma that never ceases to bedevil middle-class society: how can political order safeguard individualism without being undercut by it?

If Nietzsche clings to the need for a new mythology, then, it is not primarily for reasons of social stability. It is rather because 'without myth, every culture loses the healthy natural power of its creativity', as he writes in *The Birth of Tragedy*.[11] Myth confronts the pallid abstractions of law, morality and the state with the concrete image, thus allowing art to flourish once more. We have seen that for some earlier thinkers, mythology and the aesthetic acted as prostheses of Reason, carrying it into the heart of common experience. For the Nietzsche of *The Birth of Tragedy*, however, Reason (or truth) and the aesthetic are antithetical. It is a momentous break with a history of thought for which art and truth are inseparable. The aesthetic or Apollonian is a magnificent illusion which shields us from the Dionysian horror of human existence. Its task is to conceal the truth rather than to embody it. Tragic art is both culture and the negation of culture, as the beautiful and the terrible exist cheek by jowl. The post-human animal is he who dares to embrace the horror of meaninglessness by finding in it a chance to oust the Creator and take his own existence courageously in hand, hammering himself and the world around him into whatever alluring form takes his fancy. It is a plucking of sense from futility, beauty from terror and freedom from necessity which is familiar in tragic art.

In one sense, Nietzsche heralds the end of culture as well as the death of God. How can there be culture if the self is a fiction, objects mere spin-offs of the Will to Power, consensus despicable, the world shapeless and impenetrable, the history of civilisation a litany of grotesque accidents, morality a matter of sadistic self-violence, reality a set of partial interpretations and truth a life-enhancing illusion? In another sense, however, culture retains a supreme importance in Nietzsche's writings. Indeed, he uses the word specifically in *The Will to Power* to denote the spiritual lifestyle of the Overman. Culture as a form of life in common is cast aside so that culture as individual self-realisation may flourish all the more freely. Culture as a shared life form involves each individual internalising the law, a project that was essential in its time but must now give way to a new species of animal, one that will behave like an aesthetic artefact in bestowing the law on himself. This creature resembles the citizen of Kant or Rousseau in that he stoops to no authority that he does not fabricate for himself; he differs from him in that he pledges fealty only to the law of his own unique being. It is the emergence of this splendid specimen of post-humanity that justifies the chronicle of collective self-torture we know as morality.

One criticism of the Overman is not that he is a proto-Nazi beast out to stamp on the faces of the poor, but that he represents precious little advance on the classical culture-hero, not least for such an astonishingly avant-garde thinker as Nietzsche. He is less some latter-day Genghis Khan than a reverent, refined, strenuously self-disciplined creature, generous of spirit and magnanimous in his bearing. In fact, Goethe, who hardly qualified as a blond Teutonic beast, is lauded as a kind of *Übermensch* in *The Twilight of the Idols*. For all his scepticism of the unified subject, Nietzsche by no means rejects the ethic of self-realisation. On the contrary, he presses it to a point at which the very idea of a culture in common becomes well-nigh unthinkable. Social norms and collective mores are oppressive in themselves, a calamitous misconception which will pass straight into post-structuralism. The self as a work of art is at odds with all communal existence. The two chief senses of culture are now mutually incompatible.

One of Nietzsche's finest achievements is to demystify cultural idealism. 'How much blood and cruelty lies at the bottom of all "good things"!' he remarks in *On the Genealogy of Morals*.[12] It is a theme he shares with those other two great demystifiers of the modern age, Marx and Freud. Culture and morality are the fruit of a barbarous history of debt, torture, revenge, obligation and exploitation – in short, of the whole horrific process by which the human animal is degutted and debilitated to be rendered fit for civilised society. The toil and strife from which all precious ideas are born is what Nietzsche calls genealogy, in contrast to the consoling evolutionism of the cultural idealists. What they know as history is for him no more than 'a gruesome dominion of nonsense and accident'.[13] It is what Man needs to be cured of, not what assures him of a smooth passage into an even more bountiful future. Every advance in civility has been paid for in the coin of subjection and self-torment. Morality is born of violence and self-repression. Its home is that inward space of guilt, sickness and bad conscience which some like to call subjectivity. It represents an emasculation of the spirit, and those who cannot see beyond it (Kant, the English, religious types) are despicable eunuchs.

Like most avant-gardists, Nietzsche is a devout amnesiac. We can inaugurate the future only by a wilful oblivion to the catastrophe of the past. There is no Kantian or Schillerian vision of *Bildung* here, no faith in an upward movement through which humanity might fulfil its collective powers. As with Marx, though in a quite different sense, only through a fundamental breaking and remaking can we repair our condition. There are other affinities with Marx as well. Despite his distaste for metaphysics, Nietzsche is a full-blown theodicist when it comes to the less creditable aspects of human conduct, all of which he sees as playing their part in the future flourishing of humanity. Transcendence requires the baptism of the gutter, for the species as a whole if not for individuals. The era of the moral law may have been a disaster, but it is also an essential prelude to the advent of the *Übermensch*.[14] In a similar way, it is arguable that Marx saw capitalism, with all its wretchedness and brutality, as indispensable for the advent of socialism.[15]

Nietzsche is not, like Marx, a historical materialist, but he is a materialist after his own fashion, laying bare the unlovely origins of so much that presents itself as noble and eternal. The most sublime of ideas have their root in need, anxiety, envy, malice, rivalry, aggression and the like. He also takes over a strain of 'vulgar' materialism from Schopenhauer, who sees human history as a species of zoology and revels in a certain coarse physiological reductionism. Schopenhauer's discourse is among other things one of the pharynx and the larynx, of cramps, convulsions, epilepsy, tetanus and hydrophobia. For Nietzsche as for Marx, culture is founded on the material body. He asks himself in *The Gay Science* whether philosophy has 'not been merely an interpretation of the body and a *misunderstanding of the body*',[16] and in typically carnivalesque style notes with mock solemnity in *The Twilight of the Idols* that no philosopher has yet spoken with reverence and gratitude of the human nose.

\* \* \*

The discourse of science, whether of the nose or more pivotal matters, was to pose its own challenge to culture. For Darwin, human cultures are the accidental outcrops of processes that lack all meaning in themselves. For him as for Nietzsche and Freud, non-sense lies at the root of sense. If Schelling had sought to incorporate the natural sciences into his spiritual vision, thinkers like Comte and Spencer aimed to do the reverse. Human meanings and values were to be brought under the sway of laws which also governed the evolution of the mollusc and the motion of the planets. For naturalism and Positivism, the human spirit was no longer irreducible. There could be a science of humanity as well as a hermeneutics of it. Later, structuralism would play its own part in querying the centrality of culture, treating all such life forms as mere variations on the abiding laws of a universal mind. There are also those for whom psychoanalysis can be seen as a science of the human subject.

As the nineteenth century unfolds, the concept of culture begins to shed its innocence. A suspicion that was already stirring in Jean-Jacques Rousseau's writings – that the price we pay for civilisation is too high, that refinement for the few means distress for the many – begins to intensify. In Rousseau's view, the arts and sciences have been by and large agents of moral corruption. There can be no civilisation without vanity, luxury, indolence and degeneracy. Friedrich Schlegel, in common with some other Romantics, upbraids culture for estranging us from Nature. The desires it breeds in us are tainted at source. Human aspirations are by no means an unequivocal good. It is no longer possible to suppose with the more libertarian Romantic that desire turns morbid only when it is thwarted by some external force. It is not simply by virtue of their suppression, alienation or one-sidedness that our powers tend to fester. On the contrary, they are infiltrated by a certain sickness from the outset. Desire is a perverse, semi-pathological force, one which looks forward with self-lacerating pleasure to the prospect of its own demise. The later modern era thus glances back over the heads of the Romantic libertarians and rationalist *philosophes* to the pre-modern idea of Original Sin – a notion which is absent in Marx, but which Freud will reinvent in his own post-Augustinian idiom.

The Fall up from Nature to culture is a fortunate one, but it involves wreaking a certain ferocious violence upon ourselves. There is a defectiveness or amnesia at the core of our being without which there could be no creativity. From Nietzsche to Adorno, the benefits of civilisation are not denied, but it is 'the horror teeming under the stone of culture' that increasingly clamours for attention.[17] In the era of Auschwitz, the word that had come to signify the most complex form of human refinement – culture – is also bound up with the most unspeakable debasement. 'Whatever [the historical materialist] surveys in art and science,' Walter Benjamin comments in an illustrious passage, 'has a descent that cannot be contemplated without horror. It owes its existence not just to the efforts of the great geniuses who fashioned it, but also in greater or lesser degree to the anonymous drudgery of their contemporaries. There is no cultural document that is not at the same time a record of barbarism ... [cultural history] may well increase the burden of the treasures that are piled up on humanity's back. But it does not give mankind the strength to shake them off, so as to get its hands on them.'[18] Georg Simmel is another who finds something burdensome about this cultural booty. Culture in his view is Spirit in objectified form; but in modern times it comes to overwhelm subjective existence, assuming an autonomous logic of its own in glacial indifference to human purposes. Human beings now stagger under an oppressive surplus of culture, rather than wilting for lack of it.[19]

Benjamin's ambivalent assessment of culture is that of Marxism as a whole. In scorn of all primitivism, it sings the praises of civilisation, while in the face of all Panglossian progressivism it insists on the atrocious price that this achievement has extorted from humanity. Rather than denying culture, Marxism relocates it. Culture does not go all the way down, as it does for the postmodern culturalists. On the contrary, it springs from material forces which are not cultural in themselves – rather as language is the product of marks which are not significant in themselves, or as consciousness for Freud has its origins in forces which are not inherently meaningful. Besides, the culture that for Schiller and Arnold is a principle of unity is for Marx a way of masking division. Culture, in short, is too close to ideology, as well as to hard labour, to be unambiguously affirmed. Its claims to be the polar opposite of power are either deceitful or naive.

The difference between Marx and Nietzsche on this subject is not a question of whether the noble has its source in the ignoble. Both are full-blooded materialists on this score. It is a question of what one makes of the fact. From a Marxist viewpoint, it is an open question whether the fruits of civilisation can justify the barbarism that went into their making. A Marxist might claim (though surprisingly few of them do) that no profusion of future treasures could be worth the toil that has been the fate of the majority over the course of class history. How long would a future socialist order have to endure, and how vigorously would it need to flourish, to make reparation for a past which weighs like a nightmare on the brains of the living? If there is light at the end of the tunnel, what of those who perished on the tracks and were lost in the sidings, those who will not be hauled through to some political redemption but whose very names have been erased from the historical record?

For his part, Nietzsche has no doubt that civilisation is worth every cent of the savagery it has involved. In a passage excluded from *The Birth of Tragedy*, he coolly justifies the role of slavery in the genesis of ancient Greek art, and brazenly proposes that in modern times 'the misery of the laboriously living masses must be further intensified in order to enable a number of Olympic people to produce the world of art'.[20] It is not difficult to give a name to at least one member of the Olympic class. Culture is the opposite of exploitation, but it is also what legitimises it. In justifying the misery of the masses, culture is ideological in the Marxist sense of the term; but in Nietzsche's view it is not ideological in the sense that it should seek to dissemble or deny it. One of the greatest of liberal thinkers, John Stuart Mill, agreed with Nietzsche that slavery in the ancient world was justified by the political and intellectual culture to which it gave rise.

A theodicy of this kind is really incompatible with tragedy. Suffering in Nietzsche's eyes is to be affirmed as the soil from which culture springs, but it is also to be acclaimed because it is an integral part of human flourishing. Existence itself is hard, cruel and wantonly destructive, and the *Übermensch* is that erotically ambiguous being, at once macho and masochistic, who delights in inflicting pain on himself by curbing his passions. Only the spiritual castrati of various stripes fail to embrace this warrior ethic with a cry of tragic joy. For Nietzsche, Christians in particular belong to this camp, revelling in their sorrows with a macabre relish.

In fact, Christianity is arguably a more tragic creed than Nietzsche's own doctrine, precisely because it regards suffering as unacceptable. Christian faith turns on the tragic action of confronting affliction and despair in order to redeem them; but this is possible only if they are seen for what they are, not as enviable opportunities to flex one's moral muscles. The Jesus of the New Testament never once counsels the sick to reconcile themselves to their sufferings. On the contrary, he appears to regard the source of their ailments as demonic. In Gethsemane, panic-stricken at the prospect of his own impending death, he prays to be released from his fate. The fate that lies in store for him may be tragic, but it is not heroic, as it might be if suffering were thought ennobling. On the contrary, such political executions are tragic not only because pain has no merit in itself, but also because they are for the most part eminently avoidable. One thinks of Brecht's sardonic reworking of the doctrine of tragic inevitability: 'This man's sufferings appal me because they are unnecessary.' Jesus did not need to die, any more than any other political prisoner has to perish. Not to acknowledge this is to excuse the powers which impose such penalties. If some value can be plucked from suffering, well and good. But it would be preferable if one could reap one's benefits from some less distressing source. Nietzsche, by contrast, can see only cowardice in the avoidance of pain. For him, hardship has a value in itself. His tragic vision is thus at risk of making suffering appear too meaningful. Theodor Adorno was suspicious of tragedy for precisely this reason. It seemed to him to impose too much sense on the senseless, and thus to diminish its horror.[21] The very form of the art risks making its sordid content more palatable and coherent than it is.

* * *

If Marx and Nietzsche remind us of the exorbitant cost of culture, Freud is another who acknowledges the blood and cruelty that lie at the bottom of all good things. In his later writings, he posits in humanity a primary aggression which is sublimated, fused with Eros, builder of cities, and harnessed to the task of subjugating Nature in order to dredge a civilisation from it.[22] The death drive which lurks within our violence is thus cheated out of its nefarious intentions and pressed into the service of constructing a social order. But establishing that order, as well as living under it, involves renouncing gratification; and this task is taken in hand by the superego, source of the authority, idealism and moral conscience vital to the maintenance of social existence. The more civilised we become, then, the more we must forswear gratification; and the more dutifully we do so, the more the malicious superego is empowered to unleash its high-minded terror upon us. Moreover, since the craven, chronically masochistic ego reaps an obscene pleasure from being chastised, we find ourselves caught up in a morbid collusion between Law and desire, two phenomena which the naive libertarian fondly imagines to be antithetical. Wiser libertarians like William Blake harboured no such illusions.

To be gratified is thus to feel guilt, a guilt deepened by the pleasure we take in the power which punishes us. The more admirably idealist we grow, the more we stoke up within ourselves a culture of lethal self-hatred. Moreover, the more we turn our libidinal energies (or Eros) outward to the task of constructing a civilisation, the more depleted we leave these resources, so the more they can fall prey to their age-old antagonist, Thanatos or the death drive. In all these ways, there is something peculiarly self-undoing about the civilising process. If the death drive lurks within the urge to create, then what makes for civility also threatens to mar it. There is an anarchic aspect to our very rage for order.

It is possible, Freud considers, that the project of culture or civilisation demands more from us than we can properly yield, not least because the superego, being obtuse as well as vindictive, issues its ukases in callous indifference as to whether we can obey them or not. Culture is a sickeningly unstable affair. If a society fails to evolve beyond the point where the satisfaction of a minority depends on the suppression of the majority, Freud writes in *The Future of an Illusion*, it 'neither has nor deserves the prospect of a lasting existence'.[23] The political implications of the claim are dramatic. They were to become evident enough in the twentieth century and its aftermath, to which we can now turn.

# CHAPTER 6

# MODERNISM AND AFTER

As THE POWER OF religion begins to fail, its various functions are redistributed like a precious legacy to those aspiring to become its heirs. Scientific rationalism takes over its doctrinal certainties, while radical politics inherits its mission to transform the face of the earth. Culture in the aesthetic sense safeguards something of its spiritual depth. Indeed, most aesthetic ideas (creation, inspiration, unity, autonomy, symbol, epiphany and so on) are really displaced fragments of theology. Signs which accomplish what they signify are known as poetry to aesthetics and as sacraments to theology. Meanwhile, culture in the wider sense of the word retains something of religion's communitarian ethos. Science, philosophy, culture and politics, needless to say, survive the decline of religion as enterprises in their own right. Yet they are also called on to shoulder some of its offices, alongside their own proper business.

Like religion, high culture plays a double role, offering a critique of modern civilisation but also a refuge from its degeneracy. In the lineage of so-called *Kulturkritik*, the objects of its criticism were legion: science, commerce, rationalism, materialism, utilitarianism, equality, democracy and mass civilisation. 'As far as democracy in

Germany is concerned,' wrote the young Thomas Mann, 'I believe completely in its realisation: this is precisely what makes me pessimistic.'[1] This radical-conservative heritage passed from Schiller, Coleridge, Carlyle, Kierkegaard and Alexis de Tocqueville to Nietzsche, Karl Mannheim, Julien Benda, Ortega y Gasset, the early Georg Lukács, the early Thomas Mann, Martin Heidegger, D. H. Lawrence, T.S. Eliot, W.B. Yeats, F.R. Leavis and a number of other twentieth-century luminaries. In our own day, the torch has been carried by George Steiner, perhaps the last of the *Kulturkritiker*. A persuasive case can be made for the enrolment of Ludwig Wittgenstein in the ranks of these conservative cultural pessimists.[2]

There was also a left-wing version of the case, evident in the writings of the Frankfurt School. Its adherents favoured democracy but not mass civilisation; freedom and equality but not rationalism and technology. The work of Herbert Marcuse rehearses some of the familiar themes of *Kulturkritik*, but also unmasks the illusion of culture as a redemptive power.[3] In the late 1960s, a version of this cultural critique was to take to the streets. A few years later, the last of the revolutionary avant-gardes, Situationism, gave up the ghost. There were to be for the present no more large-scale couplings of culture and politics, of which Nazism had provided the most noxious example. Instead, in the period of postmodernism, a rather different animal known as cultural politics moved increasingly to the fore. Modernism, broadly speaking, had turned to culture as an alternative to politics; the postmodernist impulse, by contrast, was to conflate the two.

For the mandarins of *Kulturkritik*, ethics was to be preferred to politics, pessimism to progressivism, reverence to enlightenment, the elite to the masses, the individual to the state, community to society and the spiritual to the rational. For the early Thomas Mann, who held that aesthetics was the enemy of politics, all this boiled down to an option for the Germans against the French, at a time when the two parties were busy slaughtering each other on the battlefields of the First World War.[4] Intellectually speaking, the quarrel between the Germans and the French has been seen as one between culture and civilisation, a distinction which Freud thought quite empty.[5] His theories of sublimation, repression, aggressivity and the like cut indifferently across this divide. The distinction between ethics and politics seemed to him equally trifling when set against the internecine combat between Eros and Thanatos. As Francis Mulhern comments, Freud demonstrated 'the substantial unity of "culture" and "civilisation", and thereby undermined the rationale of the "man of culture"'.[6] Even so, though his vision of humanity is closer to Hobbes than it is to Schiller, he was *Kulturkritiker* enough himself to hold that society consisted of a few brave, disinterested souls besieged by the 'lazy and unintelligent' masses.

Few such conservative revolutionaries proved more exemplary than the German author Stefan George. Inspired by a combination of Platonism, Pre-Raphaelitism, French symbolism, aestheticism, medievalism and German nationalism, George combined a fear of Bolshevism with a belief that industrial capitalism had destroyed all traditional bonds and values. The exclusive elite of artists he gathered around him despised realpolitik and were viscerally ill-disposed to all aspects of modernity, not least democracy. George himself proclaimed the need for a prophet, the Messiah of a New Reich not easily distinguishable from himself, who would purify the race and forge a new national culture in his native land.

Refreshingly free of false modesty, he appeared as Dante at a Munich pageant in 1904, along with a young friend dressed as a Florentine page. Some of the Nazis were to adopt George as a cultural harbinger, while others were to dismiss him as decadent.[7]

From Hölderlin to Steiner, one of the most persistent motifs of this tradition has been the idea of tragedy. Why has this topic cropped up so often in the thought of modern Europe, not least when, in the long march from Georg Büchner to Henrik Ibsen, outstanding specimens of the art were notably thin on the ground? As Simon Critchley remarks, the philosophy of the tragic recurs with 'an almost uncanny persistence in the German intellectual tradition'.[8] One reason, no doubt, is that the idea of tragedy has acted as an indirect critique of modernity. It represents a memory trace of nobility in a drably bourgeois epoch, a residue of transcendence in an age of materialism. Tragic art is a question of gods, heroes, warriors, martyrs and aristocrats, rather than of the run-of-the-mill middle-class citizen.[9] The experience it records is one largely restricted to a spiritual elite. It deals in myth, ritual, destiny, guilt, high crimes, expiation and blood sacrifice rather than in cotton mills and universal suffrage. The feelings it evokes are the quasi-religious sentiments of fear, reverence, awe and submissiveness.

Tragedy is everything that modernity is not: aristocratic rather than egalitarian, spiritual rather than scientific, absolute rather than contingent, a question of destiny rather than self-determination. Far from inflating the value of Man in the manner of the middle-class progressivists, tragic art chastens him, reminding him of his sinfulness and mortality by forcing him to pass through fire. Yet in doing so it reveals in its hero a steadfastness and audacity beyond the scope of the common herd. No vulgar social hope can survive the destructive forces unleashed by this art. Yet those forces are met with a spiritual resilience more precious than any scheme for political utopia.

Suffering is not to be tided away, in the manner of the tender-minded humanitarians. The art of tragedy scorns all such moral softness. Instead, pain is to be accepted in the style of the warrior and nobleman as the ultimate test of one's mettle. Only bank clerks and shopkeepers turn tail at the sight of Medusa's heads or the foul-smelling Furies. The pain in question is not pointless, however, since tragedy is also a secular form of theodicy. The world may not make much moral or rational sense, as the shallow-minded *Aufklärer* imagines that it does, but it is possible all the same to pluck supreme value from breakdown and failure. In this way one can continue to hope without playing into the hands of the apologists for progress. Dionysus, patron of the art, is agony and ecstasy in the same person, god of obscene enjoyment but also of joy and regeneration.

The world of tragedy is dark and enigmatic, an obscurity which throws the limits of human rationality into sharp relief. Reason stands revealed as the frailest of faculties, in contrast to the demonic powers that lay siege to it. Yet this mistrust of reason is not a lapse into nihilism, since tragic art yields us at the same time a sense of cosmic order. This order must not be too palpable and schematic, which would mean a capitulation to middle-class rationalism; yet neither must it be so elusive as to suggest that the heavens mock all human endeavour. Instead, one must cling to human value while acknowledging its fragility. A path must be found between cynicism and triumphalism. With its halo of mystery and transcendence, tragedy is a reproach to the shallow rationalism of the Enlightenment. It is also a rebuke to its individualism. There can be no callow faith that Man can determine his own destiny as a free agent. No such vision can survive the implacable force of fate, the communal nature of the tragic action or the unfathomable interlocking of human destinies that it reveals. Such freedom is simply the ignorance of necessity. Tragedy dismantles the opposition between the two, refusing both an errant subjectivism and a degrading determinism. Both freedom and necessity, Schelling writes in his *Philosophy of Art*, 'are manifested in perfect indifference as simultaneously victorious and vanquished'.[10] To make one's destiny one's choice is to confound the distinction between the voluntary and the inevitable. There is hope, then, but not some bright-eyed optimism.

If the protagonist is fully responsible for his or her situation, the tragic sense is fatally weakened. We are not inclined to waste pity on those who slaughter their fathers or sacrifice their daughters in full knowledge of what they are about. The bourgeois cult of individual freedom must consequently be rejected. Yet neither is the hero a mere puppet of external forces, as the mechanical materialists regard humanity. A different ratio between free will and determination is called for. In opting to embrace necessity, the protagonist reveals a form of freedom more precious than anything one might find in the marketplace. No act can be more free than the decision to relinquish one's liberty. In making this choice, the hero pays homage to freedom at the same time as he bows to the Law. He is thus set above all vulgar determinism; yet because this is a transcendence achieved through submission, we are still invited to recognise the limits of the will. In celebrating human freedom, we also acknowledge the virtues of humility and self-sacrifice. In this sense, tragedy offers an aesthetic solution to a political and philosophical problem. It teaches us how to resolve the conflict between freedom and determinism, one that has plagued the thought of the modern age. One way it does so is by replacing a distasteful determinism with the more exalted notion of providence or the gods. In these and other ways, tragedy has served the modern age as yet another form of spilt religion, one all the more imposing for being a matter of image rather than concept. Noble-spirited souls do not respond to the theories of enlightened bourgeois philosophers by penning treatises of their own. Instead, they point triumphantly to an art form, one in which what cannot easily be said can nonetheless be shown.

It is remarkable how resilient the faith that art might prove our salvation turns out to be. It is Nietzsche's theme from start to finish. It is a hope which is able to survive the collapse of the high Victorian consensus and the carnage of the First World War. Versions of it are to be found in both Bloomsbury and *Scrutiny*, sworn enemies in so much else. Art is a fortress against an encroaching barbarism. 'Poetry,' writes I.A. Richards with stunning credulity, 'is capable of saving us; it is a perfectly possible means of overcoming chaos.'[11] F.R. Leavis speaks of confronting a crassly materialistic society with the 'religious depth of thought and feeling' to be found in great literature.[12] 'After one has abandoned a belief in God,' remarks Wallace Stevens, 'poetry is that essence which takes its place as life's redemption.'[13] 'Poetry / Exceeding music must take the place / Of empty heaven and its hymns', he writes in 'The Man with the Blue Guitar'. It is a note one can hear sounded as early as Mallarmé, for whom the proper role of art is to succeed religion.[14] Having done service for theology in its time, the aesthetic now makes a bid to supplant it. High modernism is numinous through and through, as the work of art provides one of the last outposts of enchantment in a spiritually degenerate world. Postmodernism, with its notorious absence of affect, is post-numinous. It is also in a sense post-aesthetic, since the aestheticisation of everyday life extends to the point where it undermines the very idea of a special phenomenon known as art. Stretched far enough, the category of the aesthetic cancels itself out.

The imagination as a means of grace is one of modernism's abiding motifs, from the redemptive power of memory in Proust's great novel to the priestly vocation of the Joycean artist. Henry James finds in art a form of saintly self-immolation. Epiphanies of transcendence haunt the fiction of Woolf and the poetry of Rilke. An anthropology based on death, sacrifice and rebirth underlies the most renowned of English modernist poems. Its author will argue later in his *Notes Towards the Definition of Culture* that the culture of a people must be founded on religion if it is to thrive. Not many modernist artists, however, happened to be devout Anglo-Catholics, and their preferred strategy was accordingly for culture to replace religion rather than to rest upon it. The shadow of the death of God still falls over the work of one of the most resolutely secular of twentieth-century critics, Frank Kermode, for whose *Sense of an Ending* myths, both religious and political, must give way to self-conscious fictions.

God is not exactly dead, but he has turned his hinderparts to humanity, who can now sense his unbearable presence only in his ominous absence. The mildly desperate notion of the aesthetic as a secularised form of transcendence is alive and well as late as Salman

Rushdie's Herbert Read Memorial Lecture of 1990, which rehearses a number of high-minded liberal platitudes about how the task of art is to provide us with questions rather than answers. It is not obvious that this is how Dante or Michelangelo saw the matter. Nor does Rushdie seems perturbed by the thought that if art is indeed the modern version of transcendence, an even smaller number of men and women are recipients of grace than the most rigorous Calvinist might suppose.[15]

With the advent of modernism, the two main senses of culture, aesthetic and anthropological, are increasingly riven apart. They can converge only in such imaginary worlds as Lawrence's Mexico, Yeats's Anglo-Irish estate, the organic society of the Scrutineers, Eliot's stratified Christian society, the aesthetic South of the American New Critics or Heidegger's vision of a philosophical inquiry conducted among the peasantry. (Adorno retorted that one would like to know the peasants' opinion of that.) The contest between culture as art and culture as form of life is one between minority and popular culture, which from now on confront one another as mortal rivals. Modernism is among other things a defensive reaction to the culture industry, with which it was twinned at birth. The dream of the radical Enlightenment – of a culture which would be both learned and popular, resourceful enough to challenge the reigning powers but sufficiently lucid to rally the common people to its standard – would now seem definitively over. So would the radical-Romantic hope of uniting art, culture and politics in a common project. It was a time for distinctions rather than syntheses.

\* \* \*

From Coleridge onwards, culture and civilisation have generally been seen as antagonists rather than allies. This had not always been the case. In eighteenth-century England, the ideology of commercial humanism, as G.A. Pocock has dubbed it, drew the two into close relation.[16] In fact, they are clipped together in the very word 'civilisation', denoting as it does both moral qualities and material achievements. Commercial dealings between individuals, so the theory goes, are likely to make them polished as well as prosperous, smoothing their rough edges, eroding their provincialism and angularity, and fostering a depth of mutual sympathy that will in turn render the conduits of commerce all the more frictionless and efficient. The arrogance and uncouthness of the old aristocratic order give way to *le doux commerce*. Peace and civility are good for business. *Politesse* oils the wheels of the economy. For Adam Ferguson's *Essay on the History of Civil Society*, sentiments and social relations go hand in hand, as the extension of trade and the diffusion of moral sentiments prove mutually enriching. Exchange can be spiritually as well as financially profitable, not least in that act of putting oneself in another's place which is the work of the empathetic imagination. It is no accident that Adam Smith is moralist and economist together. The merchant and the Man of Feeling are not to be treated as antitypes.

The twentieth century was to witness another mode of uniting culture and civilisation, one which could scarcely be more remote from the eighteenth-century coffee-houses. It was possible that civilisation in the sense of industry and technology could be pressed into the service of art. This, anyway, was the dream of the revolutionary avant-garde, for whom art would survive by adapting to an age of mechanical reproduction, not by seeking to resist it in the manner of high modernism. New forms of technological culture were therefore to be invented, and existing ones taken over. The wager of the Futurists, Constructivists and Surrealists, determined as they were to sup with the devil, was that history, in Marxian phrase, could progress by its bad side – that one could seize upon the technological apparatus of the existing system and harness it to revolutionary ends. You could use capitalism's techniques to subvert its forms of subjectivity. The base could be turned against the superstructure.

The experiment failed, crushed by both Stalinism and Nazism. It was only some decades later, with the emergence of postmodernism, that the two versions of culture in question could be finally reconciled. From the 1980s onward, culture in the sense of art became increasingly populist, streetwise and vernacular, while culture as a form of life was aestheticised from end to end. For the Hellenists and Romantics, the latter meant the kind of common life that was creatively fulfilling; for postmodernism, rather less euphorically, it meant a politics and economy dependent on the image. The long-dreamt-of marriage of art and everyday life, which for the revolutionary avant-garde was consummated in political murals or agitprop theatre, could be found instead in fashion and design, the media and public relations, advertising agencies and recording studios. Culture opened its arms to the everyday life that *Kulturkritik* had regarded as its nemesis.

What it gained in democratic terms, however, it abandoned in critical ones. *Kulturkritik*, with its high-minded contempt for everyday habits, was an elitist vein of conservatism; postmodernism, with its fusion of art and commerce, is a populist one. If *Kulturkritik* is too caustic in its view of the commonplace, postmodernism is too complicit. Both look askance at the way of life of the majority – *Kulturkritik* because of what it sees as its dreary mediocrity, postmodernism because it falsely assumes that consensuses and majorities are inherently benighted, and thus has an ideological preference for margins and minorities. *Kulturkritik* is disdainful of such humdrum questions as state, class, economy and political organisation; postmodernism, entranced by the liminal, aberrant and transgressive, can muster scarcely more enthusiasm for them.

Postmodernism is in many ways a postscript to Nietzsche, though a Nietzsche shorn of the quasi-metaphysical baggage – of the Will to Power, the *Übermensch* and the quasi-teleological tale of how humanity might pass from savagery to moral splendour. It also abandons his tragic vision. If *Kulturkritik* makes too much of tragedy, postmodernism is merely bemused by it. It is a post-tragic form of culture – though post-tragic in the sense that Morrissey is post-Mozart rather than in the sense that Alain Badiou is post-Marxist. It is not as if it has been hauled through tragedy in order to emerge, suitably transfigured, on the other side. In its eyes, a lack of inherent meaning in reality is not a scandal to be confronted but a fact to be accepted. Modernism involves a readiness to encounter dark, Dionysian forces, even the possibility of total dissolution, in its zealous pursuit of the truth. Postmodernism sees no such necessity. It is too young to recall a time when there was (so it is alleged) truth, unity, totality, objectivity, universals, absolute values, stable identities and rock-solid foundations, and thus finds nothing disquieting in their apparent absence. It differs in this sense from its modernist precursors, who are close enough to the original catastrophe to be still reeling from the shock waves. For postmodernism, by contrast, there is no fragmentation, since unity was an illusion all along; no false consciousness, because no unequivocal truth; no shaking of the foundations, since there were none to be dislodged. It is not as though truth, identity and foundations are tormentingly elusive, simply that they never were. They have not vanished for ever, leaving only a spectre behind them. There is no phantom limb syndrome here. Their absence is no more palpable than the absence of a hairdryer in the hands of the Mona Lisa. One would no more mourn the lack of these things than one would lament the fact that a pig cannot recite *Paradise Lost*. As Richard Rorty might put it, there is no point in scratching where it doesn't itch.

Whereas modernism experiences the death of God as a trauma, an affront, a source of anguish as well as a cause for celebration, postmodernism does not experience it at all. There is no God-shaped hole at the centre of its universe, as there is at the centre of Kafka, Beckett or even Philip Larkin. Indeed, there is no gap of any kind in its universe. This is one of several reasons why postmodernism is post-tragic. Tragedy involves the possibility of irretrievable loss, whereas for postmodernism there is nothing momentous missing. It is just that we have failed to register this fact in our compulsively idealising hunt for higher, nobler, deeper things. In any case, tragedy is thought to require a certain depth of subjectivity, which is one reason why it might appear to be lacking in Beckett. The postmodern subject is hard-pressed to find enough depth and continuity in itself to be a suitable candidate for tragic self-dispossession. You cannot give away a self you never had. If there is no longer a God, it is partly because there is no longer any secret interior place where he might install himself. Depth and interiority belong to a clapped-out metaphysics, and to eradicate them is to abolish God by rooting out the underground places where he has been concealing himself. For psychoanalysis, by contrast, the human subject is diffused and unstable yet furnished with inner depths. Indeed, the two facts are closely allied. It thus ranks among the latter-day inheritors of the tragic sense, as postmodernism does not.

Tragedy is commonly bound up with a sense of historicity. The linear nature of time means that destructive actions, once performed, are irrecoverable. Their lethal fallout can spread far beyond their origins to contaminate the future. Yet since this unrecuperability is just as true of constructive forms of action, the medium of tragic deadlock is also the arena of potential redemption. Only through time, as T. S. Eliot writes in *Burnt Norton*, is time conquered, a claim which modernism, with its suspicion of linear temporality, for the most part resists. It is true that non-linear time can also be hospitable to tragedy. The vision of temporality as endless repetition is a portrait of hell, as in Flann O'Brien's hilariously comic account of damnation, *The Third Policeman*. This is not the case, however, with the spatialised time of the postmodern, in which everything is guaranteed to return with a slight variation. Repetition may be a device for avoiding tragedy as well as generating it. This is true of the fundamentally comic worldviews of Yeats and Joyce, both of whom place their trust in cyclical time. In the gyres and spirals of the cosmos, nothing can be definitively lost.

For Romanticism, the desire that we know as history represents a kind of infinity. Modernism, by contrast, is concerned less with infinity than eternity, an enigma which is to be found at the very core of the present in some secret essence or epiphanic moment plucked from the dreary wastes of time. With postmodernism, history is reduced for the most part to commodified cultural heritage, an ever-present repertoire of inherited styles and a 'presentist' approach to the past. The finality of what has happened already is bound to cause scandal to those for whom the real must be infinitely malleable. History is too brutely given for a culture which delights in an endless array of options. It is an unwelcome reminder that our freedom in the present is constrained by the irreparable fatality we know as the past.

If postmodern culture is depthless, anti-tragic, non-linear, anti-numinous, non-foundational and anti-universalist, suspicious of absolutes and averse to interiority, one might claim that it is genuinely post-religious, as modernism most certainly is not. Most religious thought, for example, posits a universal humanity, since a God who concerned himself with only a particular section of the species, say Bosnians or people over five foot eight inches tall, would appear lacking in the impartial benevolence appropriate to a Supreme Being. There must also be some common ground between ourselves and Abraham for the Hebrew Scriptures to make sense. Postmodernism, however, is notoriously nervous of universals, despite its claim that grand narratives have everywhere disappeared from the earth, or that there are no stable identities to be found, wherever one looks. As a current of thought, it inherits most of those aspects of Nietzsche's philosophy that make for atheism; but since in its streetwise style it rejects the notion of the *Übermensch*, it refuses to smuggle in a new form of divinity to replace the old. Sceptical of the whole concept of a universal humanity, it repudiates Man as well as God, and in doing so refuses the quasi-religious consolations of humanism. In this sense, Nietzsche's warning that the Almighty will only rest quiet in his grave when Man lies alongside him is finally taken seriously.

Nietzsche himself, as we have seen, salvages a vision of the active human subject from the ruins of classical humanism. The Overman stamps his image on a world which in itself is mere flux and difference. He also brings his own desires under his dominion in much the same fashion. In this sense, Michel Foucault's doctrine of self-fashioning in his *History of Sexuality* strikes an authentically Nietzschean note. Yet it is one untypical of post-structuralism and postmodernism as a whole. For them, the flux of reality has now infiltrated the subject to the point where its unity dissolves and its agency is undermined. The postmodern subject, like the *Übermensch*, is clay in its own hands, able to change shape at its own behest; but by the same token it lacks the indomitable will with which Nietzsche's post-human animal bends reality to his demands. It is aesthetic not in the Nietzschean or Wildean sense of turning oneself into a work of art, but in the Kierkegaardian sense of lacking all unity and principle.

Since Man is no longer to be seen primarily as agent or creator, he is no longer in danger of being mistaken for the Supreme Being. He has finally attained maturity, but only at the cost of relinquishing his identity. He is not to be seen as self-determining, which is what freedom means for the likes of Kant and Hegel. The self is no longer coherent enough to be so. This is certainly one way in which postmodernism is post-theological, since it is God above all who is One, and who is the ground of his own being. It follows that if you want to be shot of him, you need to refashion the concept of subjectivity itself, which is just what postmodernism seeks to do. It is easier to accomplish this if the capitalist system happens to be in transit from the subject as producer to the subject as consumer. Consumers are passive, diffuse, provisional subjects, which is not quite how the Almighty is traditionally portrayed. As long as men and women are seen as producers, labourers, manufacturers or self-fashioners, God can never quite expire. Behind every act of production lurks an image of Creation, and one act of production in particular – art – rivals that of the Almighty himself. Not even he, however, can survive the advent of Man the Eternal Consumer.

Perhaps, then, the latter decades of the twentieth century will be seen as the time when the deity was finally put to death. With the advent of postmodern culture, a nostalgia for the numinous is finally banished. It is not so much that there is no redemption as that there is nothing to be redeemed. Religion, to be sure, lives on, since there is more to late modern civilisation than postmodernism. Even so, after a long succession of botched projects, flawed strategies and theoretical cul-de-sacs, it would not be too much to claim that with the emergence of postmodernism, human history arrives for the first time at an authentic atheism. It is true that postmodern thought pays an enormous price for this coming of age, if coming of age it is. In writing off religion, it also dismisses a good many other momentous questions as so much metaphysical illusion. If it abjures religion, it does so, as we have seen, at the cost of renouncing depth, of which it is notably nervous. It thereby abandons a good deal else of value.

It is true that postmodernism retains the odd trace of transcendence, not least in its somewhat fetishistic cult of otherness. Yet though there is otherness in plenty, there is no Big Other, no grand totality or transcendental signifier. Besides, though other cultures may be incommensurate with one's own, there is no other to culture itself. Culture goes all the way down, as God himself was once thought to do. It is a shamefaced form of foundationalism. Culture is what you cannot peer behind or dig beneath, since the peering and digging would themselves be cultural procedures. It thus operates as a kind of absolute, as culture in a loftier sense of the term did for Arnold. Yet this is culture as transcendental rather than transcendent – as the condition of possibility of all phenomena, rather than as some sacred domain beyond their orbit.

There are also traces of the transcendent in the bogus spirituality of some postmodern cultures. It is the kind of soft-centred, cut-price religiosity one would expect from a thoroughly materialist society. A muddled sense of mystery is the only form of faith to which such hard-headed societies can aspire, rather as broad humour is the only comedy with which the humourless feel at ease. So it is that those who cannot conceive of an end to Wall Street are perfectly capable of believing in Kabbalah. It comes as no surprise that Scientology, packaged Sufism, off-the-peg occultism and ready-to-serve transcendental meditation should figure as fashionable pastimes among the super-rich, or that Hollywood should turn its eyes to Hinduism. The hard-boiled who believe in nothing turn out to be the kind of fantasists who will believe in anything. It is the worldly and well-heeled who think of religion as cosmic harmony and esoteric cult, rather as the idea of the artist as a shock-haired bohemian, so James Joyce once pointed out, is the respectable burgher's view of him. Feeding the hungry is too close to filling in one's tax return for those in search of an escape from the mundane. The point of spirituality is to cater for needs that one's stylist or stockbroker cannot fulfil. Yet all this reach-me-down otherworldliness is really a form of atheism. It is a way of feeling uplifted without the gross inconvenience of God.

Andrew Wernick points out that postmodernism involves a kind of second death of God, as the various surrogates for divinity fabricated in the modern age are dismantled in their turn. The idea of society, for example, provides Durkheim with a form of transcendence, but Jean Baudrillard announces the end of the social itself.[17] The same is true of the concept of culture. If Arnold's culture is among other things a demythologised version of God, postmodernism comes up with a demystified version of culture itself. With modernism, the halo of divinity gives way to the aura of the aesthetic, which the technological art of postmodernism then dispels in its turn. The only aura to linger on is that of the commodity or celebrity, phenomena which are not always easy to distinguish. If Romanticism seeks to replace God with the fathomless, infinite, all-powerful subject, as Carl Schmitt argues in his *Political Romanticism*, postmodernism, in Perry Anderson's words, represents a 'subjectivism without a subject'.[18] If God is dead, then Man himself, who once dreamed of filling his shoes, is also nearing his term. There is not much left to disappear.

\* \* \*

One reason why postmodern thought is atheistic is its suspicion of faith. Not just religious faith, but faith as such. It makes the mistake of supposing that all passionate conviction is incipiently dogmatic. Begin with a robust belief in goblins and you end up with the Gulag. Nothing could be further from Kierkegaard's declaration in *The Sickness Unto Death*: 'to believe is to be'.[19] Nietzsche had a similar aversion to conviction, not least of the theoretical type. It was passion, not belief, that governed the greatest minds. Abstract doctrines were falsely equalising. As such, they were the intellectual equivalent of Jacobinism, socialism and Christian morality, a kind of exchange-value of the mind. There was a relation in Nietzsche's view between Kant's love of abstraction and his championship of the 'gruesome farce' known as the French Revolution. Fixed doctrines spell the death of the transient, provisional, unique and sensuously specific. Oscar Wilde, for whom truth was little more than his latest mood, thought much the same. Ludwig Wittgenstein, by contrast, did not accept that truth was a matter of opinion because the medium of opinion is language, and truth in Wittgenstein's eyes was not in the first place a linguistic affair. It was a more practical, material, institutional matter than that.

In Nietzsche's eyes, truly noble spirits refuse to be the prisoners of their own principles. Instead, they treat their own most cherished opinions with a certain cavalier detachment, adopting and discarding them at will. It is what Yeats, who like many a modernist felt the influence of Nietzsche, and for whom opinions were fit meat for bank clerks and shopkeepers, called *sprezzatura*. One's beliefs are more like one's manservants, to be hired and fired as the fancy takes you, than like one's bodily organs. They are not to be regarded in the manner of Charles Taylor or Stanley Fish as constitutive of personal identity, but rather as costumes one can don or doff at will. For the most part, as with kilts and cravats, it is aesthetic considerations which govern the donning and doffing. The left-wing historian A.J.P. Taylor once informed an Oxford Fellowship election committee that he had extreme political views, but held them moderately.

In *The Joyful Wisdom*, Nietzsche scorns what he calls the 'longing for certainty' of science and rationalism, an itch for epistemological assurance behind which it is not hard to detect a deep-seated anxiety of spirit. In his view, the compulsion to believe is for those who are too timid to exist in the midst of ambiguities without anxiously reaching out for some copper-bottomed truth. The desire for religion is the craving for an authority whose emphatic 'Thou Shalt' will relieve us of our moral and cognitive insecurity. The free spirit, by contrast, is one that has the courage to dispense with 'every wish for certainty', supporting itself only by 'slender cords and possibilities', yet dancing even so on the verge of the abyss.[20] If one believes in freedom, then this must surely include a certain freedom from one's belief in it. Whether it should also stretch to freedom from the belief that one must be free from one's beliefs is a question one may cheerfully delegate to the logicians.

It is a case that will return with the advent of post-structuralism. In an age in which the concept of certainty smacks of the tyrant and technocrat, a certain agnosticism becomes a virtue. Indeterminacy and undecidability are accounted goods in themselves. Nietzsche and his postmodern progeny thus fail to take heed of those who need a degree of certainty about their situation in order to emancipate themselves from it. Not all certainty is dogmatic, and not all ambiguity is on the side of the angels. Literary types are less likely to recognise this fact than lawyers. To be sure that one is in love, or that one's arm has just been inconveniently impaled on a spike, is not a question of sterile dogma or autocratic bluster.

Conviction suggests a consistency of self which does not sit easily with the volatile, adaptive subject of advanced capitalism.

Besides, too much doctrine is bad for consumption. It is also out of fashion because belief is not what pins society together as it welds the Lutheran Church or the Boy Scout movement together. Given its pragmatic, utilitarian bent, capitalism, especially in its post-industrial incarnation, is an intrinsically faithless social order. Too much belief is neither necessary nor desirable for its operations. Beliefs are potentially contentious affairs, which is good neither for business nor for political stability. They are also commercially superfluous. The fervent ideological rhetoric needed to found the system thus fades as it unfolds. As long as its citizens roll into work, pay their taxes and refrain from assaulting police officers, they can believe pretty much what they like. It is as if ideology no longer needs to pass through human consciousness. When asked whether he had any convictions, the Mayor of London replied that he had once acquired one for a driving offence.

The liberal state has traditionally enshrined one cardinal belief, namely that individuals should be allowed to believe what they want as long as this does not jeopardise the ability of others to do the same, or pose a threat to this doctrine itself. Otherwise, the state displays a certain constructive indifference to the views of its subjects. It is an indifference which it took a good deal of militant conviction to achieve. Places where such beliefs still play a decisive role – Northern Ireland, for example – appear atavistic or quasi-pathological. They are certainly idiosyncratic. The United States, which has always worn its ideology with embarrassing flamboyance on its sleeve, is something of an exception to this rule. It was always true of capitalism that it needed citizens who were believers at home but agnostics in the marketplace. As the system has developed, however, it has tilted decisively towards the latter. On the whole, large-scale beliefs are to be wheeled out only at times of political crisis. It is preferable for social existence to work simply by itself, without an excessive reliance on anything as capricious as individual opinion.

The faithlessness of advanced capitalism is built into its routine practices.[21] It is not primarily a question of the piety or scepticism of its citizens. The marketplace would continue to behave atheistically even if every one of its actors was a born-again Evangelical. Yet God has, of course, by no means vanished. Consumer capitalism may have scant use for him in practice, but it is still mortgaged to some extent to its own metaphysical heritage. By and large, advanced capitalism remains caught in the state of denial that Nietzsche denounces. The economy may be a rank atheist, but the state that stands guard over it still feels the need to be a true believer. Not, to be sure, necessarily a religious believer, but to subscribe to certain imperishable moral and political truths which cannot simply be derived from the size of the deficit or the unemployment statistics.

It is perfectly possible to imagine a future for the capitalist system in which its built-in atheism becomes, so to speak, official – in which, belatedly taking its cue from Nietzsche, it may throw off its *mauvaise foi* and dispense with a moral superstructure which is not only increasingly superfluous in practice but embarrassingly at odds with its own profane activities. Such a future, however, is still remote. As far as religious conviction is concerned, one does not jettison history's most formidably successful symbolic system overnight. Besides, just at the point when Western capitalism may have been edging in this direction, two aircraft slammed into the World Trade Center and metaphysical ardour broke out afresh.

Once the Cold War had been won, the West, so some of its apologists imagined, no longer stood in need of ardent convictions, grand narratives and sizeable doctrinal systems. The Death of History was accordingly promulgated, by no means for the first time. Hegel believed with becoming modesty that history had culminated inside his own head; but this merely provoked a series of later thinkers to challenge the claim, and so to perpetuate the very narrative that was supposed to have been wrapped up. Claims that history has been consummated can hardly avoid turning out to be non-self-fulfilling prophecies. Avant-gardes which seek to abolish history, for example, only succeed in augmenting it, since attempts to liquidate history are themselves historical acts. With the Death of History merchants, however, something more significant than a shop-worn theory was at stake. The triumphalism of the doctrine reflected the post-Cold-War West's increasingly high-handed political activities across the globe, one consequence of which was the unleashing of a radical Islamic backlash. The attempt to close down History had simply succeeded in prising it open again. The end of one grand narrative was the occasion for the birth of another, that of the so-called war on terror.

The irony of this is hard to overrate. No sooner had a thoroughly atheistic culture arrived on the scene, one which was no longer anxiously in pursuit of this or that place-holder for God, than the deity himself was suddenly back on the agenda with a vengeance. Nor were these two events unrelated. Fundamentalism has its source in anxiety rather than hatred. It is the pathological mindset of those who feel washed up by a brave new late-modern world, some of whom conclude that they can draw attention to their undervalued existence only by exploding a bomb in a supermarket. This is not, needless to say, a distinction between West and East.

Fundamentalism is a global creed. Its adherents are to be found in the hills of Montana as well as in the souks of Damascus. The world is accordingly divided between those who believe too much and those who believe too little. While some lack all conviction, others are full of passionate intensity. There are those who are loyal to little beyond power and profit, and there are others who, outraged by some of the consequences of this moral vacuity, tout doctrines that can blow off the heads of small children. As John Milbank writes, '[an] agnosticism designed to ward off fanaticism appears now to foment it both directly and indirectly'.[22]

Ideologically speaking, the West has unilaterally disarmed at just the point where it has proved most perilous for it to do so. Furnished with a mixture of pragmatism, culturalism, hedonism, relativism and anti-foundationalism, it now confronts a full-blooded metaphysical antagonist, one brought to birth in part by its own policies, for which absolute truths, coherent identities and solid foundations pose not the faintest problem. It is true that the West continues to believe, formally speaking, in such irrefragable absolutes as freedom, democracy and even (at least across the Atlantic) God and the Devil. It is just that these convictions have to survive in a culture of scepticism which gravely debilitates them.

Western capitalism, in short, has managed to help spawn not only secularism but also fundamentalism, a most creditable feat of dialectics.[23] Having slain the deity, it has now had a hand in restoring him to life, as a refuge and a strength for those who feel crushed by its own predatory politics. If it finds itself besieged from the outside by a murderous creed, it is also assailed from within by the rage and paranoia of those of its fundamentalist citizens left high and dry by its priorities. At the very moment when contemporary capitalism seemed to be moving into a post-theological, post-metaphysical, post-ideological, even post-historical era, a wrathful God has once more raised his head, eager to protest that his obituary notice has been prematurely posted. The Almighty, it appears, was not safely nailed down in his coffin after all. He had simply changed address, migrating to the US Bible Belt, the Evangelical churches of Latin America and the slums of the Arab world. And his fan club is steadily swelling.

As late capitalism drains the social world of meaning, culture in both major senses of the term is less able to invest everyday existence with a sense of purpose and value. On the contrary, some culture in the narrower sense of the term now shares in this general haemorrhage of meaning, along with a packaged and managed politics. It is into this spiritual vacuum that religion was able to rush, but with certain vital differences from the earlier modern period. For one thing, culture is no longer for the most part an attempt to supplant religion. From Wahabi Muslims to Southern Baptists, the two are increasingly hard to tell apart. Nor can culture and politics be regarded as opposites, in the manner of high modernism. On the contrary, it is largely for political reasons that culture in the broad sense of the term has been granted a formidable new lease of life. Forms of culture to which religious faith is central have been exploited and humiliated by the West, and it is not easy to distinguish the cultural, religious and political in their response to this onslaught. The wit who proposed that one should give up religion when it starts to interfere with one's everyday life had it exactly wrong. It is when such faith is bound up with one's everyday existence that it starts to matter, which is truer in Tehran than it is in East Grinstead. If religion ranked high in the priorities of the Enlightenment, it was not least because of its political importance. Much the same is true of radical Islam.

With the advent of the Enlightenment, science and Reason sought to inherit some of the authority of religion. With radical Romanticism, it was art rather than Reason which aimed to usurp that sovereignty, or at least to supplement it. Art was the paradigm of a new style of reasoning. It was this, not some widespread passion for music or painting, which made aesthetics so pivotal an affair in post-Enlightenment Europe. There were those for whom art was also the model for a radical politics, taking up the world-transformative mission that orthodox religion had largely abdicated. From nationalism to the avant-garde, an explosive mixture of politics and culture shook the foundations of the established order. High modernism and *Kulturkritik* were, among other things, reactions to this turbulent heritage. For these formations, culture was to be severed for the most part from the political, or at least to be seen as an anti-political version of it. It was an alternative to that philistine world, as it was also an alternative to religious faith.

In the meantime, however, religious belief persisted, while high culture found itself increasingly on the defensive. Revolutionary politics was equally rebuffed. In the closing decades of the twentieth century, a politics which pressed the claims of culture in ways that might topple empires – revolutionary nationalism – made way for the rather less ambitious enterprise known as cultural politics. The end of revolutionary nationalism and the onset of postmodernism spring from the same historical moment. A trio of grand narratives – religion, high culture and political revolution – appeared to have run their course. All three seemed to depend on metaphysical assumptions which could no longer be defended.

It was at just this point that metaphysics, having been deconstructed on the Parisian Left Bank and elsewhere, broke out on a global scale in the form of religious fundamentalism. Nor was this illogical. The identity politics by which postmodernism set such store were bound to rope in questions of religious identity as well, however awkwardly this sat with gay rights or Cornish nationalism.

The confrontation between the West and radical Islam involves a number of ironies. From the standpoint of Western modernity, the latter's refusal of any sharp distinction between politics, culture, morality and religion looms up as distinctly pre-modern. A similar blurring of boundaries, however, marks Western postmodernism, at least if one removes religion from the equation. It, too, tends to conflate politics and culture, if in a wholly different style from the radical Islamists. If the term 'cultural politics' has an oxymoronic ring for the legatees of Edmund Burke, it smacks of a tautology in postmodern company. Postmodernism tends to merge culture and morality as well, though once more in quite different mode from Islamism. It links the two realms by treating moral values as relative to specific cultures, while Islamism sees the moral and the cultural as aspects of a seamless way of life. The pre-modern and the postmodern thus find an echo in each other. In an Islamic religious faith which appears to subsume art, morality, culture and politics, the West can gaze at an image of its own earlier condition, before the great divisions of spiritual labour which characterise modernity set in. While regretting the lack of freedom inherent in this synthesis, it may also regret the solidity it lends to its opponents' sense of identity, one signally absent from its own way of life.

The ironies, however, do not end there. As the so-called war on terror took hold, it was as though the narrative recounted in this book came full circle, as an off-the-peg version of Enlightenment was recycled by the so-called new atheism in the years immediately following the terrorist assault on the United States.[24] No sooner had postmodernism dismissed Reason, truth, science, progress and objectivity as so many authoritarian delusions than they were being invoked once again by an alarmed liberal intelligentsia in pursuit of an ideology rather more substantial than anything that postmodernism had to offer. The new atheism was by no means born in the ruins of the World Trade Center, but it was spurred into fresh urgency there. There was a need for a new, militant defence of Western civilisation, given the menace now looming from the East. One such rationalist scourge of religion, the American Sam Harris, despite appearing to believe that his people are the most morally righteous ever to have walked the earth, was prepared in the wake of 9/11 to consider a pre-emptive nuclear strike resulting in the deaths of 'tens of millions of innocent civilians' against Muslim states found developing nuclear weapons.[25] This, one should note, is the voice of civilisation in its polemic against barbarism. Harris appears to regard himself as a liberal, which makes one wonder what unpleasant surprises his more right-of-centre colleagues may have in store for the Muslim world. A new form of Western cultural supremacism was abroad, though the terms of an older supremacism were now reversed. God was now on the side of barbarism, and unbelief on the side of civilisation. What stood in the path of Western progress was not the West's own problems but the Neanderthal doctrines of others.

The new atheism was probably right to claim that modern societies, whatever they themselves might imagine, no longer need religion as an ideological crutch. Some Enlightenment thinkers, as we have seen, had urged this case long before. Modern men and women do not for the most part derive their morality from the supernatural. Nor does reason need the crutch of mythology, as the radical Enlightenment was aware. This is not because it can go it alone, naked and self-reliant, unencumbered by image, fable, experience, intuition and sensuous particularity. It is because any authentic rationality must already encompass such matters. If it does not, it will fail to be fully reasonable. What rationalism from d'Alembert to Dawkins is loath to acknowledge is that human rationality is a corporeal one. We think as we do roughly because of the kind of bodies we have, as Thomas Aquinas noted. Reason is authentically rational only when it is rooted in what lies beyond itself. It must find its home in what is other than reason, which is not to say in what is inimical to it. Any form of reason which grasps itself purely in terms of ideas, and then fumbles for some less cerebral way in which to connect with the sensory world, is debilitated from the outset.

There is a final irony to be considered. In his *Faith of the Faithless*, a title which might be used to characterise a whole current of recent leftist thought, Simon Critchley acknowledges what he sees as the limits of any entirely secularist world-view, and records his doubt that radical politics can be effective without a religious dimension.[26] It is now some on the left, not the right, who look to a religious 'supplement' to the political – partly, no doubt, in response to the spiritual vacuity of late capitalism, but also because there are indeed some important affinities between religious and secular notions of faith, hope, justice, community, liberation and the like. A range of prominent left thinkers, from Badiou, Agamben and Debray to Derrida, Habermas and Žižek, have thus turned to questions of theology, to the chagrin or bemusement of some of their acolytes.

There is a dash of pathos, not to speak of a mildly comic touch, in the spectacle of a group of devout materialists speaking in strenuously Protestant terms of the 'claims of infinity', 'heeding the call', 'infinite responsibility', and the like. If Graham Greene's fiction is thronged with reluctant Christians, men and women who would like to be rid of the Almighty but find themselves stuck with him like some lethal addiction, there are also reluctant atheists – thinkers who can sometimes be distinguished from the Archbishop of Canterbury only by the fact that they do not believe in God. They have everything of religious faith but the substance of it, rather as Edmund Burke once described some of his opponents as having nothing of politics but the passions they incite. George Steiner and Roger Scruton have both ranked among such would-be devotees at various times in their career. The agnostic political philosopher John Gray is another. Religious belief has rarely been so fashionable among rank unbelievers.

Alongside the leftist fellow travellers, there are also those defenders of capitalism who, troubled by its crassly materialist climate, are out to hijack the religious spirit in order to lend this way of life some sweetness and light. Religious faith, suitably cleansed of its primitive propositions, may figure as a kind of aesthetic supplement to an uncouth social order. The title of Francis Spufford's *Unapologetic: Why, Despite Everything, Christianity Can Still Make Surprising Emotional Sense* is symptomatic of this trend, as is Alain de Botton's unwittingly entertaining *Religion for Atheists*. There are, de Botton argues, 'aspects of religious life that could fruitfully be applied to the problems of secular society.[27] We have seen already how a number of earlier thinkers eager to press religion into the service of power have made the claim. One and a half centuries in the wake of Matthew Arnold, de Botton is still wistfully hoping that culture may wrest the baton from religion. 'We are unwilling,' he writes, 'to consider secular culture *religiously* enough, in other words, as a source of guidance.'[28] De Botton is a latter-day Arnold, as his high Victorian language makes plain. Religion 'teaches us to be polite, to honour one another, to be faithful and sober', as well as instructing us in 'the charms of community'.[29] Intellectually speaking, religion is pure nonsense; but this is hardly to the point as long as it makes for some much-needed civility, aesthetic charm, social order and moral edification. A committed atheist like himself, de Botton argues, can therefore still find religion 'sporadically interesting, useful and consoling',[30] which makes it sound rather like rustling up a soufflé when you are feeling low. Since Christianity requires that one lay down one's life if need be for a stranger, de Botton must have a strange idea of consolation. His notion of faith is not quite that of a prophet who was tortured and executed by the imperial powers for speaking up for justice, and whose followers must be prepared to meet the same fate.

Religion, then, provides a convenient way of fulfilling certain emotional needs. It can inculcate moral discipline, strengthen the social order and provide a degree of ceremonial form, aesthetic resonance and spiritual depth to otherwise shallow lives. The case is a prime instance of intellectual duplicity. It reflects a trust in the enabling fiction or redemptive lie that can be found everywhere from Nietzsche and Ibsen to Conrad, Vaihinger and J.M. Synge. Liberal-capitalist societies, as we have seen, are frequently to be found in search of a judicious dose of the communitarian spirit to offset their naturally fissiparous nature. If we are witness today to a resurgent interest in religion, it is not only because the need to believe grows more compelling as capitalist orders become more spiritually bankrupt. It is also because that bankruptcy has been thrown into high relief by the spectre of radical Islam, and thus needs to be tackled if the so-called war on terror is to be won. Rather as Arnold emptied religion of its doctrinal content for political motives, so some contemporary atheistic philosophers have become latter-day fideists, setting aside the content of religion in order to bend it to their own moral and political ends. God may be dead, but the spirit of Arnold and Comte lives on. Christian faith, however, is not about moral uplift, political unity or aesthetic charm. Nor does it start from the portentous vagueness of some 'infinite responsibility'. It starts from a crucified body.

We have seen that reluctant atheism has a long history. Machiavelli thought that religious ideas, however vacuous, were a useful means of terrorising and pacifying the mob. Voltaire feared infecting his own domestic servants with his impiety. Toland clung to a 'rational' Christian belief himself, but thought the rabble should stay with their superstitions. Gibbon, one of the most notorious sceptics of all time, considered that the religious doctrines he despised could nonetheless prove socially useful. So did Montesquieu and Hume. So in our own time does Jürgen Habermas. Diderot scoffed at religion but valued its social cohesiveness. Arnold sought to counter the creeping godlessness of the working class with a poeticised version of the Christian doctrine he himself spurned. Auguste Comte, an out-and-out materialist, brought this dubious lineage to an acme of absurdity with his plans for a secular priesthood. Durkheim had no truck with the deity himself, but thought that religion could be a precious source of edifying sentiment. The philosopher Leo Strauss held that religious faith was essential for social order, though he did not for a moment credit it himself. A philosophical elite aware of the truth of the matter – that there is no sure foundation to political society – must at all costs conceal it from the masses. If the Almighty goes the way of Olympian gods and Platonic forms, how are social order and moral self-discipline to be maintained?

There is something unpleasantly disingenuous about this entire legacy. 'I don't happen to believe myself, but it is politically expedient that you should' is the catchphrase of thinkers supposedly devoted to the integrity of the intellect. One can imagine how they might react to being informed that their own most cherished convictions – civil rights, freedom of speech, democratic government and the like – were, of course, all nonsense, but politically convenient nonsense and so not to be scrapped. It took the barefaced audacity of Friedrich Nietzsche to point out that the problem was less the death of God than the bad faith of Man, who in an astonishing act of cognitive dissonance had murdered his Maker but continued to protest that he was still alive. It was thus that men and women failed to see in the divine obsequies an opportunity to remake themselves.

If religious faith were to be released from the burden of furnishing social orders with a set of rationales for their existence, it might be free to rediscover its true purpose as a critique of all such politics. In this sense, its superfluity might prove its salvation. The New Testament has little or nothing to say of responsible citizenship. It is not a 'civilised' document at all. It shows no enthusiasm for social consensus. Since it holds that such values are imminently to pass away, it is not greatly taken with standards of civic excellence or codes of good conduct. What it adds to common-or-garden morality is not some supernatural support, but the grossly inconvenient news that our forms of life must undergo radical dissolution if they are to be reborn as just and compassionate communities. The sign of that dissolution is a solidarity with the poor and powerless. It is here that a new configuration of faith, culture and politics might be born.

# NOTES

## Chapter 1: The Limits of Enlightenment

1. The sociology of secularisation is not one of my concerns in this book. For some useful recent studies of the subject, however, see Talal Asad, *Formations of the Secular: Christianity, Islam, Modernity* (Stanford, 2003), Vincent P. Pecora, *Secularisation and Cultural Criticism: Religion, Nation, and Modernity* (Chicago and London, 2006), Charles Taylor, *A Secular Age* (Cambridge, Mass. and London, 2007), Steven D. Smith, *The Disenchantment of Secular Discourse* (Cambridge, Mass., 2010), and Bryan S. Turner, *Religion and Modern Society: Citizenship, Secularisation, and the State* (Cambridge, 2011).

2. Max Weber, 'Science as a Vocation', in H.H. Gerth and C. Wright Mills (eds), *From Max Weber: Essays in Sociology* (New York, 1946), p. 155.

3. Frank E. Manuel, *The Changing of the Gods* (Hanover and London, 1983), p. 51.

4. Quoted in James Byrne, *Glory, Jest and Riddle: Religious Thought in the Enlightenment* (London, 1966), p. 34.

5. For the importance of religion in the Enlightenment, see P. Harrison, *'Religion' and the Religions in the English Enlightenment* (Cambridge, 1990), and P.A. Byrne, *Natural Religion and the Nature of Religion: The Legacy of Deism* (London, 1989).

6. Jonathan I. Israel, *Enlightenment Contested: Philosophy, Modernity, and the Emancipation of Man 1670–1752* (Oxford, 2006), p. 102.

7. Manuel, *The Changing of the Gods*, p. xii. Those who can fight their way past its florid style may also find some useful insights in Paul Hazard, *European Thought in the Eighteenth Century* (Harmondsworth, 1954). Frank E. Manuel (ed.), *The Enlightenment* (New York, 1965) contains some classic texts by leading Enlightenment figures.

8. J.G. Cottingham et al. (eds), *The Philosophical Writings of Descartes* (Cambridge, 1985), vol. 2, p. 19.

9. Israel, *Enlightenment Contested*, p. 65. Other commentators might query some of Israel's assumptions here.

10. Ernst Cassirer, *The Philosophy of the Enlightenment* (Princeton, NJ, 1951), pp. 135, 136. See also Alistair E. McGrath: 'The strongest intellectual forces of

the German Enlightenment were . . . directed towards the reshaping, rather than the rejection, of the Christian faith' (*The Blackwell Companion to the Enlightenment*, Oxford, 1991, p. 448).

11. Malcolm Bull, *Anti-Nietzsche* (London, 2011), p. 8.

12. See Ellen Meiksins Wood, *Liberty and Property* (London, 2012), p. 242.

13. I use the singular term 'movement' here with some misgivings. It is now received wisdom that the Enlightenment was in fact a complex set of sometimes mutually inconsistent national, political and intellectual currents. Ann Thomason argues for a plurality of Enlightenments in her *Bodies of Thought* (Oxford, 2008), an intriguing study of vitalist materialism in the period.

14. See J.A.I. Champion, *The Pillars of Priestcraft Shaken: The Church of England and its Enemies, 1660–1730* (Cambridge, 1992), p. 9.

15. The universalism of the Enlightenment by no means entirely blinded it to the reality of cultural difference. Montesquieu's *Spirit of the Laws* combines universal history with a degree of cultural pluralism, as in more full-blooded fashion does Herder. Voyaging, trade, exploration and colonialism were all aspects of eighteenth-century Europe's global scope, bringing a universal Reason face to face with very different cultures in apparently good working order, and thus threatening to undermine its assumptions at just the (imperial) moment that it needed to assert them. Swift's *Gulliver's Travels*, a work which is among other things an immanent critique of the Enlightenment, meditates satirically on these matters.

16. Lucien Goldmann, *The Philosophy of the Enlightenment* (London, 1973), p. 55.

17. Israel, *Enlightenment Contested*, p. 669.

18. See Jonathan Israel, *A Revolution of the Mind* (Princeton and Oxford, 2010), p. 177.

19. See Patricia B. Craddock, *Edward Gibbon: Luminous Historian* (Baltimore and London, 1989), p. 61, n. 3.

20. See Frederick C. Beiser, *The Fate of Reason* (Cambridge, Mass., 1987), Ch. 3.

21. Frank E. Manuel, *The Eighteenth Century Confronts the Gods* (Cambridge, Mass., 1959), p. 81.

22. See Alasdair MacIntyre, *After Virtue* (London, 1981), p. 38.

23. John Gray, *Enlightenment's Wake* (London, 1995), pp. 162–3.

24. See Jürgen Habermas, *Religion and Rationality: Essays on Reason, God and Modernity* (Cambridge, Mass., 2002).

25. Seneca, 'On the Happy Life', in *Moral Essays* vol. 2 (Cambridge, Mass. and London, 2006), p. 119.

26. Gotthold Ephraim Lessing, *The Education of the Human Race* (London, 1872), p. 32.

27. For an illuminating discussion of Lessing, see Barbara Fischer and Thomas C. Fox (eds), *A Companion to the Works of Gotthold Ephraim Lessing* (Rochester, NY, 2005).

28. Henry E. Allison, *Lessing and the Enlightenment* (Ann Arbor, 1966), p. 16.

29. Quoted in David Cressy, *England on the Edge: Crisis and Revolution 1640–1642* (Oxford, 2006), p. 219.

30. Quoted by Lawrence E. Klein, *Shaftesbury and the Culture of Politeness* (Cambridge, 1994), p. 158.

31. See David Hume, *Dialogues Concerning Natural Religion and The Natural History of Religion* (Oxford, 1993).
32. Francis Hutcheson, *Inquiry Concerning the Origin of our Idea of Beauty and Virtue* (London, 1726), p. 257. Hutcheson was admittedly a Presbyterian of a peculiarly liberal or 'New Light' kind.
33. David Simpson, *German Aesthetic and Literary Criticism* (Cambridge, 1984), p. 161. For the pessimism of Schopenhauer see Terry Eagleton, *The Ideology of the Aesthetic* (Oxford, 1990), Ch. 6.
34. See Immanuel Kant, *Religion within the Limits of Reason Alone* (New York, 1960), p. 32.
35. Quoted in Antoine Compagnon, *The Five Paradoxes of Modernity* (New York, 1994), p. 9.
36. Quoted in Michael Lowy, *Redemption and Utopia* (London, 1992), p. 112.
37. Joseph Priestley, *An Essay on the First Principles of Government* (London, 1771), p. 5. For an impressively comprehensive biography of this monumental figure, see Robert E. Schofield, *The Enlightenment of Joseph Priestley* (University Park, Pa. 1997),
38. See Antoine-Nicolas de Condorcet, *Sketch for a Historical Picture of the Progress of the Human Mind* (London, 1955), Ch. 10.
39. Ellen Meiksins Wood stresses the darker underside of the Enlightenment in her *Liberty and Property* (London, 2012), p. 305,
40. Hans Blumenberg, *The Legitimacy of the Modern Age* (Cambridge, Mass. and London, 1983), Part 1. Blumenberg distinguishes between secular ideas of progress and Christian eschatology, pointing out that the former is thought to be immanent in history whereas the latter breaks into it from some transcendent sphere. Most Christian theologians would in fact view the eschaton as both immanent and transcendent. The New Testament deploys both kinds of imagery to describe it: the yeast in the bread but also the thief in the night. Blumenberg also risks confusing eschatology with apocalypticism, not least when he mistakenly suggests that the characteristic Christian attitude to the coming of the kingdom is one of fear rather than hope.
41. Carl Becker, *The Heavenly City of the Eighteenth-Century Philosophers* (New Haven, 1932), p. 31.
42. Ibid., p. 163.
43. Ibid., p. 31.
44. Isaiah Berlin, *The Age of Enlightenment* (Oxford, 1979), p. 29.
45. Margaret C. Jacob, *The Radical Enlightenment* (London, 1981), p. 46.
46. Peter Gay, *The Enlightenment: An Interpretation* (New York, 1966), vol. 1, p. 9. Exactly in what sense these thinkers were revolutionaries is left unclarified.
47. See Roy Porter, *Enlightenment: Britain and the Creation of the Modern World* (London, 2001), p. 10.
48. The species of double truth I have in mind is not to be confused with the doctrine that what we must subjectively take to be true – the freedom of the will, for example – can nonetheless be scientifically shown to be false. On this subject, see Karsten Harries, 'The Theory of Double Truth Revisited', in Ricca Edmondson and Karlheinz Hulser (eds), *Politics of Practical Reasoning* (Lanham, Md., 2012).
49. Hume, *Dialogues Concerning Natural Religion and The Natural History of Religion*, p. 153. Pascal preaches a version of the double truth thesis, though with regard to

the origins of political power rather than religion: 'The truth about the [original] usurpation,' he writes, 'must not be made apparent: it came about originally without reason and has become reasonable. We must see that it is regarded as authentic and eternal, and its origins must be hidden if we do not want it soon to end' (*Pensées*, Harmondsworth, 1966, pp. 46–7).

50. Taylor, *A Secular Age*, p. 240.

51. Condorcet, *Sketch for a Historical Picture of the Progress of the Human Mind*, p. 109.

52. Ibid., p. 175.

53. A.O. Lovejoy, *Essays in the History of Ideas* (Baltimore, 1948), p. 67.

54. Frederick C. Beiser, *Enlightenment, Revolution, and Romanticism* (Cambridge, Mass. and London, 1992), p. 109.

55. Karl Schlechta (ed.), *Friedrich Nietzsche: Werke* (Munich, 1954), vol. 1, p. 166.

56. Friedrich Nietzsche, *The Joyful Wisdom* (Edinburgh and London, 1909), pp. 355–8.

57. Becker, *The Heavenly City*, p. 31.

58. Quoted in Manuel, *The Changing of the Gods*, p. 62.

59. See Hume's 'Natural History of Religion', in Antony Flew (ed.), *David Hume: Writings on Religion* (La Salle, Ill., 1992).

60. See David Fate Norton, 'Hume, Atheism, and the Autonomy of Morals', in A. Flew et al. (eds), *Hume's Philosophy of Religion* (Winston-Salem, NC, 1986), p. 123. It should be noted that this view of Hume's opinions depends upon taking Philo in the 'Dialogues Concerning Natural Religion' as voicing sentiments close to Hume's own. See also David O'Connor, *Hume on Religion* (London, 2001). The subject is also exhaustively investigated by J.C.A. Gaskin, in *Hume's Philosophy of Religion* (London, 1988), who argues that Hume seems to have believed in some form of intelligent cosmic design, but not in anything resembling the God of Christianity.

61. For de Maistre's polemics against the French Revolution, see his *Considerations on France* (Cambridge, 1994), with an Introduction by Isaiah Berlin. It is notable that Berlin's judgement on this extreme right-wing advocate of tyranny is considerably milder than his comments elsewhere in his work on left-wing champions of despotism. Some illuminating essays on de Maistre as stylist are to be found in Carolina Armenteros and Richard A. Lebrun (eds), *The New enfant du siècle: Joseph de Maistre as a Writer* (St. Andrews, 2010).

62. Edward Gibbon, *The Decline and Fall of the Roman Empire* (New York, 1932), vol. 1, pp. 25–6.

63. Jacob, *The Radical Enlightenment*, p. 25. For an excellent account of the conflict between the radical and moderate wings of the Enlightenment, see Israel, *A Revolution of the Mind, passim*.

64. For accounts of Toland, see Robert E. Sullivan's admirably erudite *John Toland and the Deist Controversy* (Cambridge, Mass., 1982). See also Robert Reed Evans's excellently detailed monograph *Pantheisticon: The Career of John Toland* (New York, 1991), and for a briefer portrait, J.G. Simms, 'John Toland (1670–1722), a Donegal Heretic', *Irish Historical Studies* vol. 16, no. 63 (March, 1969).

65. For Toland's Protestant triumphalism, see his *Anglia Libera* (London, 1701), a hymn of praise to English liberty. For his political contradictions, see Philip McGuinness, 'John Toland and Eighteenth-Century Irish Republicanism', *Irish*

*Studies Review* (Summer, 1997) and David Berman, 'The Irish Counter-Enlightenment', in R. Kearney and M. Hederman (eds), *The Irish Mind* (Dublin, 1984). See also my own account of Toland in Terry Eagleton, *Crazy John and the Bishop* (Cork, 1998), Ch. 2.

66. G.W.F. Hegel, *The Phenomenology of Mind* (London, 1949), p. 582.

67. Frank M. Turner (ed.), John Henry Cardinal Newman, *Apológia Pro Vita Sua and Six Sermons* (New Haven, 2008), p. 216.

68. Gerald Robertson Cragg, *The Church and the Age of Reason 1648–1789* (Harmondsworth, 1960), p. 161.

69. Quoted in Isaiah Berlin, *The Roots of Romanticism* (London, 1999), p. 44. For an informative study of Hamann, see the same author's *The Magus of the North: J.G. Hamann and the Origins of Modern Irrationalism* (London, 1993), as well as his *Against the Current* (Oxford, 1981), Ch. 1. Hamann was a powerful influence on Kierkegaard, as Berlin points out.

70. There were, however, plenty of Enlightenment thinkers who were empiricists rather than rationalists, and who therefore found the origins of reason in experience. For Ernst Cassirer in his *Philosophy of the Enlightenment*, the movement is in general much more empiricist than rationalist.

71. George di Giovanni (ed.), *Friedrich Heinrich Jacobi: The Main Philosophical Writings and the Novel 'Allwill'* (Montreal and Kingston, 1994), p. 513.

72. Fredric Jameson, *Valences of the Dialectic* (London, 2009), p. 187.

73. For an illuminating study of religious 'enthusiasm', see Lawrence E. Klein and Anthony J. La Volpa (eds), *Enthusiasm and Enlightenment in Europe, 1650–1850* (San Marino, Calif: 1998).

74. Ludwig Feuerbach, *The Essence of Christianity* (New York, 1989), pp. 10–11.

75. Louis Dupré, *The Enlightenment and the Intellectual Foundations of Modern Culture* (New Haven, 2004), p. 9.

76. See in particular Allen Wood (ed.), *J.G. Fichte, Attempt at a Critique of all Revelation* (Cambridge, 2010).

77. See The Earl of Shaftesbury, *Characteristics* (Gloucester, Mass., 1963), and his 'An Enquiry Concerning Virtue or Merit', in L.A. Selby-Bigge (ed.), *British Moralists* (Oxford, 1897). See also Stanley Grean, *Shaftesbury's Philosophy of Religion and Ethics* (Ohio, 1967); R.L. Brett, *The Third Earl of Shaftesbury* (London, 1951) and E. Tuveson, 'Shaftesbury and the Age of Sensibility', in H. Anderson and J. Shea (eds), *Studies in Aesthetics and Criticism* (Minneapolis, 1967).

78. Lawrence E. Klein, *Shaftesbury and the Culture of Politeness* (Cambridge, 1994), p. 55.

79. Max Horkheimer and Theodor Adorno, *Dialectic of Enlightenment* (Stanford, 2002), p. 19.

80. James P. Browne (ed.), *The Works of Laurence Sterne* (London, 1873), vol. 3, p. 311.

81. See Francis Hutcheson, *Thoughts on Laughter, and Observations on the Fable of the Bees* (Glasgow, 1758). For the eighteenth-century cults of benevolism and sentimentalism, see Eagleton, *Crazy John and the Bishop*, Ch. 3. See also Louis I. Bredvold, *The Brave New World of the Enlightenment* (Ann Arbor, Mich., 1961), Ch. 3.

82. Di Giovanni (ed.), *Friedrich Heinrich Jacobi*, p. 517.

83. Richard Price, 'A Review of the Principal Questions in Morals', in Selby-Bigge (ed.), *British Moralists*, pp. 106–7.

84. Seamus Deane, *Foreign Affections* (Notre Dame, Indiana, 2005), p. 62.
85. For Hutcheson's ethical theory see Terry Eagleton, *Heathcliff and the Great Hunger* (London, 1995), Ch. 3.

## Chapter 2: Idealists

1. For the state as a form of displaced divinity, see the nineteenth-century Catholic reactionary Joseph de Maistre: '[the state] is a true religion: it has its dogmas, its mysteries, its ministers . . . it lives only through national judgement (or reason), that is to say, through political faith, which is a creed'(quoted by Vincent P. Pecora, *Secularisation and Cultural Criticism* (Chicago and London, 2006), p. 108). Carl Schmitt reflects on the theological derivation of concepts of political sovereignty in his *Political Theology*. As far as the quasi-divinity of personal relations goes, the Bloomsbury Group, which held that such relations were among the highest human values, was the spiritual descendant of the Evangelical Clapham Sect, with which Virginia Woolf's father Leslie Stephen was associated. See Noel Annan, *Leslie Stephen: The Godless Victorian* (London, 1984), pp. 152–62. Both groups were marked by a strong spirit of elitism.
2. Fredric Jameson, *A Singular Modernity* (London, 2012), p. 163.
3. Peter Hallward, *Badiou: A Subject to Truth* (Minneapolis and London, 2003), p. 7. Badiou also makes the common mistake of imagining that a statement such as 'God is One' is a mathematical proposition.
4. The remarkable scope of the work of Herder, part *Aufklärer* and part herald of later trends, with its synthesis of history, theology, philosophy, aesthetics and the natural sciences, is exemplary in this respect. See Wulf Koepke, *Johann Gottfried Herder* (Boston, 1987), Ch. 1.
5. Nicholas Boyle, *Who Are We Now?* (Notre Dame, Ind. and London, 1998), pp. 163 and 202.
6. Andrew Bowie, *An Introduction to German Philosophy* (Cambridge, 2003), p. 94.
7. Habermas, *Religion and Rationality* (Cambridge, Mass., 2002), p. 73.
8. See M.H J. Abrams, *Natural Supernaturalism* (New York, 1971).
9. Søren Kierkegaard, *The Sickness Unto Death* (London, 1989), p. 100.
10. See John Neubauer, *Novalis* (Boston, 1980), p. 34.
11. F.W.J. Schelling, *System of Transcendental Idealism* (Charlottesville, Va., 1978), p. 34.
12. Ibid., p. 35.
13. F.W.J. Schelling, *Abyss of Freedom* (Ann Arbor, 1997), p. 93. For a perceptive recent account of Schelling's thought, see Matt ffytche, *The Foundation of the Unconscious* (Cambridge, 2012). A highly original reading of Schelling is to be found in Slavoj Žižek, *The Indivisible Remainder* (London, 1996), a study which views the philosopher as a materialist precursor of Marx.
14. See Terry Eagleton, *The Ideology of the Aesthetic* (Oxford, 1990), Ch. 8.
15. T. E. Hulme, *Speculations* (London, 1987), p. 118. Romantic theory, M.H. Abrams comments, retains 'traditional Christian concepts and the traditional Christian plot, but demythologised, conceptualised . . .' (*Natural Supernaturalism*, New York, 1971, p. 91).
16. The phrase is David Simpson's, in his Introduction to *German Aesthetic and Literary Theory* (Cambridge, 1984), p. 15. A valuable introduction to Schelling's

thought is to be found in Joseph L. Esposito, *Schelling's Idealism and Philosophy of Nature* (Lewisburg, Pa. and London, 1977).

17. Schelling, *System of Transcendental Idealism*, p. 8.

18. Fichte, *Science of Knowledge* (Cambridge, 1982), p. 248.

19. For a study of Fichte's thought, see Anthony J. La Volpe, *Fichte: the Self and the Calling of Philosophy 1762–1799* (Cambridge, 2001), a work which drastically downplays his nationalism. The anarchist thinker Max Stirner also preached a philosophy of absolute egoism. Someone once wondered what Mrs Stirner thought about that.

20. Fichte, *Science of Knowledge*, pp. 98 & 99.

21. Frederick C. Beiser (ed.), *The Early Political Writings of the German Romantics* (Cambridge, 1966), p. 5 (translation slightly amended).

22. Ibid.

23. Jürgen Habermas, *The Philosophical Discourse of Modernity* (Cambridge, 1987), p. 89.

24. See Frederick C. Beiser, 'The Paradox of Romantic Metaphysics', in Nikolas Kompridis (ed.), *Philosophical Romanticism* (London, 2006).

25. Johann Georg Hamann, *Writings on Philosophy and Language* (Cambridge, 2007), p. 63.

26. Ibid., p. 79. For a useful essay on Hamann, though one somewhat overweening in its claims for his centrality, see John Milbank, 'The Theological Critique of Philosophy in Hamann and Jacobi', in J. Milbank, C. Pickstock and G. Ward (eds), *Radical Orthodoxy: A New Theology* (London and New York, 1999).

27. Max Horkheimer and Theodor W. Adorno, *Dialectic of Enlightenment* (Stanford, 2002), p. 8.

28. David McLellan (ed.), Karl Marx, *Grundrisse* (London, 1973), p. 31.

29. Horkheimer and Adorno, *Dialectic of Endightenment*, p. 20.

30. F.W.J. Schelling, *The Philosophy of Art* (Minneapolis, 1988), p. 75.

31. McLellan (ed.), Marx, *Grundrisse*, pp. 30–1.

32. Frank Kermode, *The Sense of an Ending* (New York, 1967), p. 41.

33. Jürgen Habermas's, *Legitimation Crisis* (London, 1976) has some bearing on this issue.

34. See F. R. Leavis (ed.), *Mill on Bentham and Coleridge* (London, 1950).

35. Benjamin Disraeli's *Coningsby* trilogy and Carlyle's *Past and Present* respectively exemplify these fantasies.

36. See, for example, Schelling, *The Philosophy of Art*.

37. Johann Gottfried von Herder, *Reflections on the Philosophy of the History of Mankind* (Chicago and London, 1968), p. 99.

38. David Hume, *Essays Moral, Political, and Literary* (Oxford, 1966), p. 170.

39. For some of Herder's thoughts on these questions, see I. Evrigenis and D. Pellerin (eds), *Another Philosophy of History and Selected Political Writings* (Indianapolis, 2004). See also his 'On the Modern Uses of Mythology', in *Johann Gottfried Herder: Selected Early Works, 1764–1767* (Pennsylvania, 1992), as well as the informative essays on his work collected in Hans Adler and Wulf Koepke (eds), *A Companion to the Works of Johann Gottfried Herder* (New York, 2009).

40. See in particular 'Eckbert the Fair', in H. von Kleist, L. Tieck and E.T.A. Hofmann, *Six German Romantic Tales* (London, 1985). See also the stories by Tieck in Carl Tilley (ed.), *Romantic Fairy Tales* (London, 2000). For a study of Tieck, if an

excessively uncritical one, see William J. Lillyman, *Reality's Dark Dream: The Narrative Fiction of Ludwig Tieck* (New York, 1979).

41. Herder, *Reflections on the Philosophy of the History of Mankind*, p. 31.

42. For Herder's Enlightenment background, see A. Gillies, *Herder* (Oxford, 1945), a commentary which holds somewhat rashly that 'no man has penetrated so deeply into the springs of human affairs' as the subject of his monograph (p. 91). A valuable essay on Herder's historicism is to be found in A.O. Lovejoy, *Essays in the History of Ideas* (Baltimore, 1948).

43. A point made in Frederick C. Beiser, *Enlightenment, Revolution, and Romanticism* (Cambridge, Mass. and London, 1992), p. 196.

44. M. Chisholm (ed.), Johann Gottlieb Fichte, *The Vocation of Man* (Indianapolis and New York, 1956), p. 3. Robert Adamson, *Fichte* (Edinburgh and London, 1881) remains in some ways an admirably lucid, comprehensive study.

45. Georg Lukács, *History and Class Consciousness* (London, 1971), p. 187.

46. G.W.F. Hegel, *The Phenomenology of Mind* (London, 1949), p. 143. Hegel's views on art are to be found chiefly in his *Aesthetics: Lectures on Fine Art*.

47. See Perry Anderson, *A Zone of Engagement* (London, 1992), p. 291.

48. David Roberts, *Art and Enlightenment* (Nebraska and London, 1991), p. 10.

49. Immanuel Kant, *Critique of Judgement* (Oxford, 1952), pp. 127–8.

50. For a stylish, superbly erudite account of this subject, see Nicholas Halmi, *The Genealogy of the Romantic Symbol* (Oxford, 2007).

51. Friedrich Schiller, 'On the Necessary Limitations in the Use of Beauty of Form', in *Collected Works* (New York, n.d.), vol. 4, pp. 234–5 (translation slightly amended).

52. See Eagleton, *The Ideology of the Aesthetic*, Ch. 1.

53. See Terry Eagleton, *Heathcliff and the Great Hunger* (London, 1995), Ch. 2.

54. Friedrich Schiller, *Collected Works*, vol. 4, p. 200.

55. Friedrich Schiller, *On the Aesthetic Education of Man* (Oxford, 1967), p. 25. For useful studies of Schiller's aesthetics, see Georg Lukács, *Goethe and His Age* (London, 1968), Chs 6 and 7; S.S. Kerry, *Schiller's Writings on Aesthetics* (Manchester, 1961); and Margaret C. Ives, *The Analogue of Harmony* (Louvain, 1970).

56. Friedrich Schlegel, *'Lucinda' and the Fragments* (Minneapolis, 1971), p. 150.

57. Schiller, *On the Aesthetic Education of Man*, p. 219.

58. See Schiller, 'On the Necessary Limitations in the Use of Beauty as Form', in *Collected Work* (New York, n.d.), vol. 4, pp. 234–5.

59. Schiller, *On the Aesthetic Education of Man*, p. 215.

60. For a refutation of this case, see Perry Anderson, 'The Antinomies of Antonio Gramsci', *New Left Review* no. 100 (November 1976–January 1977).

61. Nicholas Halmi, *The Genealogy of the Romantic Symbol*, (Oxford, 2007), p. 2.

62. Ibid., p. 151.

63. Schiller, *On the Aesthetic Education of Man*, p. 147.

64. Ibid., p. 27.

65. Samuel Taylor Coleridge, *On the Constitution of Church and State* (Princeton, NJ, 1976), p. 43.

66. See Johann Gottlieb Fichte, *Address to the German Nation* (Chicago and London, 1922).

67. See H.C. Engelbrecht, *Johann Gottlieb Fichte* (New York, 1933), p. 34.

68. Quoted in John Colmer, *Coleridge: Critic of Society* (Oxford, 1959), pp. 158 and 148. Colmer's account of the later Coleridge's rather absurd political views is a remarkably sanitising one.

69. Quoted in Colmer, *Coleridge: Critic of Society*, p. 138. An excellent study of Coleridge's theoretical interests is Paul Hamilton, *Coleridge and German Philosophy* (London, 2007).
70. Quoted in Halmi, *The Genealogy of the Romantic Symbol*, pp. 125–6.
71. Quoted in Philippe Lacoue-Labarthe and Jean-Luc Nancy, *The Literary Absolute* (New York, 1988), p. 68.
72. David Lloyd and Paul Thomas, *Culture and the State* (New York and London, 1998), p. 65. This useful study suffers from a certain Anglocentrism. Fichte is mentioned only once, and Herder not at all.
73. It is notable that two of the classic English studies of nationalism – Ernest Gellner's *Nations and Nationalism* (Oxford, 1983) and E.J. Hobsbawm's *Nations and Nationalism since 1780* (Cambridge, 1990), both written by authors who hailed from the heart of Europe, have almost nothing to say about the Idealist and Romantic provenance of so much nationalist thought.
74. Proinsias Mac Aonghusa and Liam O Reagan (eds), *The Best of Pearse* (Dublin, 1967), p. 4. The four characteristics in question are traditionally thought to be peculiar to the Roman Catholic Church.
75. Though Marilyn Butler points out that *Lyrical Ballads*'s sympathy for the common life is in no sense specifically Romantic. It belongs essentially to the eighteenth-century neoclassical cult of the popular ballad and the simple, elemental life. See her *Romantics, Rebels and Reactionaries* (Oxford, 1981), p. 58. For continuities in Germany between neoclassicism and Romanticism, see Azade Seyhan, 'What is Romanticism and Where Did It Come From?', in Nicholas Saul (ed.), *The Cambridge Companion to German Romanticism* (Cambridge, 2009).
76. Quoted in Beiser, *The Early Political Writings of the German Romantics*, p. 15. For an innovative study of Novalis, one which focuses on his semiotic theories and views him as a species of proto-postmodernist, see W.A. O'Brien, *Novalis: Signs of Revolution* (Durham, NC and London, 1995).
77. Elie Kedourie, *Nationalism* (Oxford, 2000), p. 65. Kedourie's comment must be taken in the context of his unswerving hostility to the political phenomenon he is examining.
78. Quoted in Bowie, *An Introduction to German Philosophy*, p. 48.
79. See John Gray, *Black Mass* (London and New York, 2007).
80. Fredric Jameson, *Marxism and Form* (Princeton, NJ, 1971), p. 117.
81. Fredric Jameson, *The Political Unconscious* (London, 1981), p. 285.
82. Fredric Jameson, *Valences of the Dialectic* (London, 2009), p. 286.
83. Karl Korsch, *Marxism and Philosophy* (London, 2012), p. 75.

## Chapter 3: Romantics

1. For studies of Romanticism and religion, see Daniel White's admirably detailed *Early Romanticism and Religious Dissent* (Cambridge, 2006), and Gavin Hopps and Jane Stabler (eds), *Romanticism and Religion from William Cowper to Wallace Stevens* (Aldershot, 2006), a useful if rather too Byron-centred collection of essays.
2. Friedrich Schlegel, *'Lucinda' and the Fragments* (Minneapolis, 1971), p. 167.
3. Novalis, *Fichte Studies* (Cambridge, 2003), p. 168.
4. Ibid., p. 167.

5. Margaret Mahoney Stoljar (ed.), *Novalis's Philosophical Writings* (Albany, NY, 1997), p. 23.
6. David Constantine, *Hölderlin* (Oxford, 1988), p. 315. Ronald Peacock's brief study *Hölderlin* (London, 1938) speculates that the united *Volk* that Hölderlin desired might finally have become a reality. The date of the book's publication is significant in this respect.
7. Quoted in Frederick C. Beiser (ed.), *The Early Political Writings of the German Romantics* (Cambridge, 1966), p. 11. There is a relation between this viewpoint and so-called Romantic irony, a topic investigated in Azada Seyhan, *Representation and its Discontents* (Berkeley and Los Angeles, 1992), Ch. 3.
8. Philip Barnard and Cheryl Leser (eds), Introduction to Philippe Lacoue-Labarthe and Jean-Luc Nancy, *The Literary Absolute* (New York, 1988), p. xv.
9. See Terry Eagleton, *The Ideology of the Aesthetic* (Oxford, 1990), Ch. 6.
10. For a valuable study of this key text, see G. Molnar, *Novalis's 'Fichte-Studies':The Foundations of his Aesthetic* (The Hague, 1970).
11. J.G. Fichte, *Science of Knowledge* (Cambridge, 1982), p. 93.
12. An excellent account of these matters is to be found in Andrew Bowie, *Aesthetics to Subjectivity: From Kant to Nietzsche* (Manchester and New York, 1990), Ch. 3. For Schlegel in particular, see Leon Chai, *Romantic Theory* (Baltimore, 2006), Ch. 2.
13. George Eliot, *Adam Bede* (London, 1963), p. 154.
14. For a section of Scheiermacher's work, see Andrew Bowie (ed.), Friedrich Schleiermacher, *Hermeneutics, Criticism and Other Writings* (Cambridge, 1998).
15. M.H.J. Abrams, *Natural Supernaturalism* (New York, 1971), p. 119.
16. For an account of the Romantic imagination, see James Engell, *The Creative Imagination: Enlightenment to Romanticism* (Cambridge, Mass. and London, 1981).
17. The distinction can also be found in the late medieval and early modern periods. See Stuart Clark, *Vanities of the Eye: Vision in Early Modern European Culture* (Oxford, 2007).
18. See Geoffrey Hartman, *Wordsworth's Poetry* (New Haven, 1964), probably the finest study of the subject ever to be published.
19. See Terry Eagleton, *Trouble with Strangers* (Oxford, 2009), pp. 208–11.
20. Quoted in Beiser, *The Early Political Writings of the German Romantics*, p. 9.
21. Peter Gay, *The Enlightenment: An Interpretation* (London, 1966).
22. Marilyn Butler, *Romantics, Rebels and Reactionaries* (Oxford, 1981), p. 36.
23. Quoted in Lawrence E. Klein, *Shaftesbury and the Culture of Politeness* (Cambridge, 1994), p. 199.
24. For Shaftesbury on the ancient world, see ibid., pp. 146–9 and 200–6.
25. Frank M. Turner, *The Greek Heritage in Victorian Britain* (New Haven and London, 1981), p. 2. See also Harry Levin, *The Broken Column: A Study in Romantic Hellenism* (Cambridge, Mass., 1932). See also E. M. Butler, *The Tyranny of Greece over Germany* (Cambridge, 1935).
26. Samuel Henry Butcher, *Some Aspects of the Greek Genius* (London, 1891), pp. 45–6.
27. F.W. Schelling, *The Philosophy of Art* (Minneapolis, 1989), p. 41.
28. 'Pagan and Mediaeval Religious Sentiment', in R.H. Super (ed.), *Matthew Arnold: Lectures and Essays in Criticism* (Ann Arbor, 1962), p. 230.

29. For some illuminating commentary on the subject, see Dieter Henrich, *The Course of Remembrance and Other Essays on Hölderlin* (Stanford, 1996).
30. Turner, *The Greek Heritage in Victorian Britain*, p. 5.
31. Quoted in Richard Jenkyns, *The Victorians and Ancient Greece* (Oxford, 1980), p. 43.
32. For the most complete account, see Frank Kermode, *The Romantic Image* (London and New York, 1957). For a critical assessment of this work, see Terry Eagleton, 'The Politics of the Image', *Critical Quarterly* (Spring, 2012).
33. As far as motion which is also abstention from motion goes, Eliot apparently had in mind among other things taking the lift in Russell Square Underground station, the station nearest to his place of work at Faber and Faber.
34. Nicholas Boyle, *Goethe: The Poet and his Age* (Oxford, 2000), vol. 2, p. 68.
35. David Constantine, *Early Greek Travellers and the Hellenic Ideal* (Cambridge, 1984). p. 134. Jennifer Wallace has some perceptive comments on the cult of Greece in her *Shelley and Greece: Rethinking Romantic Hellenism* (Basingstoke, 1997).
36. Isaiah Berlin, *The Roots of Romanticism*, (London, 1999) pp. 16–18. These particular antitheses do not exhaust Berlin's own extensive list.
37. Carl Schmitt, *Political Romanticism* (Cambridge, Mass. and London, 1986), p. 4.
38. I refer to Romanticism as a movement or current for pure convenience. It was, of course, a complex, multiple set of artistic and intellectual trends.
39. A.O. Lovejoy, 'On the Discrimination of Romanticisms', in *Essays in the History of Ideas* (Baltimore, 1948), p. 231.
40. For a leisurely, delightfully undemanding account of Romanticism's relation to the French Revolution, see Howard Mumford Jones, *Revolution and Romanticism* (Cambridge, Mass., 1974).
41. Quoted in Isaiah Berlin, *Against the Current* (Oxford, 1981), p. 17.
42. It is unfortunate that Williams's study largely edits out those aspects of this tradition that he himself finds politically unpalatable. Its chapters on Coleridge, Carlyle and Lawrence in particular are exemplary of this drastically selective vision. The result is a seriously one-sided account, however brilliant and path-breaking.

### Chapter 4: The Crisis of Culture

1. Bruce Robbins, 'Enchantment? No, Thank You!', in George Levine (ed.), *The Joy of Secularism* (Princeton and Oxford, 2011), p. 91.
2. See Terry Eagleton, 'Eliot and a Common Culture', in Graham Martin (ed.), *Eliot in Perspective* (London, 1970).
3. Matthew Arnold, *Culture and Anarchy* (London, 1924), pp. 10–11.
4. Frederic Harrison, 'Culture: A Dialogue', *Fortnightly Review* (November, 1897).
5. Arnold, *Culture and Anarchy*, p. 33.
6. Ibid., p. 7.
7. See F.W. Bateson (ed.), *Matthew Arnold: Essays in English Literature* (London, 1965), p. 206.
8. Ibid., p. 37.
9. Ibid., p. 199.
10. Ibid., p. 70.

11. Ibid., p. 165.
12. Ibid., p. 45.
13. Walter Kaufmann (ed.), *Basic Writings of Nietzsche* (New York, 1968), p. 111.
14. Ibid., p. 112.
15. Matthew Arnold, *God and the Bible* (London, 1924), p. 6.
16. Matthew Arnold, *Literature and Dogma* (London, 1924), p. vi.
17. Arnold, *God and the Bible*, p. xi.
18. See Park Honan, *Matthew Arnold: A Life* (New York, 1970), pp. 126–7.
19. As far as a popularly accessible religion goes, Arnold has a particular affection for St Francis of Assisi, a saint whom he regards as having founded 'the most popular body of ministers of religion that has ever existed in the Church' (R.H. Super (ed.), *Matthew Arnold: Lectures and Essays in Criticism*, Ann Arbor, 1962, p. 223).
20. Arnold, *Literature and Dogma*, p. xiii.
21. Ibid., p. xxvii.
22. This is not in fact the case. In Catholic Ireland in the 1960s, at the height of a controversy over contraception, pharmacists could be found expounding the natural law.
23. Ibid., p. 110.
24. Ibid., p. xiv.
25. For an outstandingly learned study of Paul's politics, see Bruno Blumenfeld, *The Political Paul: Justice, Democracy and Kingship in a Hellenistic Framework* (London, 2001).
26. Ibid., p. 81.
27. Ibid., p. 18.
28. Arnold, *God and the Bible*, p. x.
29. Ibid., p. 37.
30. Quoted by Charles Taylor, *A Secular Age* (Cambridge, Mass. and London, 2007), p. 385.
31. Arnold, *Literature and Dogma*, p. 51.
32. Arnold, *God and the Bible*, p. xii.
33. Quentin Skinner, *Machiavelli* (Oxford, 2000), p. 71.
34. Matthew Arnold, 'The Bishop and the Philosopher', *Macmillan's Magazine* (January, 1863).
35. Lionel Trilling, *Matthew Arnold* (New York, 1949), p. 211.
36. See R.H. Super (ed.), *Matthew Arnold: On the Classical Tradition* (Ann Arbor, 1960), p. 4.
37. Friedrich Schlegel, *'Lucinda' and the Fragments* (Minneapolis, 1971), p. 200.
38. Karl Marx and Friedrich Engels, *Karl Marx and Friedrich Engels, on Religion* (Moscow, 1955), p. 42.
39. A useful selection of Feuerbach's writings is to be found in Ludwig Feuerbach, *The Fiery Brook: Selected Writings* (London, 2012).
40. Taylor, *A Secular Age*, p. 320.
41. Georg G. Iggers (ed.), *The Doctrine of Saint-Simon* (New York, 1972), p. 222. The work is a collection of lectures by Saint-Simon's disciples.
42. Ibid., p. 241.
43. For an excellent study of the movement, see Frank E. Manuel, *The New World of Henri Saint-Simon* (Cambridge, Mass., 1956). See also Georg G. Iggers, *The Cult of Authority: The Political Philosophy of the Saint-Simonians* (The Hague, 1970).
44. Iggers (ed.), *The Doctrine of Saint-Simon*, p. 247.

45. Andrew Wernick, *Auguste Comte and the Religion of Humanity* (Cambridge, 2001), p. 100. Wernick's study is far too intelligent and theoretically sophisticated for its unpropitious subject.
46. Emile Durkheim, *The Elementary Forms of the Religious Life* (Oxford, 2001), p. 18. I do not mean to suggest that Durkheim is to be ranked politically with Comte. For studies of his thought, see Jeffrey C. Alexander, *The Antinomies of Classical Thought, vol 2: Marx and Durkheim* (Berkeley and Los Angeles, 1982); Steven Lukes, *Emile Durkheim: His Life and Work* (Stanford, 1985); and W.S.F. Pickering, *Durkheim's Sociology of Religion* (London, 1994).
47. See Jonathan I. Israel, *Enlightenment Contested: Philosophy, Modernity, and the Emancipation of Man 1670–1752* (Oxford, 2006), p. 678.
48. Durkheim, *Elementary Forms of the Religious Life*, p. 320.
49. See Richard Dawkins, *The God Delusion* (London, 2006).
50. See Louis Althusser, *For Marx* (London, 1969) and 'Ideology and Ideological State Apparatuses', in Louis Althusser, *Lenin and Philosophy* (London, 1971).

## Chapter 5: The Death of God

1. Arthur Schopenhauer, *The World as Will and Representation* (New York, 1969), vol. 2, pp. 581 & 349. For an unusually positive assessment of this thinker by a fellow German pessimist, see Max Horkheimer, *Critique of Instrumental Reason* (New York, 1974), Ch. 4.
2. Max Weber, 'Science as a Vocation', in H.H. Gerth and C, Wright Mills (eds), *From Max Weber: Essays in Sociology* (New York, 1946), p. 155.
3. For Strauss's thought see *Natural Right and History* (Chicago, 1953) and *What is Political Philosophy? and Other Studies* (Glencoe, Ill., 1959).
4. Gilles Deleuze, *Difference and Repetition* (London and New York, 1994), p. 58.
5. Ludwig Feuerbach, *The Essence of Christianity* (New York, 1989), p. 21.
6. See Friedrich Nietzsche, *Daybreak* (Cambridge, 1982), p. 83.
7. See Slavoj Žižek and Boris Gunjević, *God in Pain* (London, 2012), Introduction.
8. Andrew Wernick, *Auguste Comte and the Religion of Humanity* (Cambridge 2001), p. 83.
9. Bruce Robbins, 'Enchantment? No, Thank You!', in George Levine (ed.), *The Joy of Secularism* (Princeton and Oxford, 2011), p. 91.
10. For a classic study of the theme of the death of God in nineteenth-century literature, see J. Hillis Miller, *The Disappearance of God* (Cambridge, Mass., 1963). Miller's study, much influenced by the Geneva school of phenomenology, is one of the finest, most original works we have on the literary writing of the period.
11. Walter Kaufmann (ed.), *Basic Writings of Nietzsche* (New York, 1968), p. 135.
12. Ibid., p. 498.
13. *Beyond Good and Evil*, ibid., p. 307.
14. For this Nietzschean teleology, one largely set aside by postmodern readings of his work, see Terry Eagleton, *The Ideology of the Aesthetic* (Oxford, 2000), Ch. 9.
15. See Terry Eagleton, *Why Marx Was Right* (New Haven and London, 2011), Ch. 3.
16. Friedrich Nietzsche, *The Gay Science* (New York, 1974), p. 35 (my italics).
17. The words are Adorno's, in his *Prisms* (London, 1967), p. 260.
18. Walter Benjamin, 'Eduard Fuchs, Historian and Collector', in *One-Way Street and Other Writings* (London, 1979), pp. 359–61.

19. See Georg Simmel, 'The Concept and Tragedy of Culture', in David Frisby and Mike Featherstone (eds), *Simmel on Culture: Selected Writings* (London, 1997).
20. Quoted in Andrew Bowie, *Aesthetics and Subjectivity: From Kant to Nietzsche* (Manchester and New York, 1990), p. 224.
21. See Theodor Adorno, *Noten zur Literatur* (Frankfurt am Main, 1974), p. 423.
22. See in particular Sigmund Freud, *Civilisation, Society and Religion* (Harmondsworth, 1985). Freud's original title for the work employed the term 'Culture' rather than 'Civilisation'. See also Norman O. Brown, *Life Against Death* (London, 1968).
23. Sigmund Freud, *The Future of an Illusion*, in Sigmund Freud, *Civilisation, Society and Religion* (Harmondsworth, 1985), p. 192.

#### Chapter 6: Modernism and After

1. Thomas Mann, *Reflections of a Nonpolitical Man* (New York, 1983), p. 364. For a survey of *Kulturkritik*, in its historical context, see Fritz K. Ringer, *The Decline of the German Mandarins* (Cambridge, Mass., 1969).
2. See Neil Turnbull, 'Wittgenstein's *Leben*: Language, Philosophy and the Authority of Everyday Life', in Conor Cunningham and Peter M. Candler (eds), *Belief and Metaphysics* (London, 2007).
3. For the latter critique, see 'The Affirmative Character of Culture', in Herbert Marcuse, *Negations* (Harmondsworth, 1972). Marcuse's classic study of cultural degradation is *One-Dimensional Man* (1964).
4. See Mann, *Reflections of a Nonpolitical Man*, p. 364.
5. See Sigmund Freud, *Civilisation, Society and Religion* (Harmondsworth, 1985), p. 184.
6. Francis Mulhern, *Culture/Metaculture* (London, 2000), p. 28.
7. See H.R. Klieneberger, *George, Rilke, Hofmannsthal and the Romantic Tradition* (Stuttgart, 1991), and Jens Rieckmann (ed.), *A Companion to the Works of Stefan George* (Rochester, NY, 2005).
8. Simon Critchley, *Ethics, Politics, Subjectivity* (London, 1999), p. 219.
9. For a critique of this conservative conception of tragedy, see Terry Eagleton, *Sweet Violence: The Idea of the Tragic* (Oxford, 2003), especially Ch. 3.
10. F.W.J. Schelling, *Philosophy of Art* (Minneapolis, 1989), p. 251.
11. I.A. Richards, *Science and Poetry* (London, 1926), pp. 82-3.
12. F.R. Leavis, *Two Cultures? The Significance of C.P. Snow* (London, 1962), p. 23.
13. Wallace Stevens, *Opus Posthumous* (New York, 1977), p. 158.
14. A subject discussed by Jacques Rancière in *Mallarmé: La politique de la sirène* (Paris, 1996), p. 80.
15. See Salman Rushdie, 'Is Nothing Sacred?', in *Imaginary Homelands: Essays and Criticism 1981-1991* (London, 1991). For a study of the redemptive capabilities of literature, see Leo Bersani, *The Culture of Redemption* (Cambridge, Mass. and London, 1990).
16. See G. A. Pocock, *Virtue, Commerce, and History* (Cambridge, 1985). For a critical commentary, see Terry Eagleton, 'Deconstruction and Human Rights', in Barbara Johnson (ed.), *Freedom and Interpretation* (London, 1993).
17. See Andrew Wernick, *Auguste Comte and the Religion of Humanity* (Cambridge, 2001), Ch. 8. For the dissolution of the social, see Jean Baudrillard, *In the Shadow of the Silent Majorities* (New York, 1973).

18. Perry Anderson, *In the Tracks of Historical Materialism* (London, 1983), p. 54.
19. Søren Kierkegaard, *The Sickness Unto Death* (Harmondsworth, 1989), p. 126.
20. See Friedrich Nietzsche, *The Joyful Wisdom* (Edinburgh and London, 1909), p. 287.
21. For a discussion of this question, see Michel de Certeau, 'Believing and Making People Believe', in *The Practice of Everyday Life*, vol. 1 (Berkeley, 1984).
22. John Milbank, 'Only Theology Saves Metaphysics', in Peter M. Candler Jr. and Conor Cunningham (eds), *Belief and Metaphysics* (London, 2007), p. 475.
23. For the role of neoliberalism in helping to create the conditions for religious militancy, see David Harvey, *A Brief History of Neoliberalism* (Oxford, 2005).
24. See in particular Richard Dawkins, *The God Delusion* (London, 2006), Sam Harris, *The End of Faith: Religion, Terror, and the Future of Reason* (London, 2004), Christopher Hitchens, *God Is Not Great* (London, 2007), and Daniel Dennett, *Breaking the Spell: Religion as a Natural Phenomenon* (London, 2007).
25. See Harris, *The End of Faith*, p. 129.
26. Simon Critchley, *The Faith of the Faithless* (London, 2012), pp. 24–5.
27. Alain de Botton, *Religion for Atheists* (London, 2012), p. 19 (my italics).
28. Ibid., p. 111.
29. Ibid., pp. 63 and 66.
30. Ibid., pp. 11–12.

# INDEX

NOTE: Page numbers followed by *n* and a number refer to information in a numbered note.

# Index

# Index

# Index